CREATIVE DRAMA IN THE CLASSROOM

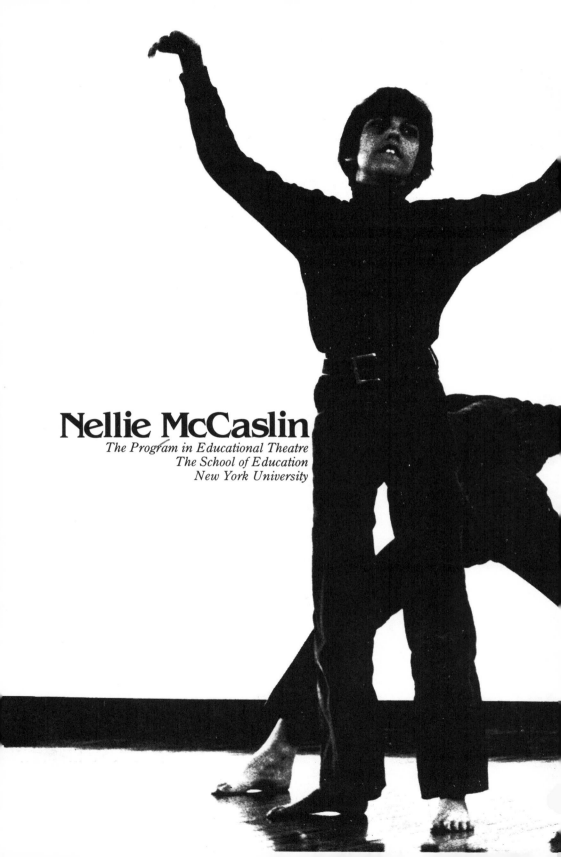

Nellie McCaslin

The Program in Educational Theatre
The School of Education
New York University

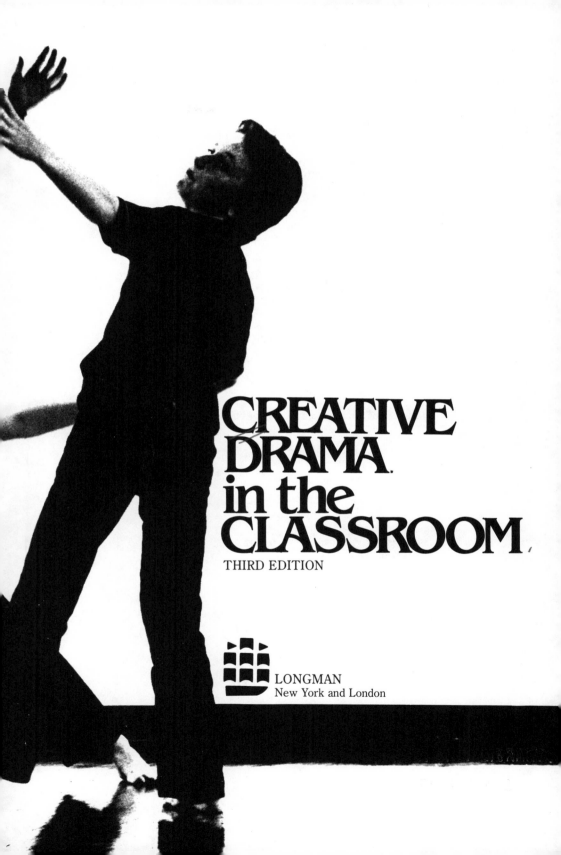

CREATIVE DRAMA in the CLASSROOM

THIRD EDITION

LONGMAN
New York and London

Creative Drama in the Classroom
Third Edition

Longman Inc., New York
Associated companies, branches, and representatives
throughout the world.

Developmental Editor: Gordon T. R. Anderson
Editorial and Design Supervisor: Judith Hirsch
Design: Antler & Baldwin, Inc.
Manufacturing and Production Supervisor: Kris Becker
Composition: A & S Graphics, Inc.
Printing and Binding: The Maple Press

Manufactured in the United States of America

9 8 7 6 5 4 3 2 1

Library of Congress Cataloging in Publication Data

McCaslin, Nellie.
    Creative drama in the classroom.

    First-2d ed. published under title: Creative dramatics
in the classroom.
    Bibliography: p.
    Includes index.
    1. Drama in education.   I. Title
PN3171.M25   1980   792'.07   79-15867
ISBN 0-582-28139-3

Dedicated to all of those friends and colleagues,
both here and abroad, whose work I admire
and whose friendship I cherish.

ACKNOWLEDGMENTS

"The Little Scarecrow Boy" by Margaret Wise Brown. From *Fun and Frolic*, revised edition, by Margaret Wise Brown, published by D.C. Heath and Co., 1955. Copyright by Margaret Wise Brown. Reprinted by permission of Albert E. Clarke, III.

"The Magic Stones" by Aviva Layton. From MAGOOK #5, copyright © 1979 by MAGOOK Publishers Ltd. Arranged for creative playing by Nellie McCaslin. Reprinted by permission of MAGOOK Publishers Ltd.

"The Old Man and the Goombay Cat" by Kitty Kirby is published for the first time in this book. Copyright © 1980 by Kitty Kirby.

"Jump or Jiggle" by Evelyn Beyer. From *Another Here and Now Storybook* by Lucy Sprague Mitchell. Copyright, 1937, by E. P. Dutton and Co., Inc. Renewal, © 1965 by Lucy Sprague Mitchell. Reprinted by permission of the publisher, E. P. Dutton.

"Merry-Go-Round" by Dorothy Baruch. Permission granted by Bertha Klausner International Literary Agency, Inc.

"Halloween" by Geraldine Brain Siks. "Halloween" (p. 32) in *Children's Literature for Dramatization: An Anthology* by Geraldine Brain Siks. Copyright © 1964 by Geraldine Brain Siks. Reprinted by permission of Harper & Row, Publishers, Inc.

"Sing a Song of Seasons" by Alice Ellison. Copyright © 1964 by Alice Ellison. From *Children's Literature for Dramatization: An Anthology* by Geraldine Brain Siks. Reprinted by permission of Alice Ellison Brain.

"Imaginings" by J. Paget-Fredericks. From *Green Pipes* by J. Paget-Fredericks, published by The Macmillan Company, 1929.

"Some One" by Walter de la Mare. Reprinted by permission of The Literary Trustees of Walter de la Mare and The Society of Authors as their representative.

"My Shadow" and "The Wind" by Robert Louis Stevenson, published by Charles Scribner's Sons.

"Mobile" by David McCord. From *All Day Long* by David McCord, by permission of Little, Brown and Co. Copyright © 1965, 1966 by David McCord.

"The Negro Speaks of Rivers" by Langston Hughes. Copyright 1926 by Alfred A. Knopf, Inc. and renewed 1954 by Langston Hughes. Reprinted from *Selected Poems of Langston Hughes*, by permission of Alfred A. Knopf, Inc.

"The Old Wife and the Ghost" by James Reeves. From *The Blackbird in the Lilac* by James Reeves, published by Oxford University Press (1952). Reprinted by permission of the publisher.

"Rimouski" by Shirley Pugh. From *In One Basket* by Shirley Pugh. Copyright © 1972 by Shirley Pugh. Reprinted by permission of Anchorage Press of New Orleans.

CONTENTS

FOREWORD

What is a theatre historian doing, writing a foreword for a book on creative drama in the classroom? Well, if there is anything at all that a theatre historian knows, it is that theatre has taken many forms, and that it has been put to many uses throughout the centuries in which it has been a mirror of the societies that have produced it. Theatre has always been the most *human* of the art forms; by the very nature of theatre, humanity in all its diversity has been both the material and the method of the art. Theatre has served to make life meaningful for performers and for audiences (the only two constants in theatre) by affording them the opportunity to reflect on their lives in progress, and to deepen their perceptions of themselves and their world. It has taken all knowledge for its province and, at its best, has added to that knowledge both understanding and sympathy.

Now, as these subsequent pages will affirm, creative drama is primarily concerned with one side of the theatrical equation—the performer. It is not aimed at an audience; it is done for the sake of the participants. But its goals are the same as those of theatre: to increase understanding, to sharpen perceptions, to make active and operative the social nature of humanity, to bring the participants into active contact with the best that has been thought and said throughout human history, and to explore the nature of being human. Though no one would pretend that creative drama *is* theatre, since it eliminates from primary consideration half the theatrical equation—that is, the audience—it is, nevertheless, a social art in its own right and in the best sense. Theatre, of course, is a highly complex performing art, demanding rigorous training and high skill of its several contributing artists. Creative drama, on the other hand, is a process which focuses almost exclusively on the personal development of the participants. That is why it belongs in schools and classrooms which do not exist—as Brian Way states and Dr. McCaslin reiterates—to develop *actors*, but to develop *people*. There are parallels in the processes of developing people and of developing actors; creative drama techniques can be useful in the training of actors, but are not—and do not pretend to be—actor training *per se*. Theatre is one thing; creative drama is another. Yet there is a symbiotic relationship between the two, and that is why a theatre historian is interested in creative drama and is concerned about it.

In the following pages, Dr. McCaslin presents a rationale for creative dramas; she details forms and procedures, including materials and methods, and even—in a cautionary manner—deals with performances for audiences. It is a rich and sympathetic presentation, aware of the human and theatrical history which has preceded it, and exploring a variety of possibilities. Much has been changed in this new edition: processes are clarified, more ethnic sources are included, additional exercises and ideas have been listed, and a thoughtful chapter on creative drama as a teaching tool has been added. The helpful annotated bibliography has been extended and brought up to date, and many new examples of successful applications of creative drama in various settings are included. In short, what has for some years been one of the most useful of handbooks in the field of creative drama has been made into an absolutely indispensable source book. I salute the new edition.

Vera Mowry Roberts
Hunter College,
The City University of New York

PREFACE

The twelve years that have elapsed since this book first appeared have brought great changes and advances in the field of drama and theatre education. I doubt that any similar period has witnessed as much interest, discussion and controversy. In the preface to the two earlier editions, I said that the text had been written in response to questions from students and teachers regarding the use of creative drama in school and recreational programs. Some of those questions had arisen in university classes, others in workshops and in professional conferences. During the past twelve years since the original publication, I have visited many more schools and college campuses and have attended numerous meetings. I have led workshops in creative drama and have been a consultant to groups establishing arts programs. My many discussions with students, teachers, and administrators have been convincing proof of a deep and urgent need for the arts in our society, a need greater today in many respects than at any time in our history. These discussions have, at the same time, disclosed some remarkably good work being carried on in every region of this country. Some of it is being done by specialists; some, by generalists—classroom teachers who are frequently unaware of their own ability to guide children to a fulfillment through creative expression. New leadership has emerged in the past decade, and some strong and effective influences have revitalized our efforts.

In both first and second editions I made mention of the increasing number of workshops being offered under a variety of sponsorships. One important difference: today many of these workshops are made possible through government agencies and private foundations. Some consist of a single session or meeting. Others are planned as a series, ranging from as few as three meetings to all-day sessions over a period of one to three weeks. Often these workshops are focused on a single topic or theme, such as *drama therapy, drama as a teaching tool, drama in the language arts program, drama in human relations* (using drama/theatre as techniques), and *exploring creativity*, to mention only a few. There are also in-service courses for teachers, conducted along more academic lines, which are organized to include participation, demonstration, discussion, and the opportunity for reading in the field.

It has been my experience through the years that the majority of those who enroll in such workshops or classes have had little or no previous training. Participants are eager to learn, but many express feelings of inadequacy, often despite years of successful classroom teaching. Frequently asked questions are: What exactly is creative drama? How should I start? Where should it be introduced? Is it the same as role playing? What material is available? Don't I need a background in theatre? What is the difference between creative drama and drama in education, as practiced in England?

The questions are legitimate. At the same time, I am aware that many of those who question their qualifications have the primary requisites: the desire to learn, a respect for the contribution of children, and an appreciation of the theatre as an art form. Without these basic attitudes, it is doubtful whether satisfying results can ever be achieved; with them, there is every likelihood of success.

Few teachers or students have had sufficient experience in the performing arts to feel secure in the beginning. On the other hand, many who have studied formal theatre techniques have had no experience with children. There is little doubt in my mind that the creative teacher will find his or her own way sooner or later, but if the following chapters hasten the process by offering a point of view and a way of working, they will have served their purpose.

This book is intended as a simple guide for the inexperienced leader or classroom teacher—the nonspecialist—who wants to initiate dramatic activities, but who needs some practical help in getting started. The book has, therefore, been conceived from a point of view rather than organized along specific age or class levels. Its very brevity would preclude a comprehensive treatment of the interests, expectations, and goals for each grade. I believe, moreover, the educational philosophy to be essentially the same for all, regardless of the age or grade level of the participants. Indeed, recent experiments with senior adults have proved that creative drama techniques, as used with children, are equally effective in working with this older age level.

My own experience with teachers has convinced me of their awareness of the interests, tastes, and backgrounds of their pupils. What they seek is guidance in the planning of simple activities and the adaptation of material for use in creative drama and language arts classes. With this in mind, therefore, the following chapters were written.

The contents include a rationale for creative drama with specific objectives and values, some suggestions for pantomime and improvisation, play structure, and the simple basic procedures involved when a class wants to share a play with an audience. While this is not intended to be a book on play production, it recognizes the fact that groups occasionally want to put on a play, and that when this happens, new problems are posed. Suggestions for solving the problems are not meant to encourage this practice, but rather to help make the transition from process to presentation.

This third edition includes two new chapters, which, I hope, will increase its usefulness. One of these chapters deals with movement, and the other, the use of drama as a teaching tool—a new concept that differs from the more traditional and familiar methods in the emphasis placed on learning. Like the other chapters, these must be considered as little more than introductions to the subjects, but the bibliographical sources will enable readers interested in these areas to pursue them further. Other chapters have been expanded according to suggestions from readers.

The bibliography has been revised and updated. Familiarity with the literature in the field will not only help to build a better background for the teacher, but should strengthen his or her own perception and awareness. The teacher can then begin to devise original techniques, geared not to an arbitrary age or grade level, but to the individual circumstances.

A word concerning the use of the generic "he" throughout the text. The author recognizes that our field is now represented by both men and women; however, the constant use of "he or she" is awkward. After careful consideration, the decision was made to avoid this through the general use of a single pronoun. It may be noted that the title of the book has been changed from *Creative Dramatics in the Classroom* to *Creative Drama in the Classroom*, in conformity with the term preferred by the Children's Theatre Association of America.

I must at this time acknowledge the great inspiration which has come from my many friends and colleagues in the United States and abroad. In the two earlier editions I mentioned the names of persons to whom I felt particularly indebted. That list has expanded to the point that it would be literally impossible to name them all. I can only say that their thinking and their work have continued to shape my own views as their writing has contributed to our field. I should like to express particular appreciation to those persons who are pioneering in the new areas of drama therapy and drama in special education. Although teachers of the arts have recognized the value of drama for handicapped persons, little research has been done; less, written. My thanks also go to those teachers who have raised the questions that I am attempting to answer. Their desire to learn has stimulated my own further thinking, and their observations have caused me to reconsider and modify some of my earlier views. And, finally, the college students and the children, whom I have had the pleasure of teaching over the years, have demonstrated by their warm response the importance of an art which is as rewarding to the leader as it is to the group. I am grateful for the opportunity to prepare a third edition of this text.

Nellie McCaslin

New York City

CREATIVE DRAMA IN THE CLASSROOM

1

CREATIVE DRAMA: AN ART, A SOCIALIZING ACTIVITY, AND A WAY OF LEARNING

PLAY

In every human being there exists the impulse to mime and to play. Primitive societies released this impulse through tribal expressions of hope, joy, fear, desire, sorrow, hatred, and worship. What primitive man felt strongly, he danced or mimed. From his sacred play came ritual; poetry, music, and dance were a part of his play. Philosophy and wisdom found expression in words.

In ancient Greece religious celebration resulted in contests, and these contests gave birth to dramatic forms or plays. As highly organized as they were later to become, these contests could be considered the creative expression of the people, from whose ranks individual playwrights emerged. During the Middle Ages, drama had its rebirth in the Church. Authorship of the scripts is unknown, but there is proof that the performers were amateurs, whose participation was voluntary. Profes-

3

Adelphi University Children's Center for the Creative Arts, courtesy Julie Thompson. Photograph by George H. Meyer.

sionalism had no part in these plays, which served a religious and educational purpose. The involvement of the audiences was probably great as they responded to the dramatization of the Bible stories and moral tales as enacted by their neighbors. In every period of history, play has served a significant purpose, interpreting and affecting the lives of the people. "We have to concede, therefore, that civilization is, in its earliest phases, played."[1]

According to the author of this statement, our modern adult preoccupation with making a business of play has resulted in its decline, and this decline is man's loss. True play does not know professionalism, for it is a voluntary activity, based on, but different from, the business of everyday life. Joy and freedom are the hallmarks of play, with the rules and limits established by the players.

True play, though free, creates order—indeed, *is* order. Whereas man may play alone, one of the basic characteristics of play is the teamwork involved; through play, the participants are drawn closely together. Huizinga notes that dressing up is often an element of play, though it is not always included and is not necessary. Examples of play may be found in all countries of the world, at different periods in history and on every age level. Play is inherent in man, and the child early manifests an impulse to engage in it.

One has only to watch a group of children playing in an empty lot or a playground to accept the truth of these observations. The child plays almost as soon as he moves, and through his playing, he learns. In his dramatic play the three- or four-year-old tries on the roles of those about him; he observes their activities and learns by pretending to be and do. He enters the various worlds of his family and neighbors, interpreting and reenacting. First he observes; then he responds, repeating in play what has made a strong impression on him in his life. Not unlike primitive man, the young child expresses his feelings through movement and words, creating more complex situations as he grows older, with the boundaries stretched but the rules still clearly established. By the time he is ready for school he has learned much about the world he lives in, and a large part of his learning has come about through his play. As Winifred Ward observed, "Drama comes in the door of every school with the child."[2]

The impulse to play, if encouraged, can become a continuing way of learning, a medium of expression, and eventually an art form. Many teachers have realized the potential of play and have made drama an integral part of their programs. Some have rejected it on the grounds that it is frivolous and therefore unrelated to serious learning. The fact that the child gives it his

1. J. Huizinga, *Homo Ludens, A Study of the Play Element in Culture* (Boston: Beacon Press, 1955), p. 14.
2. Winifred Ward, *Drama With and For Children* (Washington, D.C.: U.S. Department of Health, Education, and Welfare, Bulletin #30, 1960), p. 1.

most serious attention escapes their notice; he is made to feel that play is unworthy and therefore something to be left outside the schoolroom door. When this happens, the joyful and creative element of his free play is extinguished, perhaps never to be rekindled. Other teachers, and it is to them that this book is addressed, ask how they can keep the play impulse alive, that it may enhance learning and thus enrich the lives of their pupils.

Jon and Rumer Godden[3], in their recollections of a childhood spent in India, speak with feeling of play, its magic and privacy. When asked, as they often were by their parents, what they were playing, the reply was generally "nothing." "Or, if that were too palpable a lie, we would give a camouflage answer like 'Mothers and Fathers,' which we never played or, with us, another improbable play, 'Shops.' . . . Yet if we had told what we were playing no one would have been much the wiser, because our plays were like icebergs, only three-tenths seen, the rest hidden, inside ourselves. It was what we thought into our play that made its spell."

Games, sports, and ritual are closely related to play. Whereas sports are like theatre and are designed for an audience, games and drama exist for the participants. Theatre games, about which we hear so much these days, were created for the actor, not for the audience. A sport is held in a particular place; a game, wherever players may assemble. As to ritual, it may be defined as the observance of a set form or series of rites. We think of the ritual as having religious significance, but it is more inclusive than that. The repetition of an act or set of acts is also ritual. This is important to remember when working with children, for their games assume a ritualistic form. Movement and chants play an important part in them. By beginning a creative drama class with the familiar—movement, rhythms, songs, or group games which all know—the leader is using ritual to draw the members together and make them comfortable.

EDUCATIONAL OBJECTIVES

One of the most frequently stated aims of education today is the maximal growth of the child both as an individual and as a member of society. In order to achieve this aim, certain educational objectives have been set up. Although these objectives vary somewhat, there is general agreement that knowledge, skills, and appreciation of the arts are essential. The modern curriculum tries to provide for each child to:

1. develop basic skills in which reading, writing, arithmetic, science, social studies, and the arts are stressed

3. Jon and Rumer Godden, *Two Under the Indian Sun* (New York: Knopf, 1966), p. 55.

2. develop and maintain good physical and mental health
3. grow in his ability to think
4. clarify his values and verbalize his beliefs and hopes
5. develop an understanding of beauty, using many media including words, color, sound, and movement
6. grow creatively and thus experience his own creative powers[4]

Although other objectives are mentioned, these six are most frequently listed in the building of programs designed for today's world and the complex problems life offers.

The most enthusiastic proponent of creative drama would not go so far as to claim that its inclusion in the curriculum will ensure the meeting of these objectives. On the other hand, many objectives of modern education and creative drama are unquestionably shared. Among the shared objectives are:

1. creativity and aesthetic development
2. the ability to think critically
3. social growth and the ability to work cooperatively with others
4. improved communication skills
5. the development of moral and spiritual values
6. knowledge of self

Before discussing creative drama in greater detail, some definitions are in order. The terms creative dramatics or creative drama (now the preferred term), play making, children's theatre, dramatic play, and role playing are used, often interchangeably, though they have quite different meanings. A definition of terms will clarify the meanings as they are used in this text.

DEFINITIONS

Dramatic Play
This is the free play of the very young child in which he explores his universe, imitating the actions and character traits of those around him. It is his earliest expression in dramatic form but must not be confused with drama or interpreted as performance. Dramatic play is fragmentary in nature, existing only for the moment. It may last for a few minutes or go on for some time. It may even be played repeatedly, if the interest is sufficiently strong, but when this occurs, the repetition is in no sense a rehearsal. It is, rather, the

4. Robert S. Fleming, *Curriculum for Today's Boys and Girls* (Columbus, Ohio: Charles E. Merrill Books, 1963), p. 10.

repeating of a creative experience for the pure joy of doing it. It has no beginning and no end, and no development in the dramatic sense.

Dramatic play may be as simple as Susan's passing of imaginary cookies to a guest when her mother is entertaining a friend at tea. The two or three minutes of spontaneous pantomime are indeed dramatic play since they involve stepping into the role of the mother and performing an often observed activity. Susan has seen how a hostess behaves and is taking advantage of an opportunity to slip into the role to see what it is like to be "mother" and do as she does.

Dramatic play may, on the other hand, follow the pattern of six-year-old Erma, who was the youngest child on the street and, therefore, the last to go to school. She had heard about teachers and lessons and longed for the day when she, too, could pack up her books in a bag and trot off after breakfast with the other boys and girls to the elementary school. When the time came, her curiosity may have been satisfied, but her fascination became even more intense. According to her family, she would return every afternoon and set up her own class in the dining room. Whether the others joined her or not, she would play for an hour or more with an improvised desk and a blackboard. She assumed, in turn, the various roles of principal, teacher, boys, and girls. Most often, however, she would be the teacher who called the roll, disciplined the children, and, to the great amusement of her mother and older sister, reenacted everything that had taken place during the day. This situation held her interest for three years, though the content varied according to her daily experiences. Other parents have described similar preoccupations, some lasting for an extraordinarily long time, until the interest waned and another took its place.

It has been stated that "dramatic play helps the child develop from a purely egocentric being into a person capable of sharing and of give and take."[5] Certainly this is true of the two examples cited. In both instances the mother accepted the play without interference, letting it continue with neither impatience nor the kind of amused attention that might have caused self-consciousness. In dramatic play the child creates a world of her own in which to master reality. She tries in this imaginative world to solve real-life problems that she has, until now, been unable to solve. She repeats, reenacts, and relives these experiences. In the book *Understanding Children's Play*, the authors observe that through this activity the child is given an opportunity to imitate adults, encouraged to play out real-life roles with intensity, to dramatize relationships and experiences, to express his own most pressing needs, to release unacceptable impulses, to reverse the roles usually taken, to

5. Ruth Hartley, Lawrence K. Frank, and Robert M. Goldenson, *Understanding Children's Play* (New York: Columbia University Press, 1964), p. 19.

try to solve problems, and to experiment with solutions. If encouraged, by providing the place, the equipment, and an atmosphere in which the child feels free to express himself, dramatic play is a natural and healthy manifestation of human growth.

According to Richard Courtney, "Play is the principal instrument of growth. Without play there can be no normal adult cognitive life; without play, no healthful development of affective life; without play, no full development of the power of will."[6]

Marie Winn writes in her book, *The Plug-in Drug*, that the child can work out difficulties through play, assuming the roles of the adults in his life, redressing grievances and reenacting scenes that have caused distress. "In play he can expose, and perhaps, exorcise, fears that he cannot articulate in any other way; more important, perhaps, is the opportunity imaginative play affords the child to become an active user rather than a passive recipient of experience."[7] In our TV world, this is an important contribution.

Creative Drama[8] and Play Making

These terms may be used interchangeably since they refer to informal drama which is created by the participants. As the name "play making" implies, it goes beyond dramatic play in scope and intent. It may make use of a story with a beginning, a middle, and an end. It may, on the other hand, explore, develop, and express ideas and feelings through dramatic enactment. It is, however, always improvised drama. Dialogue is created by the players, whether the content is taken from a well-known story or is an original plot. Lines are not written down or memorized. With each playing, the story becomes more detailed and better organized, but it remains extemporaneous in nature and is at no time designed for an audience. Participants are guided by a leader rather than a director; the leader's goal is the optimal growth and development of the players.

The replaying of scenes is therefore different from the rehearsal of a formal play, in that each member of the group is given an opportunity to play various parts. No matter how many times the story is played, it is done for the purpose of deepening understanding and strengthening the performers rather than perfecting a product. Scenery and costumes have no place in creative

6. Richard Courtney, *Play, Drama and Thought* (New York: Drama Book Specialists), p. 204.

7. Marie Winn, *The Plug-in Drug* (New York Viking), p. 95.

8. Definition of creative drama accepted by the Children's Theatre Association of America in 1977: "Creative drama is an improvisational, nonexhibitional, process-centered form of drama in which participants are guided by a leader to imagine, enact, and reflect upon human experiences. Although creative drama traditionally has been thought of in relation to children and young people, the process is appropriate to all ages."

drama, although an occasional property or piece of a costume may be permitted to stimulate the imagination. When these are used, they should not be considered mounting, or suggest production. Most groups do not feel the need of properties of any kind, and are generally freer without them.

The term "creative drama" is used to describe the improvised drama of children from age five or six and older, but it belongs to no particular age level and may be used just as appropriately to describe the improvisation of high school students. The young adult is more likely to label it "improvisation," which, indeed, it is, but the important distinction to keep in mind is that it has form and is, therefore, more structured than dramatic play. At the same time, it is participant-centered and not intended for sharing, except with the members of the group who are not playing and are, therefore, observers rather than audience.

Children's Theatre

The term "children's theatre" refers to formal productions for children's audiences, whether acted by amateurs or professionals, children or adults, or a combination of both. It is directed rather than guided; dialogue is memorized, and scenery and costumes usually play an important part. Since it is audience-centered, it is essentially different from creative drama and dramatic play. The child in the audience is the spectator and the benefits derived are aesthetic.

What does a child gain from attending good children's theatre? He gains much. First of all, there is the thrill of watching a well-loved story come alive on a stage. There is the opportunity for a strong, vicarious experience as he identifies with characters who are brave, steadfast, noble, loyal, beautiful. Emotions are released as he shares the adventure and excitement of the plot. And, finally, he learns to appreciate the art of the theatre if the production is tasteful and well done.

We are speaking now of the child in the audience, not the child in the play. While there is much that is creative and of value for the performer, it is generally agreed that participation in creative drama is far more beneficial than public performances for all children up to the age of ten or eleven. Occasionally, there is an expressed desire "to put on a play," and when this comes from the children themselves, it is probably wise to grant the request. There are times, to be sure, when sharing is a joy and a positive experience, but is to be hoped that formal play production would be infrequent. Certainly, if it is done, the production should be simple and all precautions taken to guard against the competition and tension that so often characterize the formal presentation of a play. For junior and senior high school students, however, a play is often the desired culmination of a semester's work. To deprive students of the experience would be to withhold the ultimate satisfaction of communicating an art.

Some leaders in the field believe that any performance in front of an audience is harmful because it automatically interferes with the child's own free expression. I should agree up to a point, but the theatre is, after all, a performing art, and when the audience is composed of understanding and sympathetic persons, such as parents or members of another class, it may be the first step toward communicating a joyful experience. Without question, however, very young children should not perform publicly. Those in the middle and upper grades may not be harmed if their desire, and the right occasion, indicate that the benefits outweigh the disadvantages. A performance is a disciplined and carefully organized endeavor, involving a variety of skills that children of elementary school age do not and should not be expected to possess.

I am not speaking here of the professional child actor, who, most educators agree, is in grave danger of being damaged by exploitation and the pressures of performance. The same dangers, however, are present whenever children are used for ends other than their own growth and development. When children are trained rather than guided, praised extravagantly instead of encouraged, or featured as individuals rather than helped to work cooperatively with others, they risk losing all the positive aspects of the experience. Ironically, this leads to poor theatre as well, for ensemble, that most desirable quality of good theatre, is achieved through the process of working together, not by featuring individual players.

Role Playing

This term is used most often in connection with therapy, or education. It refers to the assuming of a role for the particular value it may have to the participant, rather than the development of an art. Although all art may be considered to have certain curative powers, it is not the primary purpose of either creative drama or theatre to provide therapy or make use of drama to solve social and emotional problems. Role playing is what the young child does in his dramatic play, it is true, but it is also a tool used by psychologists and play therapists.

Acting is, in a way, an extension of dramatic play. According to Richard Courtney, "Play, acting and thought are interrelated. They are mechanisms by which the individual tests reality, gets rid of his anxieties, and masters his environment."[9]

9. Richard Courtney, *Play, Drama and Thought* (New York: Drama Book Specialists, 1974), p. 177.

Drama therapy is similar to role playing in its stated purpose. Its use assumes a problem, for which this type of treatment is indicated. Physically handicapped, mentally retarded, emotionally disturbed, and culturally disadvantaged children may derive great benefit from its use, provided the therapy is in the hands of a competent and sensitive therapist. The distinction between role playing and therapy, therefore, consists more of degree than of kind. *Role playing* may be considered preventive, in that it provides an opportunity for all children in a group to develop sensitivity toward the feelings of others, and encourages changes of attitude through understanding. *Therapy* is the dramatic technique used for its curative power in helping a patient to solve problems which frighten, confuse, or puzzle him. "It is in itself both a form of comfort and reassurance, and a way of moving on toward new attitudes about these things."[10]

A Creative Drama

The word drama is also used to mean literature. In the present context, however, it is used to mean a play that is developed creatively by a group, as opposed to the one that abides by a written script. When the dialogue is written by either teacher or children, it automatically ceases to be spontaneous drama, although it may, indeed, be a fine example of creative writing. This occasionally happens, and when it does, the results may be doubly rewarding. The play may be simple or elaborate, but if it is to be properly described as creative drama, it must be improvised rather than written.

VALUES IN CREATIVE PLAYING

There is general agreement among teachers of creative drama that important values can be gained from creative playing. Depending upon the age of the children, the particular situation, and the orientation of the leader, these values may be listed in varying order. It is the contention of this book, however, that in spite of these differences, certain values exist in some measure for all, regardless of age, circumstances, or previous experience. To be sure, the activities must be planned with the group in mind, and the emphasis placed upon the needs and interests of those involved. The five- or six-year-old needs and enjoys the freedom of large movement and much physical activity, but this should not deny a similar opportunity to older boys and girls. Adult students in early sessions gain freedom and pleasure when given an opportunity to move freely in space.

10. Peter Slade, *Child Drama* (London: University of London Press, 1954), p. 119.

The ten- or eleven-year-old enjoys the challenge of characterization and often creates with remarkable insight and understanding. The young child, however, can also create on his level, though he cannot be expected to compete with children who are older. In other words, it is not a question of assigning different values to various age levels; it is a matter of accepting basic values that exist on all levels, varying more in degree than in kind. Specifically, these values may be listed as follows:

An Opportunity to Develop the Imagination

Imagination is the beginning. In order to work creatively, it is necessary, first of all, to push beyond the boundaries of the here and now, to project oneself into another situation, or into the life of another person. Few activities have greater potential for developing the imagination than play making. Little children move easily into a world of make-believe; but as we grow older, this amazing human capacity is often ignored, or even discouraged. The development of the imagination to the point where the student responds spontaneously may take time, in some cases, but it is the first step toward satisfying participation.

The sensitive teacher will not demand too much in the beginning but will accept with enthusiasm the first attempts of the beginner to use his imagination to solve a problem. Once the player has had the fun of seeing, hearing, feeling, touching, tasting, or smelling something that is not there, he will find that his capacity grows quickly. Holding the image until he can do something about it is the next step, but the image must come first. Through drama, the imagination can be stimulated and strengthened to the student's everlasting pleasure and profit. We learn through experience. Unless we want a child to experience everything—which is, of course, impossible—we are obliged to give up the idea except by way of theatre. Through participation in drama and vicariously through attendance at plays, we can provide realistic experiences in acceptable and exciting ways.

An Opportunity for Independent Thinking

A particular value of creative playing is the opportunity it offers for independent thinking and planning. Although the drama, both informal and formal, is a group art, it is composed of the contributions of each individual, and every contribution is important. As the group plans together, each member is encouraged to express his own ideas and thereby contribute to the whole. The leader recognizes the part each child plays and the value that planning has for him. If the group is not too large, there will be many opportunities before the activity is exhausted. Thinking is involved in such questions as: Who are the characters? What are they like? What part do they play? Why do they behave as they do? What scenes are important? Why? How can we suggest this action or that place?

The evaluation that follows is as important as the planning: indeed, it is preparation for a replaying. Children of all ages are remarkably perceptive, and their critical comments indicate the extent of their involvement. A well-planned session in creative drama provides exercises in critical thinking as well as an opportunity for creativity.

Freedom for the Group to Develop Its Own Ideas

It has just been stated that through creative drama an individual has a chance to develop and grow. This is also true of the group, in which ideas are explored, evaluated, changed, and used. As a group of any age works together under sensitive and skilled leadership, the members learn to accept, appreciate, and stimulate each other. Every teacher has experienced a group in which the dynamics were such that all seemed to produce more because of their association. This is not to say that creative drama is a magic formula for successful teamwork, but it unquestionably offers a rare opportunity for sharing ideas and solving problems together. The formal play, whatever problems it may pose, cannot offer a group this same challenge. The written script imposes a structure in which free improvisation has no place. There are values in formal production, to be sure, but the major emphasis is on the product, rather than on the participants.

The strength, incidentally, that is acquired through this kind of planning and playing together is a valuable asset when, at some later date, the group decides to give a formal play. Far from limiting the players, improvisation strengthens techniques and builds individual and group rapport.

An Opportunity for Cooperation

When a group builds something together, it is learning a valuable lesson in cooperation. Social differences may be forgotten in the business of sharing ideas and improvising scenes. Teachers who guide children in creative drama cite numerous examples of social acceptance based on respect for a job well done, and the bond that develops from the fun of playing together. As an illustration, Jack entered a neighborhood class in drama which several of his third-grade schoolmates attended. It was obvious that he was an outsider, and the leader despaired of his ever becoming a part of the group. For the first three or four sessions, he contributed nothing and was chosen by no one, regardless of activity.

Then one day the children were dramatizing the story of *The Stone in the*

Road. They wanted a farmer, to drive along the road with a donkey cart. Several attempted to pantomime the action but, each time the children insisted that "he didn't look like he was really driving." Suddenly Jack, who had been sitting on the sidelines, put up his hand and volunteered to try it. The vigorous and convincing pantomime he created as he guided his cart around the stone astonished the class. His position in the group changed at that moment, and while he never became one of the leaders, he was accepted and often sought out. Working together in an atmosphere of give-and-take is an experience in democratic partnership; it provides the opportunity for the Jacks in the group to contribute their skills and have them accepted. Or, as a college student once put it, after her first experience of being in a play: "Now I know what John Glenn meant by 'we.' It was all of us working together who did it!"

An Opportunity to Build Social Awareness

Putting oneself in the shoes of another is a way of developing awareness and human understanding. By the time a player has decided who a character is, why he behaves as he does, how he relates to others, and the way in which he handles his problems, he has come to know a great deal about him. Even the very young or experienced player may glimpse insights that help him in his understanding of people and, therefore, of living. Both literature and original stories provide the player with this opportunity to study human nature.

In one class of ten-year-olds, the teacher began the morning by asking the children to think of someone they had seen on their way to school who had attracted their attention. It was suggested that the person should have interested them enough to become a character in a play. Immediately, every hand went up, and a variety of people were described. After a period of telling what they looked like, where they were, who they might have been, and what they were doing, the teacher asked the class to select three who would be good subjects for original stories. The class was then divided into three groups, six or seven in a group, and given an opportunity to make up a story centered around the person of their choice.

The first group decided upon the character Peter suggested—an old man whom Peter described sitting on the steps of his apartment building. The children decided the old man might have been a school janitor who, in his retirement, spent the morning watching the children go to school. Having reached this decision, it was no time at all until they had developed a plot in which the old man's memory of having once saved a child's life became a sudden reality: A boy had run across the street after his ball, and the old man, in an automatic reaction, had rescued him from being hit by a car. The story, with its throwback scene imposed on the present, was dramatic and exciting both to the players and to the rest of the class; more than that, however, was the warm and sympathetic portrayal of the old man. Two adults who were in the room that day have spoken many times of the scene. If the memory remained with the observers, is it not likely that the children, who created the play, must have grown in the process?

A Healthy Release of Emotion

Much has been said about the thinking, both creative and critical, that charcterizes creative drama. Another value is of equal importance: the opportunity to feel and release emotion. As children grow up, the opportunity for emotional response is too often restricted to television and movies. While there is value in being a spectator, the deep involvement of active participation is lacking.

Control of emotion does not mean suppression of emotion. It means the healthy release of strong feelings through appropriate and acceptable channels. At some time or another, all people feel anger, fear, anxiety, jealousy, resentment, and negativism. Through the playing of a part in which these emotions are expressed, the player may release them and thus relieve tension. "By permitting the child to play freely in a setting of security and acceptance, we enable him to deal satisfactorily and healthfully with his most urgent problems."[11]

Better Habits of Speech

To many teachers, a primary value of creative drama is the opportunity it offers for training in speech. There is a built-in motivation for the player wishes to be heard and clearly understood. Volume, tempo, and pitch, as well as diction, are involved in a natural way; no other form of speech exercise captures the player to the same degree or offers so good a reason for working on speech. The little girl who can barely be heard in a classroom recitation will be reminded by her fellow players to speak up or the lines will be lost. And the boy with the strident tone will also be told when his voice is too loud or inappropriate for the character he is portraying. Being, in turn, a giant, a prince, a king, an old man, or an animal, offers further opportunity for developing variation of tone and expression. In creative drama, the concern is less for a standard of speech than it is for audibility, clarity, and expression. While the teacher does not dwell on speech as the major objective, she can point out its importance, and the children will accept the validity of her suggestion.

11. Hartley, Frank, and Goldenson, *Understanding Children's Play* (New York: Columbia University Press, 1964), p. 16.

Not only articulation but also vocabulary is served through this form of oral expression. Conceptual thinking and the congitive aspect of language are encouraged when words are put into practical use. For the young child, the culturally disadvantaged child, or the student with a foreign language background, vocabulary can be built and distinctions in word meanings made clear through participation in creative drama. Even abstract learnings may come more readily when words are acted or shown.

An Experience with Good Literature

The story one plays makes a lasting impression. Therefore, the opportunity to become well acquainted with good literature, through dramatizing it, is a major value—not that every story chosen will be of high literary quality. But many will be, and the leader usually discovers that these are the stories that hold interest longest. Both folk tales and modern tales provide fine opportunities for acting. Bruno Bettelheim has advanced powerful arguments for the folk and fairy tale, a genre that has recently been questioned as to its relevance for the modern child. In addition to the narrative interest of these tales, there are important psychological reasons why they continue to have value and why they should be used, though, of course, not to the exclusion of contemporary literature. A program that includes a variety of material helps to build appreciation and set a standard for original writing. Television shows and comic books attract temporary interest; but put beside a story that has stood the test of time, these rarely sustain attention. Believable characters, a well-constructed plot, and a worthwhile theme make for engrossing drama. What better way of discovering and learning to appreciate literature?

An Introduction to the Theatre Arts

Art is said to represent the human being's interpretation of life, expressed in a way that can be universally recognized and understood. The theatre offers many examples. While creative drama is primarily participant-centered, like theatre, it deals with the basic conflicts in life and thus offers the young player his first taste of the magic and make-believe of the theatre. In his imagination, a chair becomes a throne; a stick, a wand; a change in lighting; a difference in time; and a character, a human being in whom he believes and with whom he can identify. Listening, watching, and becoming involved are required of the theatre audience. The child who is introduced to the theatre first through playing is going to look for more than superficial entertainment when he attends a performance. If we can visualize drama/theatre as a continuum, with dramatic play at one end and formal theatre at the other, we can follow a logical sequence leading from the child's earliest attempts at "make-believe" to creative drama to the finished product, in which there must also be belief.

Recreation

Implicit in everything that has been said so far, yet different and of value in itself, is the opportunity for recreation, or "re-creation," that drama/theatre affords. Under certain types of circumstances such as camp, community centers, after-school activity programs and neighborhood clubs, the highest priority of drama may indeed be recreation. Drama is fun. It exists for the pleasure of the players and it expresses free choice. It may also, in time, lead to serious work or even a lifelong avocation. Many universities today have programs in leisure studies, in which the constructive use of our increased free time is the focus. The human impulse to play makes drama one of the most popular activities in a recreation program.

SUMMARY

Creative drama, whether in the classroom or in the camp or community program, may be regarded as a way of learning, a means of self-expression, a therapeutic technique, a social activity, or an art form. Children are helped to assume responsibility, accept group decisions, work together cooperatively, develop new interests, and—particularly in a classroom situation—seek new information. Drama is the most completely personal, as well as the most highly socialized, art form we have.

The values of informal play are many, and the leader will discover these and others as the group moves and grows. Not all the values listed will be manifested at once, or perhaps ever, for the creative process is slow and takes time to develop. Also, leaders do not all hold the same priorities. They arrange them according to their situations and interests. More will be said on this point later.

It is often observed that few persons perform on their highest level. This is true of the beginning player, child or adult, who, through shyness or actual fear, needs encouragement and acceptance.

The sensitive leader recognizes this and tries to create an atmosphere of mutual trust. In his acceptance of every child and what he has to offer, the leader has taken the first big step toward building self-confidence. Freedom will follow, learning will occur, and an ordinary room will become a place in which exciting things can happen.

2

IMAGINATION IS THE BEGINNING

Imagination and creativity are two words we hear a great deal these days. Whether we are able to define them precisely, or whether we merely have a sense of their meanings, we use them freely, and in regard to a variety of people and a multitude of activities. The purist may object to the coining of such terms as "creative furniture," "imaginative setting," or "sophisticated equipment," yet our continued and widespread usage in regard to both people and products has made them household words.

The *fact* of imagination has long been recognized, but it is only recently that the *value* of imagination has been hailed. Shakespeare described imagination as the spark that makes man "paragon of animals." Today, not only the artist but also businessmen, scientists, military leaders, and educators describe imagination as the magic force that goes beyond the mastery of facts and techniques in the search for new ideas. While it is not the purpose of this book to go into the subject in either length or depth, the

19

New Canaan Country Day School, courtesy Mary Perrine. Photograph by David Brooks.

terms imagination and creativity have been used in describing the art of creative drama. Therefore, some definition is required.

CREATIVITY

Creativity may be defined in a number of ways. It may be thought of in terms of product or process, depending on whether we are concerned with the solution to a problem or the way in which the problem is solved. If creativity is interpreted as process, it is considered as a new way of seeing, a different point of view, an original idea, or a new relationship between ideas. Inventiveness and adaptation are often included in the thinking of those who believe creativity to be a way of working.

If, on the other hand, creativity is defined in terms of product, it is best illustrated by works of art (poems, stories, paintings, music, dance), scientific inventions, and new arrangements or designs. There has been great interest in the study and measurement of creativity in recent years, and a considerable body of data has appeared. One assumption accepted by psychologists doing research is that creativity is not a special gift possessed by a fortunate few, but, rather, a human capacity possessed to some degree by all men. It has been found, incidentally, that many individuals learn more if permitted to approach their studies creatively.

According to some authorities, the beginning of creative thinking may be found early in the life of the infant, in his "manipulative and exploratory activities."[1] In his awareness of human expression, gestures, and sound, the baby is first observer and then investigator. It is but a short step from here to his own experimentation, at which point he becomes creator. Drama, both informal and formal, is man's artistic creation, based on his observation of human life—selected, arranged, and heightened.

The words—observer, investigator, creator—are of particular interest to the teacher of creative drama. One leader held a discussion on the subject of creativity and imagination with a group of eight-year-olds in a creative drama class. Their dialogue ran something like this:

TEACHER: What does creativity mean to you?
PATRICIA: I think it means to make.
DENISE: No, not to make. To make up.
TEACHER: Can you explain the difference?
KENNY: Well, if a man made a pair of shoes, he'd be creating.

1. E. Paul Torrance, *Creativity*, What Research Says Series (Washington, D.C.: National Education Association of the United States, 1963).

TEACHER: Do you all agree with Kenny?

DENISE: No, I think only the first pair of shoes would be created. If the man made a lot of others like them, they'd just be made—not made up.

TEACHER: Then everything that's made is not created?

DENISE: (*sticking to her original point*) Only the things that aren't copied.

TEACHER: How do you feel about copying?

PATRICIA: You don't get any fun out of copying.

CATHY: I think it's all right to copy some things.

TEACHER: What kind of things, Cathy?

CATHY: Well, like good manners. And words. You wouldn't know what to do lots of times if you didn't have something to copy.

TEACHER: Then you don't think copying is always a bad thing to do?
                (*General agreement that it is not.*)

DENISE: Just the same, you shouldn't use somebody else's mind. You want a thing to be just yours.

ALAN: You have to know what to copy and what not to. Sometimes it's hard to know which is which.

TEACHER: How would you explain imagination? Dean?

DEAN: You think of something that isn't there.

TEACHER: Would anyone like to add to that?

BILLY: Yes, it isn't that it isn't there. It's more like you make yourself believe.

PATRICIA: You see, outside of you it isn't real. Inside your head, it's there.

TEACHER: Do you enjoy using your imagination?

JOHN: Oh, yes. Because you can make anything happen.

PATRICIA: Sometimes they're silly things. What we do isn't always good.

TEACHER: What do you mean, "not good"?

PATRICIA: I mean, some children have better ideas than others.

TEACHER: But you still want a chance to try them all out?

DENISE: Oh, yes. It's better for an idea to be yours than good.

BILLY: I think using your imagination means being creative. It means making up something that wasn't ever there before.

The discussion went on like this for some time, but it was obvious that the terms creativity and imagination held real meaning for the children. Their observations—that it is important to have ideas and the freedom to try them out—are basic to good work in creative drama.

Creativity refers both to the cognitive and the affective life and is the result of conscious and unconscious effort. In the anthology, *Essays on Creativity*, the point is made repeatedly that "ideas are born from stimulation from within and without, but such stimulation must be grasped, filtered and used."[2] Working together, students and teacher can accomplish this to the satisfaction of all. A creative act does not happen once; it is an ongoing process, which with encouragement and guidance becomes a way of life. Rollo May puts the whole thing very simply when he says that creativity is the act of repatterning the known world into meaningful new configurations.

IMAGINATION: BEGINNING EXERCISES

The first day the class meets, the leader will do well to begin with the simplest exercises in which imagination is involved. Regardless of age level, there must be an opportunity for the participants to go beyond the here and now, but they cannot, and should not, be expected to handle a story or create an improvisation. It is also wise to begin with the entire group, if space permits. This removes all thought of audience, thereby diminishing fear and self-consciousness.

How the leader begins will be determined by the age, experience, and number in the group, as well as the size of the playing space. If the group is fortunate in having a very large room, physical movement is an excellent opening exercise. Music or even a drumbeat will enhance the mood and help to focus the attention. One simple and very effective way of beginning is to have the group walk to the beat of the drum. As the group becomes more comfortable and relaxed, the beat can be changed: rapid, double time, slow, and so on. The participants, in listening for the change in beat, forget themselves and are usually able to use their entire bodies. Galloping, skipping, and hopping are fun for younger children, and good exercise for those much older. Adults find freedom and pleasure in physical movement and sit down when it is over—relaxed and better able to go on to the next assignment.

From the purely physical body movement, the teacher may move on to mood. For example, if the group has been walking to a beat, he may suggest that there is green grass underfoot. "How does it feel to you? Your feet are tired. Think what it is like to put them down on soft, cool grass. Take off your shoes. (Some will do so at this suggestion.) Walk on it. Feel it."

Soon the steps will become more flexible as the image of grass grows stronger. The teacher might suggest, next, that there is ice underfoot. "It is hard, slippery, difficult to walk on, dangerous." The movement usually changes perceptibly now as the participants imagine the difficulties of crossing

2. Stanley Rosner and Lawrence Abt, *Essays on Creativity* (Croton-on-Hudson, N.Y.: North River Press, 1974), p. 192.

an icy pavement. Muscles are tensed and bodies stiffen. It is here that one or two may lose their balance or even slip and fall down as they get into the spirit of the situation. The teacher's acknowledgment of their efforts offers encouragement and usually stimulates further invention. Imagining that they are running across hot sand, stepping over puddles, crossing a creek, wading through snow—each suggestion stretches the imagination a little more. When the exercise is over, most groups will have moved far from the first stiff, self-conscious steps without realizing when, or how, or even that they have done it.

Games, known to all the participants, might come next. Tossing a ball is a familiar activity, and the players by this time usually respond eagerly. The teacher may suggest that they are using a tennis ball, then a basketball, next a beach ball, or a ping-pong ball. The players experience little difficulty shifting from one ball to another, and have fun showing its size and weight as they throw and catch it. Lively groups sometimes drop the ball, run for it, lose it, or carry the assignment much farther than the leader suggested. Favorite activities such as flying kites, jumping rope, playing hopscotch, and playing with jacks provide other opportunities for using the imagination. How long this goes on is best left to the discretion of the teacher, who can tell when the interest begins to wane.

A pantomime of seasonal sports might be the culmination of the various exercises, and a means of tying them together. If the class is large, it may be the time to subdivide into smaller groups, with each taking a particular game or sport. However the teacher proceeds from here, he will find that imagination has been sparked and the next step will be easier. The chapter on movement includes a more detailed discussion of ways in which movement, dance, and mime can be used as both means and ends.

CONCENTRATION

If imagination is the beginning, concentration—the capacity to hold an idea long enough to do something about it—must come next. It is not enough to glimpse an idea; the image must be held long enough for action to follow. Inexperienced players of any age may have difficulty here, for self-consciousness and fear of failure are paralyzing and distracting agents. It is now that the teacher needs to encourage every effort, however small, in order to free the player of his self-doubt. This is difficult in some cases: the player may never have excelled at anything and so does not believe that he has anything worthwhile to offer. Many children, on the other hand, become involved easily. Concentration poses no problems for them because of their freedom from fear and their willingness to experiment.

Theatre of Youth, Buffalo. Courtesy Rosalind Cramer.

ORGANIZATION

Concentration and organization go hand in hand. Once the players are able to focus their attention on their material, they can get down to the business of organizing it. They have ceased to think about themselves and are ready to decide such things as who their characters are, what they are doing, and the overall form the improvisation will take. If the group is working on a story, the organization will more or less follow the plot. The characters are related to a logical sequence of events, and it is up to the players to decide how they will handle them.

If, on the other hand, the group is creating an original situation—pantomime or improvisation—a different kind of planning is involved. More guidance is required, since there is no structure to follow, but if children feel free to experiment, they come up with surprising and often delightful results.

"Organization" does not mean the imposing of a conventional form, but, rather, an arrangement of parts or material, so as to achieve order. Older groups, or groups that have had more exposure to television, movies, and theatre, are less inclined to experiment with organization although, with encouragement, they can be helped to find the challenge in "trying it another way." Organization is order, and until it exists in some form or another, the participants rarely find satisfaction in creative playing.

SELF-EXPRESSION

So far, we have been talking about exercises that may or may not be expressive. Creative drama implies self-expression, hence the necessity of the participant's involvement beyond merely imitating an action. How does he feel when the kite soars high in the air? Who is winning the ball game? How do we know? How many jacks has he won? Does he enjoy picking flowers in the woods? What are his feelings as he fishes, or rows his boat against a strong current? These are the kinds of questions we may ask as the players grow more confident.

We are not concerned with the quality of the child's performance yet; rather, we are concerned with his developing freedom and the ability to express himself. Each child has something to say, something that he alone can offer, provided he is given the opportunity and the encouragement. No one has put this any better than Hughes Mearns:

> You have something to say. Something of your very own. Try to say it. Don't be ashamed of any real thought or feeling you may have. Don't undervalue it. Don't let the fear of what others may think of it prevent you from saying it. Perhaps not aloud but to yourself. You have something to say, something no one in the world has ever said in just your way of saying it—but the thing itself is not half so important to you as what the saying will be to you. [3]

COMMUNICATION

Although communication is the responsibility of the formal theatre, and therefore not our primary concern, there comes a time when the participants want to share their work in creative drama, and this sharing involves communication skills. It has been stated that, for the younger child, public performance is undesirable; for the older child, under the right conditions, it may do

3. Hughes Mearns, *Creative Power* (New York: Dover Publications, 1958), p. 259.

no harm. But unless the class is exceptionally small, there will be periods of time when some are observers and some are participants. It is to these periods that communication pertains. This is the audience that is not an audience in the usual sense. On the other hand, the observers want to see and hear, and they become deeply involved in the situation. The participant soon learns that he must move on to the next stage of development: that of making himself clear, of being heard and understood, and of being interesting—in short, of communicating.

Communication comes about quite naturally in the discussion periods that follow each playing. One procedure, used successfully by many teachers, is the playing, discussing, replaying method. Or, to describe it more fully, the teacher begins with the story or situation, which she either reads or tells to the group. This is followed by class discussion, in which the characters are enumerated and described, the plot is reviewed, and the scenes are planned. No matter how simple the situation, it is important that it be thoroughly understood before the first playing. The group will decide which characters are necessary to the plot, which ones may be eliminated, or whether others should be added. Often a story that is excellent to read takes considerable adapting to make it good drama.

When the teacher is sure that the group has all details well in mind, he is ready to suggest playing it. Asking for volunteers usually brings a show of hands from which the teacher will choose the first cast. The players come forward, while the rest of the class remain in their seats. After they have finished the scene, the teacher leads a general discussion. This evaluation period covers the plot and the way the children have handled it. The players themselves always have criticisms to offer, but the observers also have reactions to share. Children's criticism is honest and their observations are keen. Because the observers anticipate playing the story themselves, they are as deeply involved as the players. Such questions as these help to guide the discussion:

1. Did they tell the story?
2. Was anything important left out?
3. What did you like about the way they began it?
4. Did we understand the ending?
5. When we play it the next time, what might we add or leave out?

The questions are naturally more specific when we have a particular story in mind. There will be further discussion of characters, their relationships and motives, but these usually come after a second or third playing. Finally, when the teacher feels that a number of important points have been made and the class is growing eager to resume playing, a second group is given a chance to play the same scene. This group, having the benefit of observation and discussion, will probably succeed in developing more detail and clearer characterizations. This does not necessarily happen, for the first group to volunteer may have been the stronger.

At any rate, when the second cast has finished, a new evaluation period is in order. It is always interesting to hear the different kinds of comments that this second discussion evokes. A third playing, a fourth, even a fifth may follow, depending on the interest of the children and the length of the period. It is a good idea to take the cue from them as to when to move on to the next scene. As long as the scene holds their interest, they will continue to grow in their understanding of it. The teacher will become increasingly sensitive to their involvement as they work together.

As the group gains experience, its ability to communicate increases. Younger children, because of their more limited vocabulary, communicate more easily through body movement and facial expression. Older children are not only better able to express themselves verbally but also enjoy improvising dialogue. The adult student, depending on his background and previous experience, will feel more comfortable in one medium or the other. If the teacher begins with movement and pantomime, however, he will find that dialogue flows easily once the player has overcome his self-consciousness.

PROBLEMS IN CREATIVE PLAYING

Sooner or later, the teacher of creative drama, or the classroom teacher who uses creative drama, is bound to encounter problems of one sort or another. They may be simple problems of time and space: periods that are too short; space that is inadequate; classes that are too large. These problems can be solved, though the solutions are not always easy. They call for adaptability and ingenuity on the part of the leader, and present difficulties that are discouraging and sometimes defeating. Other problems confronting the leader, even under ideal circumstances, are the individual problems he finds in the group. It has been stated many times that self-consciousness is the greatest obstacle to creative playing. Self-consciousness, or fear, takes many forms. The shy child and the show-off are the two most frequently encountered. The insensitive child is also a problem for he usually lacks friends and so finds it difficult to work cooperatively in a group. And, finally, there is the handicapped child whose physical, mental, or emotional problems pose special difficulties for the leader.

There is great interest in drama as therapy at the present time, but this is a special field for which the average teacher—even the specialist in creative drama techniques—is not trained. Every teacher is aware of the therapeutic value of the arts, even though the primary purposes are educational, social, and aesthetic. But because there are, in every group, those children (or adults) who experience real difficulty in expressing themselves, consideration must be given to their problems. If the problem is severe, it should be handled by a therapist and not the classroom teacher; in many cases, an intelligent, sympathetic effort to build self-respect and bring fun into the lives of the players can go a long way toward solving the problems.

Timidity

The timid child is the most common problem the teacher encounters, but one that creative drama can help. Such a child is usually quiet in a class, preferring to sit in the back of the room and let others do the talking. His fear of making a mistake, or even of being noticed, causes him to withdraw, even though down underneath he is eager to express his ideas and take part. He is usually not a happy child, for his feeling of inadequacy inhibits both expression and communication.

The little girl who never volunteers will need special encouragement to try doing a part, no matter how simple. The teacher who gives her this opportunity to show her peers what she can do may be taking the first step in helping her build a better self-image. If the child is successful, it will be less difficult for her a second time. The teacher will be wise to praise her warmly for whatever contribution she makes. Remember that, for the little girl, the very fact of getting up in front of the class is a big achievement.

There was eight-year-old Patty, who was referred to a Saturday-morning play group because of her excessive shyness. At first she took part only when the whole group was moving, and then because it would have been more conspicuous to remain seated than to get up with the others. After several weeks (probably five or six sessions), she did a pantomime of a child finding a kitten. Her honest joy and tenderness as she fondled its soft body drew spontaneous admiration from the other boys and girls in the class. This was the breakthrough. From that day Patty's eagerness to play was apparent. Her voice was small—inaudible at first—but grew stronger in proportion to her growing self-confidence. This was no sudden miracle; in fact, it took three years for the transformation to take place. Patty's feeling of inadequacy had been so deep-seated that many successes were necessary to convince her that she had something to offer that her peers would accept. She became not only one of the most vocal children in the group—she became an unquestioned leader. Whether she would have found her way anyhow, no one can say.

Creative drama as a technique was deliberately used, and the change during her three years in the class was striking.

Exhibitionism

The show-off is just as much in need of help as the shy child, but he rarely elicits the same kind of sympathetic attention. His problem is also one of uneasiness, and in trying to prove his importance, he does all the wrong things. His behavior will range from monopolizing the class discussion to interfering with the work of the other children (pinching, pushing, interrupting). He may deliberately use a wrong word for the sake of a laugh. He is conscious of the effect he is having, and so has difficulty concentrating on what he is doing.

An example is John, a nervous little fellow of nine, with facial mannerisms and a habit of interrupting. John was accepted by the others: he amused them. For more than a semester John's work was erratic. He seemed unable to get involved in a part for more than a minute or two, and then he would look around the room to see what effect he was having on the rest of the class. There was no sudden or dramatic incident that effected a change; rather, it was a long period of working under the patient guidance of a teacher who took every opportunity to praise his honest expression and help him to find satisfaction in getting attention legitimately. By the end of a year, John was able to work cooperatively with the group much of the time and forego showing off. His problem was still not entirely solved, but he had learned something of the give-and-take of working together, and the pleasure of recognition that comes from work that is honest.

Arline was a high school student, whose weight problem caused her great embarrassment. She expressed this by comic behavior and exhibitionistic antics. For years Arline had been the class clown, deliberately tripping, using a wrong word, or misunderstanding a simple question. In this way she made people laugh at what she did before they had a chance to laugh at the way she looked. Successful coping with her problem in this manner had created a behavior pattern that was hard to break. Through improvised drama, where there was no audience to impress, Arline gradually came to understand something of motivation and, finally, to trust and accept herself. True, the slapstick occasionally took place, but less and less often as the years passed and she was able to get the laughs for the right reasons. Beneath the clowning there was an intelligent, sensitive adolescent, who today is a successful educator. Undoubtedly there were other methods that could have been used effectively; but Arline liked theatre and elected to participate. It was obvious that through the use of creative drama she learned how to believe in herself and perhaps to lay the foundation for her future work in special education.

Sometimes the teacher may be forced to ask the disruptive child to go back to her seat. Not punishment, but the consequences of unacceptable behavior will teach her that creative dramatics demands consideration and teamwork.

The Isolate

The isolate or loner is often a child who cannot relate to the group. He or she may work hard, have good ideas, and the ability to present them effectively, but always in isolation. It must be said that this is not necessarily a problem. Indeed, it may be indicative of superior talent and high motivation. Independence is a desired goal, whereas isolation, which is the result of an inability to relate to others, is a problem. Through movement and dance all members of a group are drawn together naturally; they discover the meaning of interdependence as well as individual effort. For the person who has real difficulty in relating to his or her peers, this is a natural way of becoming a part of the group.

Insensitivity

The insensitive player is similar to, but different from, the show-off in that he is usually rejected by the others and does not understand why. His clowning brings no laughter, and he has great difficulty in making friends. He tends to reject the ideas of others and criticizes their efforts, often harshly. Playing a variety of roles may cause him to gain insights and develop an awareness of the feelings of others. Patient attention to his problem in human relations may, in time, help him to listen, and learn to accept suggestions from his peers. His is a difficult problem, but once he has begun to feel some small acceptance, he will prefer belonging to going it alone. Again, we are not talking about the extreme personality disorder but about the human being who is experiencing difficulty in working cooperatively with others.

Physical Handicaps

Children with special handicaps need special attention. Their teachers need special orientation to their special needs. While the classroom teacher may have a child who is crippled or who has a speech defect, he is not going to be equipped to practice therapy, or given time for all the help these special cases merit. If, however, he has one or two children in a group who are handicapped, he will treat them essentially as he does the others. These children need sympathy, understanding, and encouragement. The teacher must know what can be expected of them and then try to adapt the activities to their capabilities. Often such a child will be in therapy, and if the teacher can work with the therapist, he will be able to receive helpful suggestions as to his approach.

For example, Marcia, who has a cleft lip and is seeing the speech therapist regularly, will benefit from an opportunity to use speech in a legitimate and pleasurable way. The teacher will not have the time to give her all the attention she needs, but in treating her like the others and encouraging her in her efforts, he will be contributing to her social growth and, in some measure, to her treatment.

It is a common phenomenon that the stutterer often speaks fluently when cast in a play. While there is no proof that acting ever cured a stutter, the child who tends to repeat, or whose anxiety causes him to stutter, often finds relief in speaking as someone else. Regular participation in either informal or formal dramatics may have a therapeutic effect in encouraging successful oral expression.

All people gain in self-respect when their ideas are accepted and put into effect. The child with a problem has a special need for acceptance, and the teacher tries to find the best way in which he can meet it. Creative drama provides an ideal opportunity to help the timid child overcome his inhibitions; provides the show-off with a better way of getting attention; guides the insensitive child to some awareness of the feelings of others; works with the handicapped to find his avenue of self-expression; and broadens the horizons of the disadvantaged. "How drama can be used today, how the play-acting impulse can be harnessed to help people grow, to develop greater sensitivity to themselves and to their fellow human beings, to become more spontaneous and outgoing, to discard old fears and insecurities, has attracted the interest of many who are working in the various fields of human relations."[4]

Today's children are subjected to pressures and demands, which, if not greater than in the past, are certainly new and different. Not only inner city children, but the children of affluent and suburban communities reflect the changes in values and mores. The pressures they feel often result in bizarre and unpredictable behavior, causing problems for teachers and creating difficulties when freedom is encouraged. The creative drama instructor is particularly vulnerable to these problems, for she is dealing with the emotional and social, as well as the intellectual, aspects of child development.

Although freedom is essential to creativity, it is often necessary to impose restraints in the beginning, or until children become more comfortable with the group and the leader. Social mobility, broken homes, television programs, the violence in our society, and economic problems are among the causes given for discipline problems. It is not the purpose of this text to

4. Jack Simos, *Social Growth Through Play Production* (New York: Association Press, 1957), p. 16.

explore the causes, but it is important for us to be sensitive to unusual behavior and to try to deal with it with understanding, compassion, and firmness.

THE OPEN CLASSROOM

The open classroom, about which we have heard so much in the past few years, offers one of the best opportunities for small creative dramatics groups. Instead of classes of twenty-five to forty, so often found in the crowded city classrooms, this concept of learning provides both time and space for special interest groups. I have visited several open classes where small groups of children worked on favorite stories and theatre games under the guidance of assistants or student teachers majoring in the dramatic arts. In nursery school and kindergarten classes provision was made for dramatic play, and participation was encouraged. Pantomime claimed the interest of third-graders in one school, with twelve children participating at a time. Not only does the flexible physical arrangement of the open classroom accommodate the arts, but in working with fewer children at a time, the leader can accomplish more than is possible when the entire class is involved. The relaxed atmosphere also helps to free children who are intimidated by a more formal procedure. For the so-called normal child the open classroom encourages creativity and enterprise; for the child with a problem, however, it offers much more: time, space, more individual attention, and an opportunity to try out ideas in small groups. Although the open classroom is less popular today than it was ten years ago, it is still to be found, and it has great value for the teaching of creative drama.

SUMMARY

To summarize, imagination is the spark that sets off the creative impulse. Concentration (the capacity to hold an idea long enough to do something about it) and organization (the design or arrangement of the parts) are necessary to satisfying self-expression. Communication—the bridge to others—comes last, and is less the concern of creative drama than of the formal play.

In all creative work there are obstacles. These must be recognized and overcome. They may be problems of time and space, or the more difficult ones of human relations. The wise leader learns first to identify the problems and then to look for solutions. She will remember that she is neither therapist nor theatre director but teacher, guiding players, whatever their age, in the medium of informal drama. Brian Way has suggested the role of the teacher in these words:

Schools do not exist to develop actors but to develop people, and one of the major factors in developing people is that of preserving and enriching to its fullest the human capacity to give full and undivided attention to any matter in hand at any given moment.[5]

Activities and exercises are suggested, not as ends in themselves but as means to self-expression and a springboard to other more extensive projects. Some prose and poetry are also included as illustrations of what can be used and how; with a point of view and a creative approach, it is hoped that the leader will be able to find additional materials relevant to her own and the group's interests and needs.

5. Brian Way, *Development Through Drama* (New York: Humanities Press, 1967), p. 15.

3

MOVEMENT, RHYTHMS, AND DRAMATIC PLAY

Movement is a natural response to a stimulus and, therefore, an important element of drama. Indeed, movement, dance, mime, and drama merge in the expression of feelings and ideas. Theatre began with movement; its origins were closely linked with religious and magical rites. Gradually the elements of conflict, character, plot, and dialogue were added. When this happened, the theatre as an art form was born.

Early man, in attempting to order his universe, explain natural phenomena, and pray to his gods, used rhythmic movement to express himself; this, in time, became dance. An entire tribe might take part, or perhaps only the young men, or the most skilled of the dancers. As the movements were repeated, they became set and took on special meanings. These meanings were understood by both performers and spectators and were taught to the young, thus serving an educative as well as a religious purpose.

35

Adelphi University Children's Center for the Creative Arts, courtesy Julie Thompson. Photograph by George H. Meyer.

Every society has its rituals, and ritual and theatre are never far apart. Traditional garments, body paint, and masks are worn to enhance the performance. Though not theatre in our modern sense, these tribal dances are nevertheless closely akin to it in the use of body, voice, rhythm, and costume to help express strong feelings and ideas in a form the community understands.

As danced movement, therefore, drama is the oldest of the arts. Out of the rites and rituals of dance came myth; and out of myth, story or plot. It was but a short step from plot to play. The earliest theatrical performances in the western world are generally believed to have taken place in Greece along the Aegean with the worship of Dionysus, the God of Fertility. The chanting of a chorus with a leader developed into dialogue spoken by actors; by the fifth century B.C. the dramatic forms of comedy and tragedy had evolved. There were other forms of theatre before this, if theatre is defined as performance communicated through voice and action to an audience actively engaged in the experience. If, on the other hand, theatre is defined as including a body of dramatic literature, then the Greek theatre is the first and perhaps the greatest theatre known.

CHILDREN AND MOVEMENT

Like primitive man, the preschool child uses his body to express his strongest emotions and communicate his needs and desires. A child's posture, for instance, shows us how he feels, regardless often of what he may say. We read much about body language these days. This form of nonverbal communication includes any posture, reflexive, or nonreflexive movement of the body that conveys emotion to the observer. Although most of this popular writing concerns the adult, the attitudes and feelings of children are just as clearly revealed by their movements and facial expressions. A leader can learn much about the members of a group of any age from the postures they assume, their ability to relax, and the use they make of the various parts of their bodies.

A young child tends to express physically what an adult states in words. For example, when asked how a horse moves, a small child is more apt to gallop than to describe the gait. Asked the height of a very tall person, he will stand on tiptoe to reach as high as he can. Although the majority of children walk before they can talk, this early use of the body to express emotions and describe or give information is a phenomenon common to most boys and girls, regardless of their linguistic development.

In addition to these conscious and unconscious expressions, however, there is the physical pleasure that a child derives from moving, a pleasure that leads into play, dance, sports, and exercise for its own sake. Today, unfortunately, television constantly bombards the eyes and ears of children, giving information of all kinds, it is true, but at the expense of their movement experience and natural creative response. In bringing children indoors, they are made passive spectators rather than active participants in games and sports in open areas. Most children enjoy moving their bodies and discovering different ways of exploring a space. As they gain physical controls, they prefer running to walking, and they enjoy finding new methods of locomotion that are energetic and fast. Running, skipping, galloping, hopping, jumping, leaping, and rolling stretch the muscles and help the child to gain a mastery of his body as he tries out all the different things he can do with it. Because movement is so natural an expression, it is the ideal way of beginning work in creative drama. Experienced teachers of young children know this and will progress from rhythmic movement to dramatic play.

Peter Slade uses the term "natural dance" to describe dance which is not tied to a set of rules or complicated techniques but rather, is improvised and personal in style. He further identifies it as the bridge between the primitive and the sophisticated, or between natural inclination and a disciplined art form.[1]

Teachers and leaders of older groups find that their goals may be reached more easily and quickly if, instead of a verbal approach, they begin with physical activity. Actors call these activities "warm-ups" and declare them an effective way to relax and tone the muscles of their backs, legs, arms, and necks in preparation for a performance. Through rhythmic exercise a group can be drawn together and released in an objective and pleasurable way.

Rhythm, an element of movement, supplies structure and enjoyment. Rhythm is apparent in many of the games and chants of children and is the basis of music and dance. In fact, music and dance are frequently taught together through the medium of song, rhythm, and the employment of toy or rhythm instruments. This is called "music-movement" and is advocated by many educators. Dalcroze thought of using the body as a musical instrument by treating rhythm, with its roots in physical movement, as the organizer of musical elements.

Classes in movement are most successful when taught in a large room, where students have plenty of space in which to move freely. Too large an area, such as a gymnasium or a playground, on the other hand, presents problems; for large, unconfined space can lead to chaos, not freedom, dispersing the group rather than bringing it together. Therefore boundaries should be established and maintained.

Leotards, pants, jump suits, or comfortable old clothing of some kind

1. Peter Slade, *Natural Dance* (London: Hodder and Stoughton, Ltd., 1977).

should always be worn; rhythm sandals or bared feet prevent slipping on a hardwood floor. Piano accompaniment is an asset, if the leader can play or has an accompanist; if not, a drum is perfectly satisfactory. Later on, recorded music will help suggest mood and possible characterization. In the beginning, however, and for most purposes, percussion instruments are all the leader needs to give the beat and suggest or change rhythms. One advantage of the drum, incidentally, is that it permits the leader to move about freely and watch the group. This freedom of movement is not possible while playing a piano or changing tapes and records.

In a movement class it's usually a good idea to begin work with the entire group, unless it is so large or the room so small that the participants bump into each other. In that case, the leader should divide the class into two parts, working first with one, then with the other, and alternating every few minutes so as to hold the interest of all. Beginning with a large circle, the leader should beat a good rhythm for walking. When all are moving easily and without self-consciousness, the beat can be changed to something faster, such as a trot or a run. Shifting the rhythm to a gallop, a skip, a hop, a jump, then back to a slow-motion walk is not only good exercise, but it holds the participants' attention as they listen for the changes. Depending on the pupils' ages, more complicated rhythms can be added. The participants themselves can take turns beating the drum or clapping new combinations. Why rhythmic movement first? According to Marjorie Dorian, teacher of dance and author of books on the subject, it encourages spontaneous movement within a disciplined framework. This is the goal of the teacher of creative drama as well as the teacher of dance.

> The arts, through the common denominator of rhythm, can best be served by an introduction to rhythmic movement, both disciplined and expressive. Through rhythm the child experiences the dynamic changes of opposites: soft and loud, fast and slow, much and little: qualities that make us sensitive to everything around us. Through the measurement of time and space he becomes aware of the limitations that eventually give him strength to pursue other disciplines.[2]

As teachers, we have tended to think of creative drama as concerned primarily with developing intellectual and linguistic abilities, whereas we have thought of movement as concerned only with the control and use of the body. Actually, movement and body language are part of creative drama. It is the combined mental, physical, vocal, and emotional involvment that distinguishes creative drama from all other art forms and gives its special value.

2. Marjorie Dorian, *Ethnic Stories for Children to Dance* (San Francisco: BBB Associates, 1978).

Rhythmic Activities

The following activities are designed to help the student discover the drama in movement. In the early stages the leader works within the group, moving out when the participants are secure and able to move without her support. She does not *show* the groups what to do, but she supports, in every way possible, honest effort, involvement, and the development of individual ideas.

1. Take the group on a journey over a desert, across a river, up a hill, over both smooth and rough ground, over slippery rocks, through tall grass, and into an open field. Vivid imaging stimulated by rhythmic accompaniment make this a favorite game of young children and a challenge to older ones.

2. Have the group listen to different beats and then imagine what gaits or characters they suggest, which might be an Indian chief striding, an old man shuffling, a toddler, a young woman running for a train, a delivery boy with a heavy load, or a night watchman on his rounds. Try moving like these characters.

3. Do the same things with moods. Have the group first listen and then tell whether the beats sound happy, sad, proud, excited, sneaky, angry, or shy. Have the group move together to the same beats, expressing these moods.

4. "Snail" is a good beginning game for establishing a common rhythm. Have the group form a single file, each putting his or her hands on the shoulders of the person in front. The leader moves to the center of the room with the line following. Chanting "snail, snail, snail, snail," the group moves into a shell-like formation. When the players can move in no further, they reverse and move back into their original circle.

5. Rhythms can suggest people working or moving in unison. Try beats that describe the following: an assembly line, a marching band, robots, motorcycles, athletes warming up, workmen using picks, joggers, etc.

6. Not only young children but adult actors enjoy suggesting different animals through rhythmic movement. Try to find rhythms for the following:

horses	chickens	mice
cats	cranes	frogs
rabbits	kangaroos	sea gulls
snakes	monkeys	pigeons

7. An imaginative exercise that requires a little more experience is the creation of fantastic creatures. Ask the class to imagine strange or

The National Committee, Arts for the Handicapped, courtesy Wendy Perks. Photograph by John Reynolds.

fanciful animals and then to show with their bodies what the animals are like. How do they look? What are they made of? What do they eat? How do they move? Breathe? Sleep? This can be a source of fun and relaxation as well as a challenge.

8. The following is a quieting exercise to be used after vigorous movement. Sitting in a circle on the floor, the group creates different rhythms and sounds. Clapping hands, snapping fingers, tapping knees, and brushing the floor softly with the hands are among the sounds that can be made in this position. Have each child put two, then three of these sounds together in a rhythmic sequence. The group listens carefully and tries to repeat the sequence.

From Rhythms to Dramatic Play

Dramatic play, the child's earliest effort to reproduce life situations and to try out the roles of others, is based on imitation. Through imitating the actions and behavior of those around him, the young child masters reality and gains self-confidence. Movement thus merges with improvisation, as the drama takes shape. Words, the last element to be added, will be scanty at first, for the vocabulary of the preschool child is limited. As a matter of fact, much older players in creative drama classes tend to say less than they have planned and feel. Sooner or later, however, the need for words is felt; when that moment comes, natural dialogue is born. This is the reason why movement is preferred to a verbal beginning for every age level.

Virginia Koste, in her book, *Child Play, Rehearsal for Life*, observes that "Ironically one backlash of the creativity craze has been the neglect, the ignoring of imitation with all of its implications in human learning and art."[3] She urges us to restore imitation to its rightful place, for it is through observation and imitation that children learn. Knowledge of others and their ways of doing things enables children to invent new forms and create dramas and characters of their own. "Holding the mirror up to nature" is a necessary function; imitation is a fault only when it discourages inventiveness and encourages dependency and copying.

Observation and Imitation

Here is an exercise for observation and imitation that younger children enjoy. It is suggesting movement through the "——ly" game. The entire class can play it together, or one person can begin and the others follow his or her interpretation. In this way every child is assured of the opportunity to create a movement. Words might be: lazily, quickly, slowly, curiously, wearily, sleepily, noiselessly, loudly, angrily, happily, joyfully, thankfully, sheepishly, etc. Incidentally, it is also a way of learning new words.

Similar to this is the beating out of rhythms. Each child beats a rhythm for the others to follow. After each has had several turns, variations of the game can be played. One child can go into the center and begin a rhythm, change it suddenly, and tap the one who will begin the next. This has endless possibilities and is an excellent exercise for encouraging close observation and imitation.

In the preceding activities we were concerned with rhythms and the use of the body. All movement is concerned, however, with *where* and *how* the body is used.

3. Virginia Koste, *Child Play* (New Orleans: Anchorage 1978), p. 19.

A. *Where* the body moves refers to:
   a. level (high, low, medium)
   b. direction (forward, backward, left, right, in diagonals)
   c. shape of the movement
B. *How* the body moves refers to:
   a. energy (much or little)
   b. time (sudden or sustained)
   c. flow (free or tight)

The next group of exercises may be used to work on the *where* or the *how* of moving. Try the following to show *where* movement takes place.

Low movement: caterpillar, duck, seal, shallow pool of water, young plant emerging from the earth

High movement: airplane, high cloud, person on stilts, wire walker, kite

Horizontal movement: swinging bell, elephant's trunk, lion pacing in a cage, someone paddling a canoe, someone on a swing

Up-and-down movement: seesaw, plane, bird, bat, ball bouncing, elevator, falling star, Jack-in-the-box, rocket, piece of machinery

Try the following to show *how* movement takes place.

Fast movement: arrow, fire engine, express train, leaf in a storm, jet plane, speedboat, racehorse, top, skateboard

Slow movement: clock, farm horse, melting ice, tugboat, turtle, freight train pulling out of the station, movie in slow motion

Turning movement: curling smoke, merry-go-round, revolving door, spool of thread, figure skating, top

Strong, heavy movement: chopping wood, bulldozer, tank, stormy waves, digging in concrete

Soft, light movement: balloon, butterfly, flickering candle, soap bubble, kitten, kite, elf, leaf

Sharp movement: bucking bronco, cuckoo clock, cricket, grasshopper, juggler, woodpecker

Floppy, loose movement: clothes on a line, rag doll, mop, loose sail, straw hat blowing down the street, long hair blowing, flag in the breeze

Smooth movement: airplane, cat, fish swimming, syrup pouring, skating, rainbow forming, automobile on a throughway

Twisted movement: octopus, pretzel, knot, piece of driftwood, crumpled paper, tangled chain

Change in movement:
1. a candle standing tall and straight burns down to a pool of wax
2. a piece of elastic, stretched and then released
3. a paper drifting to the sidewalk, then picked up by a sudden gust of wind
4. a board slowly breaking away from the side of an old building, then falling off
5. a toy train moving rapidly, running down and stopping; then being rewound and repeating the sequence

The following images suggest being, using or doing, and feeling through movement.

Water
Being: bubbles, rushing water, rain, whirlpool, quiet pool, surf
Using: blowing bubbles, carrying water, hosing the lawn, water skiing, wading in shallow water
Feeling: weightlessness of floating, walking in water, walking against the tide

Fire
Being: bonfire blazing, forest fire raging, smoke puffing, match being lighted
Using: building a fire, putting out a fire, being warmed by a fire
Feeling: hot, warm, sleepy from a fire, choking from the smoke of a fire

Air
Being: soft summer air with only a slight breeze blowing
Using: pumping air into a tire, blowing up a balloon, breathing good, clean air
Feeling: warm air, cold air, polluted air, pleasant cool air

Try to suggest the following ideas in dance; then in pantomime. They may be expressed quite differently or they may be much the same, depending on the one moving. Each student must move as he or she feels, for there is no right or wrong way. At this stage sincere involvement is the major goal.

1. offering a prayer
   giving thanks
   asking for rain in a time of drought
2. casting a magic spell on someone
   being under a magic spell
   trying to throw off a spell

3. feeling frightened
   investigating the cause of your fear
   feeling relief at discovering that your fear was groundless
4. feeling joyful
   showing what has made you so happy
   sharing your joy with others
5. feeling very angry
   showing what has made you so angry
   resolving your anger by doing something about it

Now take one of the above ideas and combine the three parts of it so as to create a simple story.

Working with partners

The activities so far have been planned for the whole class. Working in pairs or with partners is more difficult, because the movements must be synchronized. Try the following simple exercises as a starter.

1. Have each member of the group take a partner. Have them put their hands on each other's shoulders and then push to see who is the stronger. Working with a partner in this way helps the individual move from group work to individual work without feeling self-conscious.
2. Next try the theatre game of having one person lead another whose eyes are closed. Have the class walk around the room in pairs until all are moving easily together. Reverse roles and try it again.
3. Divide the group into pairs, with one person standing at each end of the room. To the beat of the drum, they:
   (a) walk toward each other, meet and part
   (b) walk toward each other, meet and clash
   (c) walk toward each other, meet and go off together
4. Have one person begin a movement and the partner pick it up and continue it.
5. Have one person begin to make or do something and the partner complete it.

Telling stories in movement

Pure dance has no describable story. Mime, on the other hand, uses movement to narrate or describe. It varies from the classic form of mime that captures the essence of a person or action to the imitative that reproduces an action realistically and in detail. There's a trend at the present time to add sound to enhance the situation or help tell the story. This is a new direction in the art of mime and requires as much skill as silent theatre. All forms of movement and mime demand concentration, practice, and precision. In time, a personal style is developed and characterizes the work.

Myths and legends lend themselves to mime and mimetic movement. They are generally simple in plot and deal with universal themes and feelings. The more complicated the narrative, the less easy it is to dance, and therefore the greater the temptation to use words to explain it. Because of their simplicity the following stories can be told in dance, in mime or movement, or with improvised dialogue. Try telling them all three ways. Be sure that everyone is thoroughly familiar with the story before attempting to do anything with it. First beat a rhythm on the drum and have the entire group try telling the story in movement. Then, perhaps, individuals will have suggestions as to what more can be done with it.

SEWALI AND THE SNAKE

There was once in East Africa a brave young warrior named Sewali. He had heard tales of a great snake, Sesota, who killed and

National Theatre Workshop of the Handicapped, New York City. Photograph by Pat Hutchings, S.J. Courtesy of Rick Curry, S.J.

terrified his people, and he was troubled. One day Sewali went to the chief and told him that he wanted to go out and conquer the great serpent. The chief was pleased with Sewali, though he doubted that the young brave could overcome a monster that the strongest warriors had failed to capture. Nevertheless, he gave his permission for Sewali to go.

Sewali put a large jar on his shoulder and went into the jungle. When at last he reached the snake's cave, he took off his necklace and wrapped it around the neck of the jar. The great snake saw the sparkling beads of the necklace and was attracted to them. Cautiously he approached the jar. After a few minutes he glided inside it. Quick as a flash Sewali put the lid on the jar, thus imprisoning the snake. Then, dragging the heavy jar behind him, he returned to his village and proudly displayed his captive. All the people danced joyfully around the jar in celebration of Sewali's brave and clever deed, for they knew that this was the end of the feared Sesota.

THE SIX SONS OF ANANSI

The West African tales of Anansi the Spider make excellent material for both dance and dramatization. There are many of these stories, but one of the best known is the tale of Anansi's six sons.

Anansi was a clever trickster, whose popularity came from his ability to outwit others and thus help human beings. In this story, however, it is he who is in great danger and his six sons come to his rescue. They are named See Trouble, Road Builder, River Drinker, Game Skinner, Stone Thrower, and Cushion.

Anansi was lost. First to discover it was his oldest son, See Trouble. See Trouble saw his father in grave danger across the river so he went to his brother, Road Builder. Road Builder quickly built a bridge across the river, but before Anansi could cross it, he was swallowed by a huge fish. This time River Drinker came to the rescue and drank all the water. This enabled Game Skinner to cut open the great fish and rescue their father. Before Anansi could escape, however, a huge falcon swooped down and lifted him high in the air. Then Stone Thrower threw a rock, hitting the falcon, causing him to drop his prey. Anansi fell to earth, landing on the body of his sixth son, Cushion, and thus was saved.

Anansi did not know to which son he should be most grateful, therefore he implored the God Nyame to reward the one who had done the greatest deed. Nyame could not decide, either, so he took the Globe of Light into the sky in honor of the six sons of Anansi, the spider.

THE TURNIP

The old Russian folk tale of pulling up the turnip can be told completely in movement. Although the case is composed of individuals rather than groups, there are so many characters and the tale is so short that everyone in the class can have a turn. It is a very amusing situation, but also one that requires skill and control to prevent its becoming a series of pratfalls.

It was autumn and time for the turnips to be harvested. Grandfather went out to the garden and bent down to pull the first one. But this turnip was different from any turnips he had ever planted. It refused to come up! So, after trying unsuccessfully with all his might, he called his wife to help him.

When grandmother came out and saw what he wanted, she put her arms around his waist, and together they pulled and pulled. Still the turnip would not budge. Then granddaughter came out to the garden to see what was happening. Putting her arm around grandmother's waist, she pulled grandmother, who pulled grandfather, who pulled the turnip. But the turnip refused to come up.

The story continues in this way with any number of characters included, each one pulling the one before him. Sometimes it is told with the granddaughter's dog pulling her and a beetle pulling the dog, followed by a second, third, and fourth beetle all pulling at the end of the line.

Finally, when all pull together, the turnip comes up!

THE RAVEN TALES

The Raven stories of the North American Indians are excellent for either dance or improvisation on any age level. Raven was a creator of the world, but like Anansi, he was a trickster as well. Legends tell how Raven used his wits to defeat evil or greedy spirits and so help human beings in trouble. The story of how he stole the stars, moon, and sun, though complicated, can be cut down to the simple tale of a people rescued from living in darkness.

Raven, by changing himself from a bird into a human form, gained access to the house of the powerful chief, who kept the sun, moon, and stars in boxes under lock and key. Raven succeeded in persuading the unsuspecting grandfather to give him the box containing the stars. Stealthily, he took it out and tossed them to his people. But the stars alone did not give enough light, so Raven returned to the chief's house. Knowing where the boxes were hidden, he watched his chance; then, when no one was looking, he took the second box containing the moon. But it, also, gave too little light. Raven knew that the remaining box must contain the sun, so he went back for the third time to the chief's house and stole the sun.

One of the legends has it that he came to the bank of a river and asked to be helped across with the heavy box, but the people refused assistance. Finally, angered and out of patience, he released the sun. The sudden burst of brilliant light terrified the people; those wearing the skins of animals fled into the forest where they became the "forest people." Those wearing garments made of sea animals dived into the water and were thereafter known as "sea people." Those clad in bird clothing flew into the air and became the "sky people." Thus the legend of Raven's theft continues on into an explanation of how the earth, sea, and sky people came to be.

Any part of this story, or several parts of it, can be told entirely in movement; it can also be told with sound added or played with simple dialogue. One program of Raven tales, developed by university students for children's audiences, began with an explanation of the totem pole, four of which were used to mark off the playing space. Then three of the Raven tales were played with choreographed movement and dialogue. The performers wore leotards and elaborate masks, which they put on and took off as they assumed the roles of the different characters.

Following the performance, the children in the audience were invited to participate in a variety of activities suggested or stimulated by the performance: improvisation, dance, and mask-making. For the children who took part in these activities the afternoon provided rich experiences in theatre, folklore, and creative expression.

The leader can find other stories and discover what the group can do by using movement only to tell them. Nursery rhymes make good material for young children. For older children and adults, legends and myths suggest a variety of rhythms and movements. Modern situations are also good and may be preferred by older children.

SUMMARY

Movement, the basis of play, ritual, games, dance, and theatre, is a natural beginning for work in creative drama. Physically, the whole body is involved: torso, arms, legs, head, and neck. Through the use of the body, muscles are stretched and relaxed. Posture and coordination improve with regular exercise. Because the entire group can take part at one time, the possibility of self-consciousness is lessened. Persons of all ages and backgrounds usually find it easier at first to become involved through movement rather than through verbalization. This is particularly true of younger children, those for whom English is a second language, and persons with special problems and needs. Often in the rhythms and patterns of a child's movement the problems in his inner life are revealed. This is why movement and dance are recommended as treatment, serving both diagnostic and therapeutic purposes.

Imitation and observation are as much a part of movement as creativity. The leader encourages imagination but discourages the cliché. Through movement, therefore, children experience both discipline and freedom. By moving into the rituals of the group (and here the word is used in its broadest sense), a feeling of belonging is engendered. Rhythm, that underlying flow and beat, captures the mover in what was described earlier as an experience both objective and pleasurable. Taught together, rhythms and dramatic play provide a sound foundation for acting. "Dance-drama" encompasses the disciplines of both arts and is, therefore, a powerful tool for creative expression.

4

PANTOMIME:
THE NEXT
STEP

Pantomime is the art of conveying ideas without words. Children enjoy pantomime, and for the young child this is an excellent way to begin creative drama. Since many of his thoughts are spoken entirely through the body, the five- or six-year-old finds pantomime a natural means of expression. Group pantomimes of the simplest sort challenge the imagination and sharpen awareness. In kindergarten, such basic movements as walking, running, skipping, and galloping prepare for the creative use of rhythms. Music can set the mood for people marching in a parade, horses galloping on the plains, toads hopping in a field, racing cars on a track, or children skipping on a fine autumn day. In other words, rhythmic movement becomes dramatic when the participant makes use of it to become someone or something other than himself.

For older children and adults, pantomime is advocated because it encourages the use of the entire body and relieves the players of having to think of dialogue. Here,

51

New Canaan Country Day School, courtesy Mary Perrine.

also, group pantomime should precede individual work. Familiar activities such as playing ball, flying kites, running for a bus, or hunting for a lost object get the group on its feet and moving freely. If the entire class works at one time, self-consciousness disappears and involvement is hastened. Fifteen or twenty minutes of this sort of activity, changed frequently enough to hold the group's interest, makes for relaxation and readiness to move on to a more challenging assignment.

CLASS SIZE

While creative rhythms can be carried on successfully with any number, pantomime requires a group of no more than fifteen to twenty. If a class is very large, the teacher should make every effort to divide it so that half the group is involved with some other activity at that hour. Pantomime demands individual attention, and every child should be assured the opportunity of participation each time the class meets. This is true whatever the age level, for growth depends upon repeated experiences in exercises that increase in difficulty.

LENGTH OF CLASS PERIOD

The length and frequency of class meetings depend upon the situation (school, club, or camp) and the age of the players. With very young children, daily experiences for ten to fifteen minutes are ideal, whereas for older children, two or three meetings a week for forty-five minutes or an hour work out well. With club groups, the meeting may be only once a week; this is less desirable but may be the only possible arrangement. High school students and young adults can be absorbed for as long as two hours, but, in general, more frequent meetings of shorter length are preferable.

In schools where creative drama is a definite part of the curriculum, the teacher can look forward to regular meetings throughout the year. Where it is not, it will be up to the classroom teacher to introduce it whenever and however she can. She will probably use pantomime in connection with other subjects which, if imaginatively done, can be of value as a tool for teaching and a creative experience for the class.

PLAYING SPACE

A stage is generally used for formal rehearsals, whereas a large room is more desirable for creative drama. Little children enjoy moving all over the room and should be encouraged to do so. The younger the group, therefore, the larger the space required. If a large room is not available, a classroom in which all the chairs have been pushed aside will do. Space makes for freedom; a small or cramped area inhibits it. As was said in the preceding chapter, however, too large an area can present other problems, particularly for a beginning or uncontrolled group. Boundaries are needed, as the leader soon discovers; there is greater freedom where there are clear boundaries of both time and space than where neither exist. An auditorium with a stage and chairs is least desirable as a playing space for a beginning group of any age, since it inevitably leads to a concept of performance with stage techniques before the players are ready for it. Under any circumstances, seating children on the floor in a semicircle where all can see, hear, and be heard is the most satisfactory arrangement.

IMAGINATION

Whatever the space, the teacher will try to see that it is kept uncluttered and that the players are seated in a circle or semicircle around it. Having engaged in rhythms and group activities, the players are now ready for pantomime. There are many ways of proceeding, but one that has proved effective is having the class handle a small, nondescript object (such as a small box or blackboard eraser) as if it were several different items. For example, the teacher calls six or seven players to the center, hands one the object and tells him it is a diamond bracelet, the most beautiful piece of jewelry any of them has ever seen. He will than ask the players to:

1. handle it
2. look at it
3. react to it
4. pass it along to the next person

When each has had a chance to handle and react to the object, the teacher may say that it is now a kitten with very soft fur. The same group again takes it and reacts to it. The next time, it may be a wallet—dirty and torn—with nothing in it. The fourth time it is passed, it becomes a knife, or a glass of water filled to the brim, or perhaps an old and valuable manuscript. Each time it is handed around, the group invests it with more of the qualities of the suggested object. The idea, of course, is to stimulate the imagination and help the players realize that it is not the property used but their own imaginations that turn an eraser first into a bracelet, then a kitten, then a wallet, and finally a knife or a glass of water.

The observers are as interested as the players in the growing reality that develops. Depending upon the time at their disposal, the teacher may repeat the exercise with another group, or move on to a new exercise. Some of the questions that might be asked of the observers are:

1. How did we know it was a bracelet?
   "One player held it so that the diamonds sparkled in the light." "John held it as if it were very expensive." "Linda tried it on." "Charles looked for the price tag."
2. Why did we know it was a kitten the second time the eraser was passed?
   "One stroked its head." "Another girl put it close to her cheek as if it were alive." "Barbara held its legs carefully when she gave it to Lois." "They all held it as if it were soft and round."

Questions put to the players might be:

1. What did the wallet look like to you?
   "It was dark green leather." "It was old and torn." "There was a faded snapshot in the front." "It had a hole in the bottom." "It was muddy because it had been lost in the yard."
2. You were careful not to let any of the objects drop, but you handled them differently. Why?
   "The bracelet was valuable." "I didn't want it to get broken." "The kitten was alive, and that made it different from all the others." "When I jiggled the glass, the water almost spilled."

Questions like these push the players to stronger visual images and greater power of observation.

Another exercise that serves to excite the imagination is the suggestion that a table in the middle of the room is covered with a variety of small objects. Each participant must go up and pick out one thing, showing, by the way he handles it, what it is. While this is an individual exercise, it can be done with several persons at once so that the attention is not focused on a single player. By having the rest of the class seated in a semicircle, some observers will see one player and some another. This is fun for all, and what self-consciousness may have existed in the beginning will soon be gone.

CONCENTRATION

Many children will be able to concentrate on the activities, but some, for whom this is the first experience of this sort, will not, so the next step is to work on "holding the image." One good exercise is to have the class hunt for a ring that has been lost. A few minutes of searching usually involves them in the assignment. If it does not, the teacher might actually hide a ring and ask them to find it. The reality that comes with the second playing demonstrates clearly the difference between pretending to hunt and really looking. Other good group exercises for developing concentration are:

1. watching a plane come in
2. looking at a funny movie
3. smelling smoke in the woods
4. listening for the lunch bell to ring

SENSE IMAGES

The class is now ready for some specific exercises involving the five senses. This might be introduced by a discussion of the ways in which we find out what is going on around us. We see; we hear; we touch; we smell; we taste. Individuals may do the following, using no props, but trying to "see" what is suggested.

1. Enter a very large room in which you have left your sweater.
2. Go into a dark closet to look for your sweater.
3. Go into your own room to get your sweater.
4. Try to find your sweater among a dozen in the locker room.

Exercises for the sense of hearing might include:

1. hearing an explosion
2. listening to a small sound and trying to decide what it is
3. listening to a military band coming down the street
4. hearing a dance orchestra playing a popular tune on the radio

Exercises for the sense of smell might include:

1. coming home from school and smelling cookies baking in the kitchen
2. walking in the woods and smelling a campfire
3. smelling different perfumes on a counter
4. smelling something very unpleasant and trying to decide what it is

Exercises for the sense of taste might include:

1. eating a piece of delicious chocolate candy
2. trying a foreign food that you have never tasted before, and deciding you like it
3. biting into a sour apple

Exercises for the sense of touch might include:

1. touching a piece of velvet
2. touching a hot stove
3. touching or holding an ice cube
4. touching or holding some sharp nails

These are only a few suggestions, and the leader will think of many more. Whatever is suggested, however, should always be within the experience of the players. Practice in actual hearing and observation is good exercise and may be introduced either beforehand or at any point that the teacher thinks it of value. For instance, the teacher might ask the players to:

1. Close your eyes for one minute and listen to all the sounds you can hear.
2. Go to one corner of the room and describe all the things that you see.
3. Touch one object and describe it as completely as possible.

What we are trying to do is to "lead children into experiences that will involve them in touching, seeing, tasting, hearing, and smelling the things in their world. We also want them to become involved in experiences that will lead to imagining, exploring, reasoning, inventing, experimenting, investigating, and selecting, so that these experiences will not only be rich in themselves but lead to personal creative growth."[1]

PERFORMING AN ACTION

There is no right or wrong order and no prescribed length of time the group should spend on one kind of exercise. Generally speaking, the older the players, the longer the attention will be sustained, but this does not always hold true. At any rate, a pantomime guaranteed to capture the interest of every player, regardless of age, is "making or doing something." In the beginning the teacher will offer suggestions, but later, the players will have ideas of their own. Some good suggestions might be:

1. setting a table
2. baking a cake
3. feeding your dog
4. getting dressed

1. Earl Linderman and Donald W. Herberholz, *Developing Artistic and Perceptual Awareness* (Dubuque, Iowa: William C. Brown & Co., 1964), Introduction, p. x.

5. doing your homework
6. turning on a favorite TV program
7. buying a pizza and taking it home
8. riding on a crowded bus and going past your stop
9. packing your backpack
10. choosing food in a cafeteria

Again, let it be stressed that particularly in working with disadvantaged children, or with children in urban areas, the activities suggested should be those in their environments. "Washing clothes" rather than "fishing in a brook" is familiar to these children, and can, therefore, be easily imagined and acted. This, incidentally, also helps children to respect their own ideas and regard their own experiences more positively.

Pantomimes of actions will grow more complicated as the players put them into situations. The above might be inherent in such scenes as the following:

1. You are getting ready for a birthday party for your sister, and must set the table. What are you going to put on it? Are these decorations? A cake? Favors? Presents? What dishes and silver will you use? Is it a surprise? Are you alone?
2. You are baking your first cake. No one is home, so you must read and follow the recipe yourself. What will you put in it? What utensils do you need? Is it a success?
3. You have a new puppy and have come home from school to take care of it. What do you feed it? How much? How big is he? What kind of dog?
4. You are getting up on a Saturday morning. Today it has begun snowing so you must dress to go out and play. What do you wear? Is it cold? Are you excited about it? Do you take time to comb your hair? Eat your breakfast?
5. It is after dinner and you have been told to do your homework. There is a television show you would like to see, but you know you should study. What is the assignment? Do you like the subject? Is it hard? Easy? Boring? What is the show you want to see? Is anyone else in the room? What do you finally do about it?

MOOD AND FEELINGS

Somewhere along the way, feelings have crept into the pantomimes so that a specific assignment on mood will not be appropriate. The teacher may want the group to talk about feelings first, or perhaps this will come about as a result of a particularly good job one of the players has done. The teacher might even ask the class what kinds of feelings they have experienced, and their responses will often include many more than he has anticipated. Anger, fear, happiness, excitement, pride, curiosity, vanity, anticipation, sorrow, and hatred are some that seven- and eight-year-olds have enumerated.

This might be a time to break the class into groups of four or five, with each group taking one feeling to pantomime. Delightful results are always forthcoming when working on mood. One group showed excitement through a scene on Christmas Eve, when they crept downstairs to look at the tree and presents. Another asked if they could act out the story of *Pandora's Box* because it was such a good example of curiosity. Another group chose fear and set their scene in a tent at a summer camp. They were campers who heard a strange noise at night and imagined it to be a bear, but it was only their counselor coming back.

It soon becomes obvious that more than one emotion is usually involved in a situation of any length. Therefore, the next step will be to show change of mood. Situations like the following help the players to move from one mood to another.

1. You are a group of friends taking a hike in the woods. It is a beautiful day and you find strawberries and wildflowers. You stop to have your lunch, but when you are ready to move on, you discover that you have wandered from the path and are lost. Your happy mood changes to panic. Where are you? Should you go on, or turn back? Is there any familiar landmark to guide you? Suddenly one of the girls finds a broken flower lying on the ground. As she picks it up, she realizes that it is on the path, and she must have dropped it when she looked for a picnic spot. Panic turns to relief as the group starts for home.

2. A group of boys discover a cave (or it could be the basement of an empty building). They go in, curious as to what they may find. One of them stumbles over a box. The boys open it and find money and jewels. Excitement grows as they realize they have found hidden treasure. Then they hear voices; men are approaching. Terrified, the boys hide. The men go past, not seeing them. The boys stuff a few coins in their pockets and run, escaping from danger.

3. A group of people get into an elevator in a big downtown building. Suddenly it stops between floors. Their poise turns to fear as the operator pushes one button, then another, and nothing happens. Suddenly, she gets it started and the elevator moves, taking the passengers down to the ground level.

4. You are a group of children who come into your schoolroom one morning and find a monkey scampering about. First you are startled, then

amused by his antics. Finally, the man who has lost him comes in and catches him, taking him away. You are sorry to see him go as he waves good-bye to you from his owner's shoulder.

5. You are going on a field trip to which you have looked forward for a long time. You get in the bus, but the bus will not start. After a few minutes, the driver lets you know that he cannot make it go, and so your trip must be postponed. Disappointed, you get out. Suddenly the engine starts. You turn around and see the driver motioning for you to get back in. Your happiness is great because you can now go after all.

6. You are sitting in a movie. First you are watching a very dull short. How do you feel when it seems to be going on forever? Then it changes to a hilariously funny cartoon. How do you react? At last, the feature begins and you are absorbed.

Mood can be created in countless ways, among them the use of pictures, colors, light, music, and rhythms. The following ideas have been put into practice successfully with widely varying results.

1. The leader selects a picture or photograph that will evoke a strong emotional reaction. If the picture is realistic, the leader might, after all in the group have had a a chance to look at it closely, ask such questions as: Who is in the picture? Why do you think he is there? What is he doing? What does he seem to be feeling? Why do you think he feels that way?

The discussion that follows will lead into possibilities for pantomime or even improvisation, if the group is ready for it. A story can be built from the meanings and mood the children find in the picture. Instead of a composition in which persons are represented, however, a picture of a place may be shown. Country roads, city streets, the platform of a railroad station, a deserted house, a stretch of empty beach, woodlands—all are springboards if the mood evoked is one which kindles the emotions and arouses our curiosity. Where do you think this is? Why is no one around? What feelings do you have when you look at it? What is there about it that makes you feel this way?

After some discussion the leader will be ready to continue with questions leading to a scene laid in the place portrayed. Who might come along? Where is he or she going? Does he meet anyone? Anyone else? What do they talk about? Do? Feel? In very little time most groups will people the canvas with characters, often involving them in an imaginative situation laid in the scene depicted. For example, a deserted house could take the group in several different directions. It might be the site of buried treasure (still a favorite theme of eight to ten-year-old boys), important documents, or a fascinating archaeological discovery. It might, on the other hand, be the home a family has had to leave sorrowfully. Why? What has happened? Perhaps a son or daughter returns to say a last good-bye. Perhaps he or she meets a friend, finds something left behind, something meaningful. Or perhaps it is the home of a famous person, who has come back after an absence of many years to see his old neighborhood once more. Does anyone see him? Does anyone recognize him? What happens if they do? How does he feel about his home? The reception he is given? How do his old neighbors react?

2. Instead of a realistic painting, an abstract composition might be shown. Color, dark and light contrasts, design, the brush strokes—all will stimulate imaginative response. Not what the picture may *mean* but what it means to the viewer is the object of this exercise. Younger children tend to respond to the abstract composition more quickly than older players, perhaps because they do not feel the need for realistic detail and appreciate the fact that the artist's expression is direct and free like their own. Movement, rather than story, will usually be the reaction to this experience, although some children move naturally from physical movement into character.

3. As stated elsewhere, music is a powerful stimulus to creativity. Use of rhythms to suggest kinds of movement, characters, or animals is a popular and highly successful way of working. From this to the heightening of characterization is a natural next step. Actually, only the beat of a drum is necessary, although music, particularly if the leader is able to play the piano, can enrich the activity. Recordings of orchestral music are extremely effective means of establishing mood and may be used as we used pictures to stimulate the imagination. Listening, reacting, responding. A leader with no formal background in music can guide the group, not in the sense of a lesson in music appreciation, of course, but in the sense of encouraging listening and imaginative response. Again, young children seem to respond more spontaneously to music than older children, who have learned to be concerned with structure, theme, and melody. Careful selection of the music to be used is necessary. Thereafter, the procedure is much the same as that followed with the pictures. How does it make you feel? Show us. Where are you? Who are you? Are there others with you? What might be happening?

To create a story from music takes time, but after several experiences in listening and responding the group will be ready to proceed with the creation of characters, an original situation suggested by the music, and perhaps some dialogue. Again, music is the way of inducing the flow of creative energy and, because of its abstract quality, may produce a mood more readily than other stimuli.

Adelphi University Children's Center for the Creative Arts, courtesy Julie Thompson.

CHARACTERIZATION

Until now, we have been pantomiming activities and working to induce mood or feeling. The next step is characterization. Some participants will already have suggested characters different from themselves, but the teacher can use either the same exercises or new ones to start the group thinking in terms of characterization.

Again, situations involving groups are a good way to begin.

1. You are a group of people waiting for a bus on a city street. Each one of you will think of someone special to be: an elderly woman going to see her grandchildren, a businessman late for work, a girl on her way to high school, a blind man who needs help getting on the right bus, a young man beginning a new job, etc.

2. You are pilgrims who have gone to a shrine where, once a year, one wish is said to be granted. Decide who you are and what it is you want. You might be a crippled man who wants to walk again, a poet who wants very much to have his work published, a young mother who wants her sick baby to be cured. The teacher may wish to play with the group and be the statue at the shrine who indicates which wish is to be granted. This is a good situation because it offers an opportunity to work on both characterization and strong motivation.

3. You are people in a bus terminal. Some of you are going on trips, others returning; still others are meeting friends or relatives. There may be a porter, a man selling tickets, a man selling newspapers and magazines, etc. By your behavior, let us know who you are and how you feel as you wait for the buses to arrive and depart.

Some individual pantomimes stressing character are suggested:

1. You are a robber who is entering a house at night. While you are there, the people return unexpectedly. You listen and finally make your escape, having stolen nothing.
2. You are the neighborhood gossip. You have a party line, and one of your favorite pastimes is listening in on other people's conversations. This afternoon you hear some very good news, some bad news, and then some remarks about yourself and your habit of listening in on your neighbors. How do you react? What do you do?
3. You are a child who has wanted a dog for a long time. One day you overhear your parents talking about it in the next room. Your mother does not want a dog, but your father thinks it is time you had one. They discuss reasons for and against it. How do you react to their arguments and what is the final decision?
4. Two of you will be a customer and a storekeeper in a shop in a foreign country. You do not know each other's languages. The customer decides, in advance, on three things he needs to buy and tries to convey what they are to the clerk, through pantomime. Who are you? What are the three things? How does it turn out? (This is an exercise which the entire class can do in pairs.)

Another exercise is to take one action and do it as three different people. For example:

A. You go into a restaurant to order a meal.
   Do it as:
   a. a teen-age boy who is very hungry
   b. a middle-aged woman who has very little appetite and sees nothing on the menu that she wants
   c. a very poor man who is hungry but must limit his choice to what he can afford
B. You are trying on dresses in a shop.
   Do it as:
   a. a very fat woman who has trouble being fitted
   b. a young girl, looking for a pretty dress to wear to a dance

c. a secretary who is trying to find the most appropriate dress to wear on her first day at work in a new job

C. You are visiting an art museum. First you look at the exhibition as:
   a. an artist who knows the painter whose work is on display
   b. a woman who thinks she should go to museums but does not appreciate the pictures
   c. an elderly woman who has been ill and is enjoying visiting her favorite museum for the first time in many months

D. You are exercising in a gymnasium. Do the exercises first as:
   a. a young man who loves all athletics
   b. a fat man whose doctor has advised him to exercise to lose weight
   c. a child who has never seen gymnasium equipment before
   What does each do and how does he feel about it?

PANTOMIME SUGGESTED BY OTHER MEANS

Some exercises are fun to do and stimulate inventiveness, but they have nothing to do with familiar actions, mood, or characters. These are good as a change, and may be introduced any time the leader feels the group needs a new type of stimulation. Some ideas are:

1. Beat a drum and ask the group to move in any way the drum beat suggests.

2. Ask each person in the class to represent a mechanical appliance. He does not operate it, he *becomes* it. Some very imaginative results may be expected such as: a pencil sharpener, an egg beater, a lawnmower, a hair drier, a record player, etc. This is a challenging exercise, guaranteed to break down all inhibitions.

3. Give each person a color and ask that he suggest it by means of movement, attitude, or characterization. This incidentally, may be followed up with an improvisation in which the color becomes a person. For example: Mrs. White, Mrs. Black, Mrs. Blue, Mrs. Green, Mrs. Red, and Mrs. Yellow might be ladies at a tea. What are they like? How do they talk? How can we distinguish one from another?

4. Each person selects a property, and acts according to what it suggests to him. The following are usually good for stimulating imaginative reactions: a gnarled stick, a ruler, a gold bracelet, a broken dish, a sponge. Again the players do not use the properties; they become characters suggested by their qualities.

5. Be puppets. Try to imagine what it feels like to be controlled by

strings. Imagine that you are being controlled, then dropped by the puppeteer. While there is an element of characterization involved, it is the feeling of the inanimate object being manipulated that interests us.

6. Have the group listen to orchestral music. Suggest they try to identify the various instruments. Then have the children *be* the instruments—not the musicians playing them but the instruments themselves. If they are enjoying the exercise, suggest that each child select a different instrument to be until a whole orchestra has been assembled. This particular activity will probably not last longer than one session, but it is fun and a means of stretching the imagination.

7. Put up a sheet at one end of the room with the light behind it. Have the children pantomime something behind it. See what happens. The magic quality of a silhouette never fails to stimulate an immediate desire to try out ideas. This particular activity, incidentally, is an excellent one for the timid child who feels less exposed behind a sheet than he does out in the open. Practice in acting behind the sheet leads to inventiveness: What happens when the actor is close to the sheet? Far from it? Approaches or leaves it? How can a figure be exaggerated? Enlarged? How is humor obtained? Then try acting out nursery rhymes and stories in shadow.

8. The leader discusses growth and growing. From this it is suggested that the group conceive of themselves as seeds, buried deep in the earth. It is dark and they are quiet. Then spring arrives with rain, sun, and wind. What happens to the seeds? Do they break through the earth? Can we feel them push and grow? As summer comes, the plants grow taller. What are they going to be—flowers or trees? Tall, short, bushy, weak, or strong? Feel the warm rain, the hot sun, the breeze blowing, the final push to maturity. Poetry written about the springtime ties in well with this exercise.

9. Either the teacher or the class composes a story in which a variety of sounds are listed and described. It is great fun to act out the sounds and/or what is making them. For example, one child wrote the following narration for the others to act.

I woke up in the morning to the sound of my ALARM CLOCK going off. I opened my CLOSET DOOR which squeaked. Then I turned on the FAUCET and the water made a rushing sound in the sink. After that I ran downstairs to breakfast. The coffee was PERKING in the pot. The BACON was frying in a pan. The TOAST popped up in the toaster. The RADIO was playing but the MUSIC was drowned out by the STATIC.

Outside I heard my father MOWING the lawn and an AIRPLANE was flying low overhead. It was going to be hot and my mother turned on the FAN. Suddenly down the street I heard the noise of the SCHOOL BUS, its engine chugging. I ran out the front DOOR, which slammed and I ran down the walk, my SHOES clattering. My DOG barked as I climbed aboard a very noisy BUS.

Such an exercise as this stimulates awareness as well as imagination in the attempt to suggest or reproduce sounds and the objects making them.

10. Mirror images are popular and great fun for actors of all ages. Two players face each other, one being himself and the other his mirror image. Whatever the person does, his image must reproduce precisely. With practice this can become a skilled performance, challenging to the players and fascinating to those watching. Greater awareness as well as the ability to work together are developed in the process. Older groups may ask to repeat this exercise from time to time, realizing the possibilities for technical improvement.

11. Older players often find the following exercise rewarding. Imagine yourself shut up in a box. How large is it? Can you stand up? Move around? Get out? Let us see the box—its sides, floor, top. Suppose the box becomes larger? What do you do? It grows smaller. What happens to you then?

This is an exercise which may be repeated many times with the players improving their technique as they try to imagine and suggest in every way possible the experience of being encased in a box.

12. The following exercise is for older children or adults. Each member of the group writes a letter of apology for something he has done or might have done. Then the leader asks two players to go to the telephone. One gives the apology and the other whatever response he feels is appropriate. Next, the first player faces the other person and makes his apology in person. Finally, he reads the original letter aloud, and the group comments on which apology has the greater reality, how the two improvisations have gone, and why. This is an interesting exercise, which may be carried out with each member of the group, time and interest permitting.

As the group progresses, organization improves, and situations often develop into simple plots. The players are learning to use their entire bodies to express ideas and are ready to add dialogue. Although improvisation, or informal dialogue, is the subject of the next chapter, the teacher will want to alternate exercises in pantomime and improvisation. No matter how advanced the group, pantomime is always good to work on from time to time because of the type of practice it offers.

STARTING PLACES

The following *situations* are suggested as starting places to set children thinking. The younger or less experienced the group, the more preliminary work in the form of pantomime and discussion is needed. Group pantomimes related to the situation will stimulate movement; whereas discussing the topic and asking questions about it helps to stir the imagination. When all seem to be ready, divide the class into several small groups to develop simple narratives. Each group will come up with its own ideas as to plot and characters. This can be a one-time activity or the beginning of a creative play done entirely in pantomime.

> a beggar comes to the door
> a house is for sale
> the tallest sunflower in town
> a magic sandal
> a bracelet in an alley
> a puppy in a box left in a doorway

Starting places may also be *locations*. See what the class can do with some of these, again beginning with pantomimes as warm-ups and discussion questions to start the flow of ideas. When everyone is ready to begin work, divide the class into groups to develop narratives to be told through mime.

Making a Machine

There are many variations on this exercise, which has great appeal for older students. One way of beginning is for the leader to start a regular beat and ask one person to come into the center of the room and begin a movement. When the movement has been stabilized, a second person comes forward with another movement that relates to the first. This continues until as many as a dozen players become parts of a machine, each one contributing a movement that is coordinated with the rest. The effect can be interesting and dynamic when all players are working together.

This exercise may be made more interesting by adding sounds. Each player makes a noise appropriate to her movement. When all parts of the machine are moving rhythmically together, the sounds enhance the effect. This exercise requires imagination, inventiveness, concentration, cooperation, and the ability to sustain both sound and movement until the mechanical quality is established. The machine can run indefinitely, or it can break down, either stopping or falling apart.

The group may also start with a particular machine in mind (threshing machine, wrecking equipment, ice cream machine, sewing machine, etc.); or a machine may develop from the activity of the players. As a group gains experience, the results will become more precise and sophisticated. Incidentally, this is a technique that can be incorporated effectively into an improvisation, and it is often far more interesting than the use of conventional props.

Some teachers find that acting a story while it is read aloud is a good transition from pantomime to dramatization. Many stories can be done in this way, though some lend themselves to it better than others. One story, which has met with success with more than one group, is included here as an illustration. It is *The Little Scarecrow Boy*.[2]

THE LITTLE SCARECROW BOY
MARGARET WISE BROWN

Arranged for creative playing by Aurand Harris

Once upon a time, in a cornfield, there lived a scarecrow (he enters and takes his place), and his scarecrow wife (she enters and takes her place beside him), and their little scarecrow boy (he enters and joins his mother and father).

Every day of the world old man scarecrow would go out into the cornfield to make faces at the crows. (He crosses the room and takes up his position in the cornfield.) And every day of the world little scarecrow boy would want to come, too. (He goes to his father and pulls at his coat.) And every day of the world, old man scarecrow would say:

> No!
> No, little boy,
> You can't go.
> You're not fierce enough to scare a crow.
> Wait until you grow.

(He shows how high little scarecrow boy will have to grow. The little boy is discouraged and returns to his mother.)

So, little scarecrow boy would have to stay home all day and just grow. (His mother holds up her hand to the height he will have to grow. First he stretches his neck, then he stands on his toes and finally he jumps but he does not reach her hand.) Every morning when the sun came up (the sun crosses the room, smiling happily), old man scarecrow went out to the cornfield. He waved his arms and made terrible faces.

2. Margaret Wise Brown, *Fun and Frolic* (New York: D. C. Heath & Co., 1955).

Every day the crows cried, "Caw! Caw! Caw!" (The crows fly in and circle around the corn, then one by one each crow sees old man scarecrow, screams, and flies away.) He made such terrible faces that the crows would fly far, far away.

Every night, when the sun went down (the sun walks back across the playing space, smiling happily) old man scarecrow would go home (he goes to the mother and the little boy), and there he would teach little scarecrow boy how to make fierce faces. (He makes a face and the little boy imitates it.) One—two—three—four—five—six. Old lady scarecrow would clap her hands and whistle through her teeth at the looks of them.

One day after the little boy knew all six of his father's terrible faces so that he could make them one after the other, he decided to go out into the cornfield by himself and frighten a crow. (The scarecrows have closed their eyes in sleep.) So the next morning, before the sun was up, or old man scarecrow was up, or old lady scarecrow was up, little scarecrow boy got out of bed. (He steps forward cautiously.) He dressed and went quietly . . . (he takes one step) . . . quietly . . . quietly . . . quietly out of the house and over to the cornfield. He stood in his father's place. (He takes his father's position in the cornfield.)

It was a fine morning and the sun came up. (The sun crosses the stage, smiling.) Far away over the trees, crows flew around and around. Little scarecrow boy waved his arms through the air. He had never felt fiercer in all his life. (The little boy waves his arms and makes faces.) In the distance the "caws" of the crows were heard. (The leader enters and all of the crows fly in, circling the corn. One crow at a time sees the little boy, screams and flies off. Only the leader is left and he is not afraid. He starts toward the little scarecrow boy.)

"Oh!" said little scarecrow boy, and he made his first fierce face. Still came flying the big crow.

"Oh, Oh!" said little scarecrow boy and he made his second fierce face. Still came flying the big crow. He made his third fierce face. "Oh, oh, oh!" It was time to go. (He jumps down and runs in a circle, covering very little ground but running hard. The crow flies after him.)

So, little scarecrow boy ran and ran. Then he stopped. He made his fourth fierce face. Still came flying the big old crow. He ran and he ran and he made his fifth fierce face. Still came flying the big old crow. Little scarecrow boy had only one face left now. So he stopped. He held his arms wide above his head and he made his sixth fierce face. (As he makes his sixth face, the old crow stops, backs up, then turns and flies off.)

Whoa! The old crow stopped and then backwards flew through the air, feathers flying everywhere, until there wasn't even the shadow of a crow in the cornfield. A scarecrow at last!

(Meanwhile, old man scarecrow walks to his side.) Then little scarecrow boy saw a shadow in front of him and he looked around. There beside him stood his father. Old man scarecrow was proud of his little boy and shook his scarecrow hand. (They shake hands.) Old lady scarecrow was proud of her little boy, who could make all six fierce faces. (She pats him fondly.) And when little scarecrow boy grew up, he was the fiercest scarecrow in all the cornfields in all the world.

This is a somewhat shortened version of the story, with action suggested by one group of children. All took turns playing the different parts and had a grand time creating fierce faces. One child read the story while the others acted it in pantomime. The scarecrows offered an opportunity to experiment with physical movement in addition to simple characterizations. Stories read while acted help the more timid or inexperienced children to follow the plot and feel the sense of accomplishment that comes from successful dramatization.

SUMMARY

Pantomime, while good practice at any time, is usually the most satisfactory way of beginning work in creative drama. Although it is not necessary to follow a prescribed program of exercises, it is easier for many groups to begin with familiar activities and then move on to mood, or feeling, and finally characterization. By starting with movement and then pantomime, the players learn to express themselves through bodily action, without the additional problem of dialogue. Younger children accept this as a natural means of expression, and older children and adults find it easier to begin with pantomime than with improvisation or formal acting. Pantomime sharpens perception and stimulates the imagination as players try to remember how actions are done and what objects are really like, as to size, weight and shape. Recalling emotion demands concentration and involvement: How do you feel when you are happy, tired, angry, excited, anxious, etc.? Close observation of people is a means of developing believable characters whose bearing, movement, and gestures belong to them and whose behavior seems appropriate. Although pantomime is considered here as a medium of expression, it may become an art form in itself. Mimes like Marcel Marceau have demonstrated its power to communicate with people of all ages and backgrounds, when a high level of artistry is achieved.

5

IMPROVISATION: CHARACTERS SPEAK

Improvisation is difficult at first. Dialogue does not flow easily, even when it has been preceded by much work in pantomime and a thorough understanding of the situation or story. With practice, however, words do begin to come, and the players discover the possibilities of character development when oral language is added. Dialogue is apt to be brief and scanty at first, but usually begins to flow rapidly once the children become accustomed to it. Players, aged seven and older, enjoy the opportunity of using words to further a story and more fully describe the characters they are portraying. It is a good idea to begin with simple situations so as to get accustomed to using dialogue before attempting more ambitious material.

Many of the situations suggested in the previous chapter on pantomime can be used, although they were designed with movement in mind. Frequently, children will begin to add dialogue of their own free will, as they

71

feel the need of expressing ideas in words. When this happens, the leader accepts it as a natural progression from one step to the next. Younger children, players for whom English is a second language, or older students who lack self-confidence, will usually wait until they are urged to try adding dialogue. The teacher will not expect too much and will accept whatever is offered, knowing that more will be forthcoming the next time. The author recalls a sixth-grade class that was acting *The Story of Roland*. Although fond of the story and well oriented to the background, the first time it was played, one scene went like this: "Hello, Roland."—"Will you marry me?"—"Why, Roland, I'd love to." The final playing, after several had tried and discussed it, was a charming scene with all the necessary exposition and appropriate vocabulary.

Since even the simplest stories present complications for the beginner, some preliminary exercises are suggested. The purpose here is to give emphasis to dialogue rather than to the memorization or plot. Sometimes just one scene of a story can be improvised to advantage. The teacher will feel his way, and if the interest is sustained better with excerpts from favorite stories, he may prefer them to exercises.

Sounds, incidentally, can stimulate imagination and lead the listener to the creation of an improvisation. For example, the teacher can beat a drum or tambourine, knock, ring bells, or make any other kind of sound. This works particularly well with younger children but is a good exercise to use from time to time with those who are older.

SIMPLE IMPROVISATIONS
BASED ON SITUATIONS

The following improvisations may be done with various age levels, although the backgrounds of the players will determine the appropriateness. In some cases, the situations are better for older players.

1. You are a group of people in a subway station. It is six o'clock in the evening. In the center is a newsstand, at which newspapers, magazines, and candy are sold. It is run by a woman who has been there for many years. She knows the passengers who ride regularly, and is interested in them and all the details of their daily lives. Decide on who you are going to be—a secretary, an actress, a businessman, a cleaning woman, a shopper, a policeman, a teenager, a stranger in town, etc. Then let us know all about you through your conversation with the proprietor of the newsstand, while you are waiting for your train.

2. The scene is a toyshop on Christmas Eve. It is midnight, and the owner has just closed the door and gone home. At the stroke of twelve the toys come alive and talk together. They may consist of a toy soldier, a rag doll, a beautiful doll, a clown, a teddy bear, a jack-in-the-box, etc. Let us know by your conversation and movements who you are and why you were not sold.

3. You are a committee from your school, assigned the job of selecting a gift for your teacher, who is retiring. Each of you has an idea of what you think is appropriate, and you have only a certain amount of money to spend. The scene takes place in a large gift shop. Let us know who you are and what you want to buy. What is the decision you finally make?

4. This improvisation is good on a high school or college level. The scene is a meeting of the student council. You have the job of questioning a student who is reported to have stolen the examination questions for a history class. She is brought before you, and you ask her questions. What is each one of you like? How do you handle the situation? Is she guilty or not? What is your final decision and what do you do about it?

5. This improvisation is also probably better for older students, although it has been done by ten- and eleven-year-olds. You are a group of people returning for your thirty-fifth reunion from high school or college. Who are you? What has happened to you since you last saw each other? Have you been happy, successful, or unsuccessful? Let us know all about you through your conversation.

6. You are a group of young women in a suburban community. One of you has invited the new neighbor in to meet the rest of the group. Coffee is served and you talk together. All seems to be going well when the hostess notices that an expensive silver tray is missing from her coffee table. One by one, you begin to suspect the newcomer. Why do you suspect her? Did she take it? Is it found? Where? If she took it, why did she? Let us know what each one of you is like by your reaction to this situation. How does it turn out?

7. This improvisation is good with children. You are a group of children in an apartment house. It is Valentine's Day, and you are gathered in the front hall to look at and count your valentines. You see one child in the building going to her mailbox, and you notice that she did not receive any. How do you feel about this? What is each one of you like? Do you decide to do anything about it? If so, what do you do?

8. You are a group of children who live near a very cross, elderly woman. She chases you away from her property whenever you come near it. This particular morning, you see that someone has broken

her fence and ruined many of her flowers. For the first time you feel sorry for her. What do you do? How does she react to you? Do you all agree as to whether you should help her? Do your actions change her attitude toward children?

9. A new child has entered your class at school. He does not speak English, and some of the children laugh at him. When recess comes, you all go out to the playground. How does each of you treat him? How does he react to you? You are all different so you will each feel differently toward him. Do you finally take him in, or do you exclude him? Try changing roles so that different players have the experience of trying the part of the new child. Does the improvisation change as you all think more about the situation?

10. The scene is a small bakery. One of you is the owner, one of you a child who helps him on Saturdays, and another is a beggar. It is not busy this particular morning so the owner goes out for coffee. While he is gone, a beggar comes into the shop and asks for some bread. The girl (or boy) knows that she should not give away the bread but she feels sorry for the old man. What do they say to each other? What does the owner say when he comes back? Try changing parts in this improvisation to see if it will turn out differently.

IMPROVISATIONS SUGGESTED BY OBJECTS

Not only situations and stories motivate improvisation; some very imaginative results can be obtained by the use of objects or properties. Try some of the following suggestions as springboards.

1. An object (any object) is put in the center of the circle where all the players can see it. Look at it, without speaking, for three or four minutes. Try to think of a story about it. Where might it have come from? How did it get here? What does it make *you* think of? Each of you will have an original story to tell; tell it.

2. This time, divide the class into groups of three or four. An object is presented, and each group is asked to make up an improvisation about it. Perhaps the property is a wooden spoon. When used with one class, the following ideas were suggested and these situations improvised.

   a. The scene was a settler's cabin over one hundred years ago. The family had very few household items and so they prized each one. Among them was a wooden spoon. In this scene it was used to stir batter for cornbread, and then washed and put carefully away.

b. The scene was a museum, and the spoon a relic from the Indians who once inhabited the region. The characters were the curator of the museum and two children who were visiting it. The curator answered their questions by telling the history of the spoon.
c. The scene was a cave. Three boys were hiking and found the spoon. They used it to dig, and discovered an old box of coins that had been buried there. They took the old spoon home with them for good luck.
d. The scene was an industrial arts class. The boys were making things of wood, and a blind boy carved the spoon. It was so well done that the teacher said he would display it as one of the best things made in his class that year.
e. The scene was a dump. The old wooden spoon was the speaker as he told the other pieces of trash how he had been used and handed down from one generation to the next. Finally his family became rich and threw him away because they considered him too old and ugly to be of further use to them.

Any object can function as a springboard, and no two groups will see it in exactly the same way. Among the kinds of properties that suggest ideas are:

a velvet jewelry box	an old hat
an artificial rose	a cane
a foreign coin	a quill pen
a feather duster	an old dog leash
a bell	

An improvisation with unusual interest was developed from a whistle by a very imaginative group of ten-year-olds. They decided that it was a policeman's whistle, made of silver and bearing an inscription. They laid the scene in his home on the day of his retirement from the force; the characters were the policeman, his wife, and his grandson. The policman came in that evening, took off his whistle, looked at it nostalgically a long time, then laid it on the supper table. His grandson, coming into the room at that point, begged him to tell the story again of how he had received it. As the story began, there was a throwback scene, in which the policeman was rescuing a child from burning in a bonfire many years before. He was honored for his bravery and given an inscribed silver whistle, which he treasured for the rest of his life. At the finish of the story, the throwback scene faded and some neighbors came in with a cake and presents for him. The improvisation was effective both in its good dramatic structure and the reality of the characterizations.

Not every group is able to develop an improvisation to this degree, but occasionally one will, and when it happens, it is an inspiration to the rest of the class. Incidentally, it is nearly always the result of the play's having been based on familiar material so that the players are sure of the dialogue and can identify easily with the characters. Again, respect for their background and acceptance of the ideas that come out of it not only make for comfort but also bring forth ideas that the teacher probably would not have thought of. Children of foreign background have a wealth of material on which to draw, but too often it remains an untapped source because they have been made to feel that it is unworthy of consideration. Both the stories they have been told and the details of their everyday life contain the basic ingredients of drama. For example, one group of boys, who lived in a housing project, played a scene in an elevator. The situation was simple but had reality. Two boys, having nothing to do, decided to ride up and down in the elevator, angering the tenants and almost causing a tragedy because one man on a high floor was ill and waiting for the doctor. Whether or not this had been an actual experience the teacher did not know, but the situation contained reality, humor, and drama, with characters who were believable.

One final example of the use of properties was an improvisation done by a group of high school girls. They had been asked by the teacher to empty their purses and select the six most unusual or interesting objects. The objects they finally chose were a newspaper clipping, a snapshot, a lipstick in a Japanese case, a key ring with a red charm, a pocket knife, and a purse flashlight. Within minutes they had created a mystery, prompted by and making use of every one of the properties they selected. There were six players, and their preparation time was approximately ten minutes.

IMPROVISATIONS FROM COSTUMES

Similar to the use of props, and equally effective in stimulating ideas, are pieces of costume. Such garments as hats, capes, aprons, shawls, tailcoats, and jewelry will suggest different kinds of characters. Innumerable examples could be given of situations that grew from characters developed this way. For example, to one boy, a tailcoat suggested a musician, down on his luck and playing his violin on a street corner for pennies. A feathered hat helped a little girl create a lady of fashionable pretensions, and become a comic character in her extravagant dress and poor taste. A shawl suggested witches, grand-mothers, people in disguise, or a scene laid in very cold weather.

It is wise for the teacher on any level, working anywhere, to keep a supply of simple and sturdy costumes available for this kind of use. If children experience difficulty in getting into character, a piece of a costume may some-times be all that is needed to provide the necessary incentive. Costume used in this way is not dressing the part, but an aid to more imaginative thinking.

IMPROVISATION FROM CHARACTERS

In an earlier chapter, an illustration was given of an improvisation created from a character. This is a successful method of starting, as well as a way of encouraging, observation. If the group is small and has had some experience, original monologues are good practice and fun for the players. If the class is large, however, this is probably not a wise assignment, unless the monologues are kept short.

To create from a character, the teacher can ask each member of the class to think of a particularly interesting person he has noticed that day, or sometime during the week. This is followed by questions as to:

who was he?
what was he doing?
did he have anything to say?
how did he dress?
how old was he?
what special thing about him attracted your attention?

One girl offered as a character a woman who served the hot vegetables in her school cafeteria. Although the woman was bad-tempered, the girl had observed that she was always extremely generous in her servings and did her job more efficiently than anyone else. The group, which chose her as a heroine for their story, decided that she might have been a refugee. Because she had experienced hunger during that period in her life, she was determined that all plates would be generously filled, now that food was available. Her irritability they attributed to her own unhappy experiences and her separation from her family. The scene that the children improvised, using this particular character as an inspiration, was thoughtful, sympathetic, and interesting to the class.

Another improvisation based on an actual person was the story of an elderly woman whom one child noticed every day, sitting on the front porch of her house. The group, which chose her for a heroine, decided that she was really very rich but miserly, and was saving her money for the day when her son came home. They agreed that he had gone into the army several years before and had not returned. Although he had been reported missing, his mother clung to the hope that he would come back some day, and so she sat on the porch—waiting by day, and counting her money by night. The group decided to have him return, so the story had a happy ending.

A fantasy was the result of another character study. Two of the children described a well-dressed old man whom they saw coming home every morning around eight o'clock. They decided that he must have an interesting occupation and so made him a wizard, who helped the good people and punished the evil through the power of his magic cane. This became a modern fairy tale filled with highly imaginative incidents.

IMPROVISATIONS FROM CLUES

Older players enjoy creating improvisations from clues. The following exercises can be done to build characters. With these clues, what kinds of persons do you imagine? In an improvisation, create a character who is suggested by:

raw vegetables	hat
cane	fur piece
book	checkbook
Coca-Cola	belt
hair dryer	stick
television	bag

The following exercise is good for experienced players. Select a place where a number of strangers might gather. This could be an air terminal, a bus stop, a grocery store in the morning before it opens, a parking lot, a picket line. One person enters and is soon joined by another. They get into a conversation. Another comes in and then another, until a large group has assembled. The class can decide in advance who each will be; or, what is harder, come into the group as the character, making those already there decide who he is. This has wonderful possibilities for character study and simple plot development.

BIOGRAPHY

Biography is a suggestion for older players. The leader chooses a character (real or fictional) and describes him or her briefly. After some general discussion, the class is divided into five or six small groups, each representing a period in the character's life. Each group then plans its interpretation of the character at a given point in time. The periods could be:

birth to age six
six to twelve years
the teens
the twenties
the thirties or forties
later life
old age

Courtesy Creative Arts Team (CAT), New York University.

Obviously, the characters in the first scene would have to be members of the family, neighbors, or others. The character, about whom the scenes are built, need not actually appear in each one, but the scenes must be related in some way to her life. This is an excellent way to study a character; if an historical person is used, it will lead to research. If it is not a real person, it is a challenge to the imagination. Biography implies not only the character but other significant persons in her life.

IMPROVISATIONS FOR TWO

Try to imagine yourself in the following situations:

1. You receive a letter in the mail, telling you that you have won first prize in a poster contest. Tell your mother the good news.
2. Your dog has been hit by a car. When you come home from school, your mother meets you and tells you what has happened.

3. You have been warned not to go down a dark street by yourself at night. This evening, however, you are in a hurry and decide to go anyway because it's a shortcut. About halfway down the block you hear footsteps behind you. You look over your shoulder and see someone hurrying toward you. You hurry, also; so does the other person. You decide to slow up; so does the person who is following you. By this time you are frightened, but it's too late to turn back. You start to run and so does he. You run faster; so does he. Finally, you reach the corner, but the light has turned red. As you stand there alone waiting for it to change, a friend comes up. It was the friend who was following you, but neither of you recognized the other, and both of you had been running to get to the brightly lit corner. You have a good laugh when you discover each other.
4. You are trying on shoes to take to camp. The clerk does not have what you want and tries to sell you something else. Should you take his suggestion?
5. You are moving to a new neighborhood today. Your best friend comes around to say good-bye to you. Although you are looking forward to your new home, you are sad to leave the old neighborhood. What do you say?
6. Your aunt, whom you have never met, has come for a visit. You answer the door. What is she like? What do you say to each other?
7. You have found a kitten that you want very much to keep, but your mother has said you cannot have a pet. Try to persuade her that the kitten needs a home.
8. A salesman comes to the door. He insists on demonstrating a vacuum cleaner, although you tell him you have one. How do you handle the situation?
9. You have been wanting ice skates for your birthday. Your grandmother, who always selects the right presents, comes to the door with a box in her hands. When you open it, you find it contains stationery. What do you say to each other?
10. You wore your sister's bracelet on a picnic, and when you get home, discover you have lost it. Now you must tell her what happened.

EXERCISES FOR THREE

1. You and your friend are going to the playground. Your little sister wants to go with you, but if she does, you cannot go into the area reserved for older children. What do you do?
2. You are delivering papers. You throw one toward a house, but instead

of landing on the porch, it breaks a window. Both the man and his wife come to see what has happened.

3. You and your friend find a five-dollar bill on the sidewalk. You want to keep it, but at this moment a woman comes down the street looking for something. You are certain she has lost it. What do you do?

4. You tried out for a leading part in a play but were put in the chorus. You try to be a good sport when you talk to the teacher and to the girl who was cast in the part you wanted.

5. Your mother has just given your old rag doll to your younger cousin, who is visiting you. Neither of them knows how much the doll means to you. You try to pretend it is all right.

6. You see the girl across the aisle cheat on a test when the teacher steps out of the room. She suspects that there has been cheating and asks you and the girl to stay after class so she can find out about it. What does each one of you say and do?

7. You are delivering flowers for a neighborhood florist. On this particular day you are carrying a very large plant, and you lose the address. You think you remember it, however, so you go to what you hope is the right door. It is the wrong address, but the person who answers the door accepts the plant, then discovers the mistake. You have left by that time. How do all three of you work things out?

8. Three of you are getting refreshments ready for a party. It is said that "too many cooks spoil the broth." This happens when all of you put salt in the chocolate pudding, thinking that it is sugar and needs sweetening. This can be a very funny situation. How do you handle it?

9. You are falsely accused of cheating on an examination. You are angry and upset. The three persons involved are your teacher, the principal of the school, and you.

10. Your two best friends are running for president of your class. You meet on the playground. What do you say? How do you handle the situation?

11. You are in a laundromat, waiting for a washing machine. One is ready, except that the person who put the clothes in it has not returned for them. One woman tells you that you have a right to remove the clothes and use the machine. Another says that you should wait, because the owner is coming back in a few minutes. Meanwhile, you are in a hurry. What do you decide to do? Does the person who left the clothes return soon? How does the situation turn out? (This has several possible endings.)

12. You are at the checkout counter of a supermarket. The cashier is checking off your items when you realize that you forgot to get the

milk. You run back for it. This annoys the person behind you. Then you discover that you don't have enough money to pay the bill so you have to return some items. By this time the cashier and two people behind you are annoyed. You put the things back on the shelves and return, but when you pick up your shopping bag, which the cashier has packed for you, it splits open. Now you are angry, too. This makes everyone laugh, including you; suddenly the annoying situation becomes funny!

OTHER SUGGESTIONS

Unfinished stories can also be used to stimulate thinking. If the teacher introduces a character and sets the scene, the group is given the problem of completing the story. Although this is more an exercise in plotting, the action is motivated by the character: an interesting character makes for an interesting plot.

One club group showed an unusual interest in holidays, so the teacher used this as a springboard for the entire year. She brought in stories about Hallowe'en, Thanksgiving, Christmas, New Year's Day, Valentine's Day, St. Patrick's Day, April Fool's Day, Memorial Day, and the Fourth of July. Sometimes the group acted out the stories she read to them; sometimes they made up stories of their own, suggested by the occasion. One day they observed that there was no holiday in August. The result was an original play, which they called *A Holiday for August*. It was to be a festival of children's games, which developed into a particularly attractive summer pageant. August was the narrator, who began by telling of his disappointment that no one had ever thought to put a holiday in his month. At the conclusion, he expressed his joy that the children had made him special with a festival of games played in his honor.

IMPROVISATIONS WITH PROBLEMS FOR DISCUSSION

The following situations involve problems. Older players may enjoy first improvising them, then discussing the options with the rest of the class.

A. You are in a gift shop in a terminal. Over the glass and china counter there is a sign that says if you break anything, you will have to pay for it. Your sweater sleeve accidentally catches a glass dish, and it falls to the floor and breaks. It is so noisy in the terminal that no one sees or hears it. What are you going to do?
   a. Go to the clerk with the broken pieces and explain what happened.
   b. Decide to do nothing, hoping you can get away with it.

B. Your class is competing in a play festival. The group about to go on is very good. Suddenly you see their most important prop lying on the floor outside the stage door. You realize that if they lose it, they won't be able to replace it, and any substitute prop will probably upset the actors. What are you going to do?
   a. Pick up the prop and give it to the stage manager.
   b. Hide the prop in a trash basket, in an effort to make them do less than their best.

C. You are invited to a party in a very beautiful home. Your mother says you should dress up, but your friends say they are going to wear blue jeans. One of them says she has no dress clothes. What will you do?
   a. Try to persuade your friends to dress up.
   b. Dress up; then change into blue jeans at the last minute.
   c. Wear your best clothes and find that everyone else is dressed casually.
   d. Try to help the one who has nothing dressy to wear.

D. You are buying a birthday present for your sister or brother. You know exactly what she or he wants. You find two different gifts, one cheap and the other expensive. You also see something you want for yourself. If you buy the expensive item, it will take all your money. If you buy the cheap item, there will be enough money left for you to get what you want, too.
   a. You decide on the expensive gift.
   b. You decide on the cheap gift and get yourself what you want as well.

E. Just before a game you fall and hurt your knee. You don't know whether it's going to ruin your playing or not. What do you do?
   a. Say nothing about it and play. The knee lets you down.
   b. Explain and stay out of the game. The team is angry and upset.

F. There has been a bad flood in your neighborhood, and many families have had to leave their homes quickly. Your mother invites some people to stay in your house till the crisis is over.
   a. One of them is a boy or girl you dislike.
   b. You have to give up your room to a family.
   c. You decide to help in any way you can.

IMPROVISATIONS BASED ON STORIES

The most popular and, in many ways, most satisfactory form of improvisation for children is based on good stories. While making up original stories is a creative exercise, a group endeavor rarely achieves the excellence of a story that has stood the test of time, or has been written by a fine author. This is a way of introducing literature, and when it is well-chosen, offers good opportunities for acting. Chapters 6 and 7 illustrate the ways in which both simple and more complicated stories have been approached.

Good stories on any level should have literary quality, worthwhile ideas, correct information, and dramatic values. Children up to the age of ten and eleven like fairy tales and legends. Older children may still enjoy these but tend to prefer adventure, biography, and stories of real life. Frequently the latter, because of their length, will have to be cut, or the incidents rearranged. This is a learning experience which, if the group has had some experience, should not be too difficult.

Sometimes groups will want to act plays they have seen. This can be a worthwhile activity, though the tendency is to try to do it exactly as it was presented on the stage. Nevertheless, it can be a valuable period of time spent with a good piece of literature and is to be preferred to the reproduction of television shows or enactment of stories from comic books.

In order to present the right story, the leader must, first of all, know the group well. One leader, who was later to achieve remarkable success, told of her first experience as a young teacher at a settlement house in a disadvantaged urban area. Nothing she brought to the children in her drama group captured their interest. Improvisaton seemed an impossible goal, though the group was alert and lively when she saw them on the street. Finally she hit upon the idea of asking them to tell her stories they knew. Hesitantly at first, then willingly, legends and family anecdotes came. She tried them. Not only was the material a success—the group doubled in size. Parents began to look in. Before the end of the year, an activity that had seemed doomed to failure became the most popular in the settlement. Some years later, the drama department was to achieve nationwide recognition as an arts center. The search for material had led to the children themselves. Their cultural heritage, and their creative use of it under intelligent and sensitive guidance, was the first step.

The leader should prepare for improvisation of the story in advance, but avoid any preconceived ideas as to how it should be done. Improvisation is a group project with ideas contributed by both children and leader. The teacher is ready to offer suggestions but must be equally receptive to those of the players.

He should not expect the product to be perfect. Improvisation is never twice the same, and while repetition usually leads to greater fluency and richness of detail, each performance does not necessarily "top" the preceding one.

PUPPETRY

Although puppetry as an art merits a book in itself, the limitations of space and content preclude more than the most elementary discussion. It is, however, another, and excellent, medium of expression. Many teachers discover that children can often respond through puppets when they are unable to perform themselves. The puppet, an extension of the self, serves as a mask, enabling the player to gain a freedom he cannot achieve when acting a part. Behind the puppet stage, the timid child can lose his inhibitions and enter into the drama without self-consciousness. Puppetry, therefore, is a valuable medium when:

1. The players are self-conscious.
2. The room is inadequate for free movement.
3. The teacher knows something about puppetry or is able to work with the art department in the making of puppets.
4. The children themselves cannot move.

The last point is illustrated by the work of a young man who worked with bedridden children in a hospital. He devised stages for each bed so that the children could play stories together, with each child manipulating his own puppet. Though this would come in the category of creative drama for the handicapped, it is cited as an example of an imaginative approach to a problem that many teachers would have pronounced impossible.

A puppet stage and puppets that function have many of the values of creative drama. Dialogue is not memorized, and the players must be thoroughly acquainted with their material in order to present it. Puppetry is a highly creative activity, in that not only the drama but the puppets themselves are made by the players.

Actually, anything movable can be a puppet—ruler, pencil, tool, toy, brush and comb, or even a broom! Whatever works will qualify, though, admittedly there is added value in having children make puppets of their own of a manageable size. If a group has certain stories or situations in mind, they will want to design puppets to act in them. They may also want to make a narrator or mascot to introduce the show. This is an excellent way of communicating directly with an audience; often a puppet can get the attention of a class more readily than can a person. In fact, a puppet acting as emcee becomes a personality who can be used in many shows to introduce characters, make necessary explanations, and establish a rapport between puppeteers and audience.

There are many different types of puppets. String puppets or marionettes, rod puppets, hand puppets, and shadow puppets are some of the best known. Puppets range in size from a few inches to fourteen or eighteen feet. Some are so large they require two operators. These are unusual, though; most of the puppets we see are a foot or two high and are manipulated either by strings from above or by hands from below. As the latter are far easier to make and manage than the former, and demand much less equipment, they are most practical and popular for school use.

The use of smaller puppets simplifies matters greatly. It means, first of all, that you won't need a stage. You need only a flat surface along which to move the puppets. A covered overhead structure or elaborate equipment are not required; therefore even the youngest children can perform anywhere, indoors or out—on a park bench, desk, box, or windowsill.

A puppet show, simply done, requires little, if any, scenery. Children can, of course, make small pieces of scenery if there is time and interest. Just be sure that if scenery is made, it is secure and won't fall off the table or stage. They may want to use a few props, if necessary to the story. If so, have the children make them large in proportion to the size of the puppets. Otherwise they will be too small to be seen by the rest of the class. Also, they must be large enough to be picked up, and it is sometimes difficult for children to make tiny objects.

Papier-mâché is a good material to use for a puppet head because it can be molded into any shape and painted when it has dried. The advantage of styrofoam, on the other hand, is that it is lightweight and a hole can be scooped out for the finger of the puppeteer. Styrofoam cannot be painted as satisfactorily as papier-mâché, but it can be given a face with buttons and bits of felt. Hair and hats can be fastened to styrofoam with pins. Heads can also be made of other materials; it is interesting to try different things. Children enjoy experimenting, and often come up with delightful and inventive solutions.

There are a number of excellent books on puppetry. Consult some of the simpler ones for suggestions as to cutting patterns, making "the mouth," and "the glove." Flat puppets are also easy to make and can be very effective. They are exactly what the name implies: figures cut from a flat material like cardboard, manipulated from below, and held in profile so that they appear to have substance. One advantage of flat puppets in a classroom is that they occupy little space when packed up and put away.

There is no one right way to hold a puppet. Some puppeteers slip the index finger through the neck and into the head with the thumb and little finger acting as arms. Other puppeteers put their first and second fingers into the head. Older children have longer fingers; therefore the same position doesn't necessarily suit everyone.

Puppets can be held either in front of the operator or over his head. If the class is giving a fairly long play, it's more comfortable to work the puppet out front. This means that those who are watching will see the puppeteers, which doesn't really matter, though older children may prefer to hang a curtain between them and their puppets. This requires having a stage of some kind, where a dark, lightweight piece of cloth can be hung as a backdrop. The backdrop serves two purposes: to hide the operator and to make the puppet stand out. If the curtain is semitransparent, the puppeteer will be able to see through it without being seen. One final word; a puppet must be workable. No matter how beautifully it is made, unless it works well, it is not a good puppet.

The values in puppetry might be listed as follows:

1. Puppets provide opportunities for developing skills. Tools and materials must be handled with care in order to construct puppets that are sturdy and functional.
2. Dressing and decorating puppets requires imagination. Each puppet must become a character, first through the costume it is given, and then in the way in which it is decorated or painted.
3. Puppets require control. It takes controlled fingers to manipulate a puppet so that it can perform as the operator wishes.
4. Puppets offer an avenue of expression. Through the puppet, the operator expresses the thoughts and feelings of a character.
5. Puppets have therapeutic power. The timid or withdrawn child can find release through the puppet, whereas the aggressive child must learn to subordinate himself to the personality of the character he is presenting.
6. Puppets demand cooperation. Children learn to take turns and work together for a successful performance.
7. Puppetry is inexpensive. Delightful results may be obtained within the most limited budget. If there is no stage, a box will do until the teacher is able to construct something more permanent.
8. Puppetry can be an end in itself or a means by which other ends are reached.

ROLE PLAYING

Although it was stated in the first chapter that role playing as therapy is not the job of the creative drama teacher or the classroom teacher using creative drama techniques, some teachers have tried it with reported success. The purpose is educative rather than therapeutic, and the situations examined are common to all. Human conflicts and the ways in which problems are solved can promote social growth. Family scenes, school situations, and playground incidents give opportunity for interaction and group discussion. Discussion is the most important aspect of role playing, according to some teachers, for it is during these periods that various points of view are presented and attitudes clarified. The teacher must accept all ideas, giving the boys and girls a chance to express themselves without fear of disapproval. He will pose such questions as: How do you think the father felt? The brother? The mother? What did the man next door think when you broke his window? How do you think he felt the third time it happened? If you were he, how would you feel?

Exchanging roles is a good way to put oneself in the shoes of another, in order to understand him. One teacher gave a demonstration of role playing done with her group of junior high school girls, who lived in a neighborhood with a growing Puerto Rican population. The girls had had difficulty in accepting the newcomers, and the teacher's introduction of role playing, as a way of helping them understand the problem, led to the following improvisation. The scene was the planning of a school dance by a small clique. The committee wished to exlude the newcomers but could accomplish it only by making them feel unwelcome. This led to a serious breakdown in group relations. The period spent in playing the situation reportedly did much to restore peace and communication. The problem was faced squarely, and the girls were able to discuss their own attitudes and feelings. Later on, when the improvisation was done as a demonstration for a university class, it made a tremendous impression. The insights expressed through the honesty of the players proved the value of the experiment. The teacher did not claim to be a therapist but was an intelligent and experienced classroom teacher who was deeply troubled about a condition that was interfering with the work of the class.

Peter Slade, in *Child Drama*, summarizes the use of role playing in this way: "I would go so far as to say that one of the most important reasons for developing child drama in schools generally is not actually a therapeutic one but the even more constructive one of prevention."[1]

It must be pointed out that playing the part of a fictional character also demands identification with him and his problems. Exchange of parts gives all of the players a chance to experience both sides of a conflict. Obviously, the conflict which the group itself experiences is stronger, and the solution, if found, is of practical benefit.

SUMMARY

In summary, improvisation is the creation of a situation in which characters speak spontaneously. There are many ways of introducing improvisation, but some groundwork in pantomime is the best preparation. Once the players have achieved a sense of security in movement, they are ready to add dialogue. Dialogue does not come easily at first, but continued practice on familiar material usually induces the flow. There are many points of departure, and some of the most successful are those described in this chapter: improvisation from situations; objects or properties; sounds; characters; ideas and stories. A good program is one that makes use of all, though the teacher will be flexible in his approach, using those methods which lead to the greatest

1. Peter Slade, *Child Drama* (London: University of London Press, 1954), p. 119.

success for the group. Stories should be chosen with care and include both familiar and new material. Although the leader will probably want to start with the known, he will find this an excellent opportunity to widen horizons by bringing in good literature with dramatic content.

Role playing is a kind of improvisation, which has as its specific objective the social growth of the individuals. There may well be a place for it in the school or club program, but it must not be confused with creative dramatics as art. Both, however, are participant-centered and in that respect differ from theatre. When observed by others, improvised drama of any kind should be considered as demonstration and not as performance.

There is a great interest in improvisation today, and several professional theatre groups specialize in it. This, like the *commedia dell' arte* of the sixteenth century, is the development of improvisational theatre by adult actors to a high level of artistry. While many boys and girls are able to become involved in the playing, the purpose of improvisation with children is not to entertain them but rather to provide them with a medium of self-expression. The leader or teacher, whether working in school, camp, or club program, tries to stimulate the imagination, free the individual to create, guide the group, and build confidence. Evaluating the results with the group ultimately leads to richer performance and personal growth.

Enjoying great popularity today is *participation theatre* or *involvement drama*. This new technique, originated by Brian Way in England, permits the audience to become vocally, verbally, and physically involved in the production. Children are invited to suggest ideas to the actors from time to time during the enactment of a play. Frequently the audience, if not too large, is invited to come into the playing area to assist the cast in working out these ideas. Skillfully handled, this can be an exciting technique.

Of course, all theatre involves participation the moment the attention is captured. An audience feels, thinks, laughs, applauds, and occasionally speaks out; in our time, unlike earlier periods, adult audiences are expected to sit quietly whether the performance pleases them or not. The child audience, however, less inhibited and unschooled in these conventions, wants to do more, to become actively engaged as it suspends all disbelief. It identifies with the protagonist and participates in the action to the extent that conditions and authority permit. The younger the audience, the more natural the involvement. The point to be made here is that the *Brian Way Method* offers a new dimension in children's theatre by combining the formal with the informal in its effort to establish a closer relationship between actor and audience. The line commonly drawn between creative drama and children's theatre disappears as the spectator indeed becomes participant.

6

DRAMATIC STRUCTURE: THE PLAY TAKES SHAPE

If a creative drama teacher is going to help children create a play, he must know something of the structure and fundamental dramatic elements that distinguish the play from other forms of literature. He will not be expected to become expert at playwriting or dramatic criticism, but his enjoyment will be greater, and his guidance more helpful, if he has a basic understanding of the art form with which he is working. While there is no established formula for writing a play, particularly in this period of experimentation, there are certain elements that are necessary to its existence.

First of all, a play is to be played. Until it finds life upon a stage, it is not a play. Through the process of interpretation by actors, and the mounting by costume and scenic designers, it is born; and it will live or die according to the communication it has for an audience. It is true that some plays have been popular in their own times but have failed to speak to subsequent generations of

91

New Canaan Country Day School, courtesy Mary Perrine.

playgoers. Occasionally, but much less often, a play that is badly received when it opens finds an audience later. All too often, however, the play that fails to please in its first production is discarded before there is another opportunity to tell whether or not it communicates with even a limited audience.

There are plays that are universal and timeless in their appeal; what they have to say is as true today as when they were written, and this truth is understood by persons of all races and national backgrounds. There are other plays, however, whose messages are more temporal. Couched in the language of the day, they speak to the men and women of their own times, presenting problems both serious and comic, to which contemporary audiences respond, but to which those of another time or place are indifferent. This is not to discredit such plays, but simply to observe that, as theatre pieces, they have found success but lack the universality and timelessness of the classics. What will come out of our own time must be left to future generations of playgoers to decide. The works of George Bernard Shaw, Eugene O'Neill, and Tennessee Williams are among those that have been translated into many languages and produced widely both at home and abroad. It is too soon to tell, however, to whom they will speak in the future.

As to plays for child audiences, there are not many that meet the criteria of good dramatic literature. This is because the field is new and few professional playwrights have been attracted to it. Charlotte Chorpenning, Aurand Harris, Joanna Kraus, Flora Atkin, and Susan Zeder are among our best-known and most-produced American children's playwrights. We are not concerned with formal production or the printed script in this text; we are, however, involved with drama which older children sometimes want to carry beyond the classroom. It is here that process and product merge, and where knowledge of play structure and elementary theatre techniques are necessary. For this reason some attention is given to terminology and definition in this chapter.

Styles in playwriting change. Both the times and the theatres for which they are written affect the structure; nevertheless, certain elements identify the drama as a specific art form. Whatever our relationship to it, these are the elements of every play, whether written for adults or children.

CHARACTERS

A play involves characters. It is their conflict that holds our attention, and it is through them that the playwright delivers the message. Whether tragic or comic, lovable or despised, a character must be believable and belong to the play. Even in fantasy, a character must have reality; a witch or a ghost, for example, though unrealistic in itself, must compel our belief through the consistency of its behavior.

The hero or heroine should be someone with whom the audience can identify. Whatever his faults or human weaknesses, our sympathy must be aroused, making us care what happens. Whether he should be more good than bad is debatable, but we must accept him as real, and the actions as true.

Characters react to each other in a natural way. Though it is clearly established to whom the story belongs, there are other characters in the play who help to advance the plot through their involvement with it and their relationship to the hero, or protagonist. A skillful playwright develops character and situation through this interaction. Sometimes many characters are needed to tell a story; sometimes it is done better with one or two. The fewer there are, the greater the responsibility they have for telling the story, and the more the audience learns about them. The actor, however, must find in the most minor character the answers or clues to such questions as:

1. age of the character
2. education and cultural background
3. interests
4. occupation or profession
5. religion
6. members of the family and his relationship to them
7. social relationships
8. physical appearance and health
9. dominant mood
10. qualities of personality

Good characters are at all times consistent. If they are not, either through the writing or the actor's interpretation, we cannot believe in them. A believable character, on the other hand, has a reality that exists for the audience long after the final curtain has been drawn. Even when a character is fantastic, he must be credible.

DIALOGUE

Dialogue is the term given to the lines of the play. Good dialogue should belong to the characters, both in content and manner of speech. A nobleman will not talk like a peasant, nor will a country boy talk like a prince. While dialogue must, of course, be understood, the speech patterns of the characters must not be sacrificed. For example, a character of little education, who comes from a particular region, will use colloquial speech or appropriate dialect. Poetic dialogue has been employed during certain periods of history, but even this convention does not obscure the speech patterns and individuality of the characters.

Dialogue advances the plot. The playwright's job is to tell the story as economically as possible through the words of his characters. A soliloquy, in which only one person speaks, is a device used occasionally, but, in general, it is through conversation between two or more persons that characters are revealed and the plot is unfolded.

PLOT

The plot is the story. It may be simple or complex, internal or external, but what happens between the opening scene and the final curtain is the action we call story or plot. While tastes differ and styles change, a good plot holds the interest of the audience and is consistent. The most bizarre events must belong to it; and the outcome, whatever it may be, must seem logical.

CONFLICT

Conflict is the basis of drama, whether comic or tragic. Without conflict, there is no resolution; with conflict, the interest is sustained to the end. The successful playwright resolves the conflict in a way that is satisfying and acceptable.

THEME

The theme is the underlying thought or basic idea upon which the play rests. Not every play has a well-defined theme; it may, however, be the most important element. If there is a theme, the story both springs from and expresses it.

CLIMAX

The climax is the high point of the play. A three- or five-act play will have more than one climax, but there will always be a point at which the interest is highest. This scene usually comes somewhere near the end, after which there is an untangling, or resolution.

DENOUEMENT

This is the portion of the play that follows the climax. It may be long or short, depending upon the number of situations that need straightening out. In a children's play, the denouement and climax are often one, since children are satisfied once the conflict is settled, and long explanations at this point do not interest them.

UNITY

This is the overall term applied to the integration of the various parts of the drama, making a smooth and consistent whole. Unity may be achieved in a number of ways, such as the creation of: a single hero, a single action, a single idea, a single mood. On the other hand, a good play, no matter how many characters or episodes, can also be unified through the sensitive arrangement and organization of the various parts.

DRAMATIC IRONY

Dramatic irony is the term used for letting the audience in on a secret. Suspense is usually greater when it is employed, and many comedy scenes are funnier because of it.

STRUCTURE

Plays are described as long or short, depending on whether they are a full evening's entertainment or consist of merely one act. The number of acts in a long play varies. Though many playwrights have used the three-act form, some prefer four or five, or a series of episodes, rather than the conventional division between acts. Scenes are the divisions within acts, and usually occur when the time or place changes.

COMEDY

Comedy is defined as a play that ends satisfactorily for the hero or heroine. Comedy may be funny, but this is not essential according to this definition. Many comedies are serious, or satiric.

TRAGEDY

Tragedy is defined as a play that ends with the death or defeat of the leading character. Though fashions in playwriting change according to the times and public taste, the downfall of the protagonist places the play in the category of tragedy.

PROLOGUE AND EPILOGUE

These are the portions of the play sometimes placed at the beginning and end, to introduce it or to establish atmosphere. Such scenes are not an integral part of the play, though a narrator may appear in the prologue and also be involved in the play. Many children's plays employ narrators or are written with prologues as a means of imparting necessary information to an audience composed of different age levels and theatre experience.

NARRATOR

The narrator is a person who tells or reads an exposition that ties the incidents together. It is a useful device when an extended period of time or a variety of scenes are included, and is also a way of bridging the distance between actors and audience.

CHILDREN'S THEATRE

Children's theatre is first and foremost good theatre. In this respect, it does not differ from theatre for adults. There are, however, special requirements that must be met if the children's play is to hold their interest as well as be worthy of their time and attention. The script contains the same basic elements—characters, dialogue, plot—but not all material appropriate to the adult audience is suitable for children. Action, for example, is particularly important: the playwright, writing for children, must remember that it is more important to "show" than to "tell." Speeches should be short; long, talky dialogue is lost on the audience. Though vocabulary is necessarily adapted to the age level of the audience, it should not be oversimplified but should, rather, add enrichment and an opportunity for learning new words.

In writing an adaptation of a classic or well-known story, the playwright must make every effort to retain the essential elements of the source material

Children in South End School, Ceder Grove, New Jersey. Photograph by Lois Koenig.

so as not to disappoint or offend the audience. Characters must be believable. Fantasy and fairy stories comprise a large segment of plays written for children; nevertheless, the characters in such plays must be endowed with credibility, exhibiting a pattern of behavior that is consistent.

If the playwright has suggested difficult technical problems, he must ask himself whether they can be carried out successfully, or whether any modification of the effect will damage the play. By technical problems are meant such things as blackouts; characters who fly, disappear, or change into birds or animals; or unusual lighting and sound effects. What might be easily solved in the professional theatre can often pose an insoluble problem on the school stage, where equipment, budget, and technical assistance are limited.

Children's theatre, like adult theatre, should not depend on extravagant effects or gimmicks to stimulate interest; if such scenes are essential to the plot, however, and can be executed artistically, they will certainly add to the effectiveness. Children do not demand theatricality, but there is no question that their enjoyment is enhanced by scenes that offer excitement and color. Many children's plays call for music and dance. Therefore, the actor in children's theatre should study both so as to be able to sing, dance, fence, and master any other performance skills demanded by the play.

VALUES

Much has been said about the values of theatre for children, and basic to it is, of course, the script. The children's playwright has a special and difficult task, since he cannot anticipate the age level of the audience. The chances are that those who will be attending the play will range in age from five to twelve, perhaps a span even greater. Efforts have been made in some communities to try to control the age of the audience, either by a statement in the publicity, or by two series of plays. Age-level programming is controversial and persists as a problem with which the playwright is faced.

Children's interests change, as has been mentioned. While fairy and animal tales are popular with younger children, the eleven- or twelve-year-old prefers adventure, history, biography, and stories of real life. The attention span of the older child is longer, hence he can be absorbed for as long as two hours, in contrast to the younger child, who can probably not give full attention for more than an hour.

To the younger child, a character is all good or all bad. As he grows older, he begins to comprehend motives and can see a combination of faults and virtues, or weakness and strength, in a single person. Children identify with characters of high motives and brave deeds. Through this experience they grow, and gain appreciation for the ideals and standards by which men live. Values, therefore, are important to both young and old. Material that confirms such values as honesty, integrity, and social concern holds the interest of all, and may be presented without condescension.

In our preoccupation with ideals and values, we sometimes forget the appeal that comedy holds. Children of all ages love humor, though what is funny to the younger child—riddles, jokes, repetition, slapstick, the chase— does not appeal to his older brother or sister. Comical characters, ridiculous situations, and amusing lines are the materials of comedy, and may even teach more effectively than the serious play. Some of our social critics have used comedy to point up the defects and flaws of society.

Some criticism has been directed at those playwrights and producers who give children only the musical play. This seems to be a trend of the times, with the adult theatre having an equally large portion. However, whatever the medium—if the ingredients of taste and credibility are combined with a worthwhile idea, a hero with whom the audience can identify, action, poetic justice, substance, and literary quality, the playwright will have accomplished his purpose. Children today are exposed to so much television that they come to expect technical expertise and take spectacular effects for granted. In spite of this, however, they can be absorbed in honest work, well done and simply staged.

The following script of *The Three Wishes* is included as an illustration of a well-known children's story that contains the basic elements of a play:

a worthwhile and relevant theme
a plot that holds interest
plenty of action
characters who motivate the action
conflict
humor
a definite climax and satisfactory end

Like most folk tales, *The Three Wishes* may be enjoyed by a wide age range, though it is most popular with children under twelve. Despite the magic, it can be produced simply in classroom, club room, or camp. This is not to advocate formal productions by children of that age (the memorization of a script, long rehearsals, and performances for outside audiences); but an older group interested in giving plays for younger children would find this and other folk tales worthwhile and fun to do. Should a younger group want to perform for other classes or friends, it is more desirable for them to create a play themselves than to use a printed script. It takes longer but is well worth the time and effort. Through the process of developing a play, they will have an experience in creative writing and working with others in a variety of ways. The actual performance should be low key, regarded more as a sharing than a showing.

On the other hand, the theatre is a performing art, and children today see so many shows on television that they accept performance as a usual, rather than an unusual, occurrence. The teacher or leader should emphasize process and discourage production; nevertheless, a sincere desire to perform, on the part of the children, should be respected. "To withhold the experience," as one young teacher observed, "is like refusing them the game after they have practiced for it." According to another teacher, the most serious drawback to performance by children is the adult. Whether it is the teacher who works for a perfect product, featuring some children at the expense of others, or the adult in the audience who gives excessive praise, laughs in the wrong places, or is insensitive to the children's efforts, it adds up to exploitation. And exploitation, pressure, and boredom are destructive both to children and theatre. An occasional show need be none of these, if the adults involved handle the situation judiciously. As John Allen says of drama in schools, ". . . a school does not exist to create beautiful works of child art: what matters is the growth of the child and his ability to express himself in a variety of media."[1]

1. Allen, John, *Drama in Schools* (London: Heinemann Educational Books, 1979), p. 23.

THE THREE WISHES

(AN OLD TALE)

JOANNA, *an old peasant woman*
PETER, *her husband*
A STRANGER, *a young man with an air of mystery about him*

The scene is a small cottage. In the room are a table, chairs, a cupboard, and a fireplace. Down right there is a door leading to the outside. As the curtain rises, JOANNA, *an old woman with a discontented expression on her face, is sweeping the hearth.*

JOANNA: As if I could ever sweep all the dust and dirt from the hearth with this broom. (*She examines it.*) As many twigs fall from it as I have swept up. The old man will have to make me another, if he expects me to keep the house clean. (*She sweeps again for a moment, then stops and leans on the broom.*) Or better yet, if we had a servant girl, she could do all the cleaning. Think how that would be! To do nothing all day like our neighbor but sit in a chair by the fire and watch someone else do the work. Oh, why has the old man never earned enough to keep just one servant girl? Not five like the Duke. Nor four like our neighbor. Not even two like the simplest farmer. But one. Just one servant girl would be all I'd ask. (*She sighs.*) Oh, well, if the good man has not made his fortune yet he never will now. And we'll end our lives just as we began them—poor peasants in a cottage. (*She puts the broom in a corner and begins to set the table for supper. While she is doing this,* PETER, *her husband, comes in. He steps wearily through the doorway, then stops, leaning on a stout stick.*)

PETER: (*sniffs*) What! Supper not on the table? What have you been doing all day while I worked in the fields?

JOANNA: What do you expect with no one to help me? If we had a servant girl now, the supper would be ready and waiting.

PETER: And if I had a donkey to carry the plough, I'd not be so tired. I could climb on his back when the day's work was done and ride home in comfort.

JOANNA: A donkey? Why not wish for a horse? We could get a cart then and both of us drive out together on Sunday.

PETER: (*sitting by the hearth and continuing eagerly*) Yes, a strong brown horse like our neighbor's. I'd want one like his. Then I could plant a garden that brought in some money. In time I could buy another horse. With a team there's no telling how much we could earn.

JOANNA: Well, we haven't even one donkey. So pull up your chair and I'll have supper on the table in a minute.

PETER: (*sitting at the table*) Cabbage soup again?

JOANNA: (*bringing the pot to the table and ladling out the soup*) What did you expect? Meat and white bread like the Duke? Cabbage is the only thing in the garden.

PETER: (*eating it hungrily*) It's good. Though it would be better if you'd had a bone to cook with it.

JOANNA: A bone means meat. When have we had a roast with a bone left to flavor the soup? (*She sits down and tastes her soup. Then she takes a piece of bread.*) White bread now, instead of black. That would help.

PETER: White bread with butter, eh, wife?

JOANNA: (*eagerly*) When I stopped at our neighbor's today with the basket of cabbages to sell, I caught a glimpse of the kitchen. Such things as they were fixing for dinner! Cakes, butter, cream, and a goose roasting on the spit.

PETER: Ah, well, we are poor folk, Joanna. We could wish till the end of our days and nothing would come of it. (*At this moment a voice is heard from the fireplace.*)

STRANGER: Nothing would come of it? Are you sure, Peter? Are you sure, Joanna?

PETER: Who was that?

JOANNA: Was that you, Peter?

PETER: (*getting up*) I'd swear I heard a voice.

STRANGER: (*coming out of the fireplace*) And so you did. (*He brushes off his clothes.*) Now, then, what was that you were saying?

PETER: (*startled*) Oh, nothing. Nothing important.

STRANGER: Come, now, Peter, Joanna. You were wishing for a well-stocked larder, I think.

JOANNA: Well, yes, we were.

STRANGER: Are you sure that's all that you wish for?

PETER: (*eagerly*) Oh no. If I had a donkey now—

JOANNA: Not a donkey, Peter, a horse. So we could ride in a carriage together.

PETER: And plough a garden that went from here to that forest.

STRANGER: I'll tell you what. I've been listening to the two of you for some time and I'm about to make you a gift.

PETER: What kind of a gift?

JOANNA: Who are you? And how did you come here?

STRANGER: Let's say I'm a stranger who heard you in passing.
            (*He walks around the table and they look at him in wonder.*)
            Oh, I'm not a rich man, if that's what you're thinking.
            Though I do have strange powers.

PETER: What kind of powers?

STRANGER: I'll show you. Yes, I'm going to give you three wishes.

PETER: (*repeating the words after him, stupidly*) Three wishes?

STRANGER: Yes. But I must warn you, you'll have only three wishes
            between you. So watch out you don't waste them.

PETER: (*joyfully*) You mean, if I wished for a donkey, I'd get one?

JOANNA: No, Peter, a horse, not a donkey.

STRANGER: Sh! That's what I mean. Be careful. When you've used the
            three wishes up, there'll be no more of them. Think of what
            you want most.

PETER: And they'll be granted, no matter how great the request?

STRANGER: They'll be granted, never fear. But only the three. So
            watch out, Peter.
            (*The STRANGER moves back to the hearth and disappears as
            the old couple talk excitedly together.*)

PETER: Did you hear that, Joanna? Why, I can wish for a team of horses
            with a carriage to boot!

JOANNA: And a house!

PETER: Or a castle! With a kitchen as big as this room.

JOANNA: Filled with all sorts of good things to eat. (*She turns to speak
            to the STRANGER.*) Must we use all three wishes at once or
            can we save one for— Why, where has he gone? He's not
            here, Peter.

PETER: (*rubbing his eyes*) Vanished as suddenly as he appeared. Do you
            suppose we just dreamed this?

JOANNA: No, of course not. How could we both dream the same thing?
            And at the same time? He must have gone out the door while
            we were talking. Let's go after him.
            (*The two old people go quickly to the door but do not see him.*)

JOANNA: He's nowhere in sight. You go down the road, Peter. He may
            have gone round the bend.

PETER: All right. (*He disappears from sight, calling.*) Hey, hey, there!

JOANNA: Gone before we even had a chance to thank him. He was
            standing right here. (*Puzzled, she stands in the middle of the
            room for a moment.*) We might have asked him to supper. I

wish we'd— (*She claps her hands over her mouth*.) Just in
time. Now, then, what to wish for?
(PETER *comes in the door and goes to his chair*.)

PETER: Not a sign of him anywhere. You don't think, wife—

JOANNA: That we only imagined him? No, I don't. He said he had magic
powers. Therefore, why couldn't he disappear like smoke in
the breeze? (*She has an idea*.) Up the chimney, perhaps?
(*She goes to the hearth and looks up the chimney*.)

JOANNA: Not there, either. Come, Peter. Let's sit down and think of
three things to wish for.

PETER: Well, I still think a horse would be—

JOANNA: Sh! Remember what he said. Don't wish till we've thought of
everything we need. I'd say a house, instead of this cottage.

PETER: Or a castle with barns—

JOANNA: And servants—

PETER: And fine dresses for you—

JOANNA: And a gold-headed cane for you to lean on when you're tired.

PETER: Wait! We can't waste a wish on a cane. Why not wish me young
and strong again? Then I'd have no use for a cane.

JOANNA: (*excited*) Both of us young again, Peter! As we were when we
first moved into this cottage. My hair would be black. And
when I put on my fine clothes, I'd be as beautiful as the
Duke's daughter.

PETER: We mustn't be hasty. Let's eat our soup and then after supper,
we'll decide. (*He takes a spoonful of soup*.) It's cold.

JOANNA: And why shouldn't it be? Sitting out in these bowls. (*She takes
a spoonful*.) Oh, I wish we had sausage to go with it.
(*No sooner has she said the words than a sausage is on her
plate*.)

PETER: Oh, Joanna, see what you've done! Only two wishes left!

JOANNA: I didn't mean to do it.

PETER: (*angrily*) You've thrown away one third of our fortune, Joanna. I
wish that sausage were on the end of your nose!
(*At once the sausage is hanging from her nose. She puts her hands
up and feels it*.)

JOANNA: Peter!

PETER: I'm sorry, Joanna. I was angry. I didn't think. Here, let me pull
it off.

JOANNA: It's stuck tight. I'm trying.

PETER: (*Going over to her, he pulls and pulls*.) It certainly seems to be
stuck there. Come, let's both pull.

(They both pull but the sausage refuses to budge.)
It seems as if the harder we pull, the faster it sticks. I have it! I'll cut it off.

JOANNA: No, Peter. You might cut my nose.
(Peter gets a huge knife and comes toward her.)

PETER: I'll be careful. Let me try.

JOANNA: *(running away from him)* No, no. Leave me alone.

PETER: Perhaps if I cut it off just below—about here?

JOANNA: I don't want even half a sausage on the end of my nose. *(Wailing.)* Oh, Peter, what shall I do?

PETER: Just one wish left. Shall it be a house or the horses and carriage?

JOANNA: I can't go about with a sausage hanging on my nose. No matter how rich we were, people would laugh.

PETER: We could tie a scarf over your face.

JOANNA: Every time I stepped out of the house?

PETER: Perhaps no one would notice—

JOANNA: Oh, Peter, how would you like to have a sausage hanging down over your chin?

PETER: It may go away.

JOANNA: It won't, I know. Oh, Peter, there's just one thing to do.

PETER: You mean—

JOANNA: Yes. To wish it off. Are you willing?

PETER: I guess you're right. *(They look at each other.)* We were both foolish.

PETER
JOANNA: *(together)* We wish the sausage off her/my nose.
(Miraculously the sausage comes off in JOANNA's hand.)

JOANNA: There. *(Sadly.)* All three wishes gone. And we're no better off than we were.

PETER: Except, perhaps— Come, wife, let us eat our supper and be grateful that no more harm was done. After all, we do have soup in our bowls—

JOANNA: And a roof over our heads—

PETER: And strength enough to work in the fields.

JOANNA: And each other.

PETER: And, who knows, perhaps some day he will come again. The next time— *(He and JOANNA look at each other and laugh.)*
(The curtain falls)

The business of the sausages, incidentally, provides excellent material for pantomime, and it is suggested that this part be improvised by itself.

Myths, legends, and folk tales are particularly good for creative playing. In the first place, these stories have been told and retold over the years so that the story line is clear and easily followed. Characters are generally well-defined, have complete relevance to the plot, and, even in the case of the supernatural, have credibility. The theme is usually strong, for one generation has passed the tale along to the next, carefully, if unconsciously, preserving the values of the culture. Primitive creation myths, explaining natural phenomena, are particularly good today in the face of our expanding body of information about the universe and the new kinds of questions we are asking.

A group might dramatize a well-known myth or legend, or, through the study of legendary material, develop a play of its own. A holiday, for instance, often has an interesting origin, which would make good material with which to construct a play. Hallowe'en is a good example.

Hallowe'en

Of all the holidays, Hallowe'en must certainly be one of the top favorites of children. Their fascination with the supernatural, the dressing up in fanciful and grotesque costumes, the parties, games, tricks, and treats (all to be forgiven in the spirit of the occasion) make for a holiday with appeal for every age. Even the commercialization of Hallowe'en in the form of ready-made costumes, masks, crepe paper decorations, and packages of candy corn in the supermarket have not spoiled its appeal, though it has perhaps shifted the emphasis. At any rate, Hallowe'en as a suggestion for dramatizing is guaranteed to elicit an enthusiastic response from the most resistant group. Let's take a look at Hallowe'en to see what some of the possibilities are.

Its roots go back to antiquity, thus providing a rich source of information for playmaking as well as the fun and the social activities associated with its celebration. As a holiday, therefore, Hallowe'en enjoys great popularity because it offers interesting content, action, and an opportunity for dressing up. Fifth and sixth graders, with the help of the teacher, can learn about play structure through the process of building a creative drama from source material.

The customs associated with Hallow'en spring mostly from three distinct sources: pagan, Roman, and Christian. The strongest influence was probably the pagan. Each year the Druids of Northern and Western Europe celebrated two feasts—Betane, on the first of May, and Samhain, on the thirty-first of October. The latter was a fall festival, held after the harvest had been gathered, thus marking the end of summer and the beginning of winter. Their new year began on November first, so that Hallowe'en was actually New Year's Eve. Fortune-telling was a popular custom on this holiday, as people were eager to learn what the new year held.

The Druids believed that the spirits of persons who had died the previous year walked the earth on this night. They lighted bonfires in order to frighten away the evil spirits. It is thought that the candle in a pumpkin is a descendent of this custom. One legend has it that a rogue named Jack was caught playing tricks on the devil. As punishment, Jack was doomed to walk the earth forever, carrying a pumpkin lantern to light his way.

In order to ward off evil spirits and also to imitate them and so frighten others, many persons took to the wearing of costumes and masks. This led to playing tricks, mixing fun with fear and superstition.

In Rome the festivities were mainly in the form of feasts honoring the goddess of fruits, Pomona. When the Romans invaded Britain, they took their customs with them. The traditional use of fruits and vegetables (apples, corn, nuts) may be derived from this intermingling of celebrations.

During the Middle Ages the Christians observed All Saints' Day, which fell on November first. The eve of that day was October thirty-first, which became known as Hallowe'en, or hallowed evening. There is little, if any, Christian significance left; for most people it is a secular celebration, retaining only the outward trappings of ancient customs and rituals. Witches, ghosts, goblins, cats, bats, and pumpkins come to mind when we hear the word Hallowe'en. (Recently, collecting money for UNICEF has replaced the traditional "treats" in many communities.) Because so much information is available and much of it not generally known, Hallowe'en is a good choice for a program that can be researched, improvised, written, and, if desired, performed for the enjoyment of others. The tasks involved would be:

1. Looking up information about Hallowe'en (the amount dependent on the age of the group and the time that can be devoted to it).
2. Improvising legendary material with the greatest appeal for the children.
3. Developing a program or play by the group based on the information found.
4. (Optional) Writing a script that has come out of the research and improvisation.

Should this prove to be something the children want to perform for others, it will lead naturally into the next stage: a play for an audience. What we are concerned with here, however, is an understanding of dramatic structure, obtained through the process of creating an original play or group project. Later, if the group so desires, it might try creating a myth of its own. Children enjoy thinking of ways to explain phenomena, sayings, or characters for which they have no ready answers. Because an activity of this sort involves creative writing as well as creative playing, it is a way in which drama can be integrated naturally into the curriculum. Younger children might want to find their own explanations for such things as the Man in the Moon, Groundhog Day, Jack Frost, candles on a birthday cake, or perhaps local jokes and customs. Older children find intellectual stimulation in the study and dramatization of myths and legends. They may also want to try their hands at the writing of original science fiction. Our space age, far more familiar and acceptable to young people than we often realize, can be a powerful force for imaginative writing. The study of dramatic structure, through the creation of an original plot, is a sound and rewarding experience.

7

BUILDING PLAYS FROM SIMPLE STORIES

When the group has had some experience with pantomime and improvisation, it will be ready to attempt a story. Groups of all ages welcome this next step and often have suggestions of their own to offer regarding favorite stories or material from other classes which they want to dramatize. Regardless of how well they may know the story, there is still some preliminary work to be done before improvisation begins. The teacher, well acquainted with the group by this time, knows the kind of material that will have an appeal and present the fewest difficulties. Success is important to future work, and the leader will want to select a story that he is relatively sure the group can handle.

There is a wealth of good literature readily available, which both group and leader can enjoy and find worthy of their efforts. The stories and poems included in this and the two following chapters is illustrative of the kinds of material groups of all ages have used successfully.

109

New Canaan Country Day School, courtesy Mary Perrine.

Suggestions are offered as to ways in which it may be presented and handled. It should not be inferred that these are the only or even the best ways of using the material; they are merely illustrations of the thinking done by some groups.

Folk tales, legends, and fables are recommended material for use on all levels, though different age groups view them in respect to their own maturity and experience. For younger children, stories should be simplified in the telling, whereas in working with older children, greater emphasis can be given to characterization. Meanings and insights come with experience as well as age; hence a really good story spans many age levels.

When the teacher has decided upon an appropriate story, he must decide whether it is better told or read. In general, telling the story is preferable because it establishes a closer rapport with the audience and gives the leader a chance to observe the listeners' reactions, and clarify, as he goes along, any points that appear to puzzle them. This means that he must be thoroughly familiar with the material; in fact, the beginning teacher will do well to practice telling the story aloud before he presents it to the group. This will add to his own self-confidence and help him develop greater variety and color in his presentation. A good voice and clear diction are certainly assets, but even more important is the teacher's ability to involve himself in the material so that the story comes alive to the listeners. He will probably find it easier to establish contact if he sits down, with his audience gathered closely around him.

Experience in telling stories helps the teacher to avoid such pitfalls as forgetting parts and having to return to them out of sequence. He will soon learn to proceed in order, holding the climax until the end, including as many details as his listeners are able to handle, and as are necessary to the story. He will avoid condescension, and will adapt his vocabulary to the age and background of the group, taking advantage, at the same time, of opportunities to introduce new words and explain ideas that are strange or foreign. With a little practice, most leaders can develop an effective storytelling technique, which stimulates enthusiasm for dramatization.

After the story has been told, and all questions answered, the children are ready to begin planning how they will handle it. A discussion should include a review of the plot and descriptions of the characters. When the leader feels that the group has the details well in mind, he will suggest that they try playing it. Asking for volunteers is a good way of starting: this gives the stronger ones a chance to try it first, and the more timid an opportunity to become better acquainted with it before taking their turns. Casting is done on a voluntary basis the first two or three times. Later on, the leader may suggest that other children try various parts. For instance, he might say, "Lynne hasn't had a chance yet. How would you like to try the princess this time?" Or, "John has been the cobbler. Let's give Alan a chance to play it. And you, John, be one of the townsfolk." Or, "I know David has a strong voice. How about letting him be the giant?"

In other words, it is the development of each participant that concerns us. Later on, when the group is ready to play the story for the last time, the leader might suggest those children who have brought the greatest reality to each part, but this is as close as we come to type casting.

The situation may be played any number of times, but the replaying should not be interpreted as rehearsal. It is hoped, of course, that with each playing, the story will gain in substance and depth; that there will be deeper insights; and that the participants will develop greater freedom and self-confidence. The discussions preceding and following each playing are important aspects of creative dramatics, for it is during these periods that some of the most creative thinking takes place. Some questions that might precede the first playing are:

1. What do we want to tell?
2. Who are the people?
3. What are these people really like?
4. What are they doing when we first meet them?
5. Where does the first scene take place?
6. What kind of a house do they live in?

After the scene has been played once, more specific questions can guide the discussion. These might be:

1. Did they tell the story?
2. What did you like about the opening scene?
3. Did the people show that they were excited? (Angry, unhappy, etc.)
4. When we play it again, can you think of anything that would improve it?
5. Was anything important left out?

In the course of a year, there are often delightful results, and both the leader and group may honestly wish to share them with others. There is no reason why this should not be done, provided public performance was not the original intention. More often, however, the initial results will be crude and superficial. Dialogue will be scanty, despite the most careful planning. To the experienced leader, this does not represent failure. It is an early stage in the development of the group, and may, at that point, indicate real progress. Acceptance of the effort, therefore, does not mean that the leader is satisfied to remain at this level but, rather, that he recognizes the efforts that have been made and is aware of the values to those who have taken part. As he works with the group, he will become more selective in what he accepts but, in the beginning, he will accept all ideas because they have been offered. It is important for every member to feel that his ideas are worthy of consideration. In time, even eight- and nine-year-olds will learn to distinguish between contributions that advance the play and those that distract or have little to do with it.

The following stories have been chosen for inclusion here because of their simplicity. Most groups are familiar with them, and like them, and need only to be refreshed as to the details. The first, *Caps for Sale,* is popular with younger children, but equally interesting to older children, and even adults, because of the underlying theme. Very young children enjoy being monkeys, and like to take turns acting the Peddler. Older children, however, quickly see a parallel between human behavior and the behavior of monkeys, hence find in this simple tale a meaning worthy of their thought and effort. Although *Caps for Sale,* or *The Peddler and His Caps,* is very well known, a brief synopsis of the story is included.

CAPS FOR SALE

There was once a little old man who made caps. All year long he worked at them: red caps, pink caps, yellow caps, blue, green, and purple caps, caps with feathers and caps without. Every so often, when he had made a large enough number of caps to sell, he would put them in his pack and take them around to the villages. This particular morning he decided that he had plenty of caps to peddle, and since it was a very fine summer day, he took himself off. His cries of "Caps for Sale" roused the townsfolk, and soon many of them were trying on caps and selecting the ones they wanted to buy. Butchers, bakers, shoemakers, mothers, children, and even the mayor himself, gathered around the little Peddler, trying on caps and admiring their appearances. Finally, the mayor, who had found nothing to his liking, took off his cap and tossed it back to the Peddler, suggesting that he come again some other day. "Not today, Peddler. Come back another time."

Reluctantly, all of the townsfolk followed his example, echoing the mayor's words that he return another day. Realizing that he could sell no caps in this village, the little Peddler departed. Before long, he passed by the edge of a woods, and feeling very sleepy, decided to lie down and rest. Soon, however, he fell fast asleep, his hats lying on the grass beside him. Now it happened that this part of the woods was inhabited by a band of monkeys. Monkeys are curious little fellows, and finding the Peddler asleep under a tree, they decided to investigate the contents of his pack. First one, then another, cautiously approached. When they saw that the Peddler was wearing a cap on his head, the monkeys tried the caps on their own little heads. Then they scampered a distance away, chattering excitedly, for they were very much pleased with themselves. The sound of the chattering soon awakened the Peddler. He reached for his pack and was astonished to find it empty. Greatly puzzled, he looked about him to see where the caps might have gone. Suddenly he saw the monkeys. He called to them, pleasantly at first, and asked them to give back his caps. They only chattered, "Chee, chee, chee," pleasantly, in reply.

Then he shook his fist at them and demanded his caps, but they just shook their fists back. Angrily he stamped his foot at them but they only stamped their little monkey feet at him in return. He begged, and they begged; he moved a few steps away, and they moved a few steps away. Suddenly it occurred to him that the monkeys were doing everything he did. With a sweeping gesture, he removed his own cap and tossed it to the ground at his feet. Immediately all of the monkeys removed their caps and threw them down to the Peddler. He gathered his caps up as quickly as possible, then made a low bow and thanked the monkeys for returning them. Chattering happily, the monkeys also bowed; each was pleased with the trick he thought he had played on the other.

When the leader has finished telling the story, he will be wise to review the plot to make certain that it is clearly understood. From here on, there are many ways of proceeding. He may ask where the story begins, and how many scenes the group sees in it. They may suggest two, three, four, or even five, though they usually come to the conclusion that three main scenes are necessary. These are:

1. The Peddler starts out on his travels.
2. He arrives in the village.
3. He stops to rest in the forest.

Some groups imagine a road running all around the room, with the three scenes laid in different areas. This enables the Peddler to move from one place to another, and gives him an opportunity to talk to himself as he walks along. Since no scenery is used in creative dramatics, such an arrangement is perfectly feasible. Incidentally, one advantage of a large room in dramatizing this story is the amount of freedom it provides the players: they are not limited by the rows of seats or traditional stage area. When playing in an auditorium, however, the succession of scenes will follow a more conventional pattern, unless there is an apron (area in front of the curtain) to accommodate some of the action.

In discussing how the Peddler's occupation might be introduced, one group may suggest that he have a wife with whom he can talk over his plans for the day at breakfast. Another group may give him a helper; another, a son; and still another may insist that he lives alone and so, has him talk to himself.

Whether or not his trip down the road is considered a separate scene depends on the importance the group attaches to it, but the next major scene is certainly the village in which the Peddler attempts to sell his caps. One of the advantages of a story of this sort is the opportunity for characterization afforded by the villagers. As any number of villagers may be included, there is an opportunity for many children to take part. The mayor is always a favorite, though other delightful characters may be created; a shoemaker, a mother, a small boy, a farmer, a young girl, and a milliner are examples. The playing of this scene will be long or short, depending upon the characterizations and the fun the children have with it. Again, if a road is used to suggest the Peddler's travels, he will move along to a place designated as a part of the forest. If the group is small, the same children who were villagers can be monkeys. If the group is large, however, there is ample opportunity for others to play the monkeys. One of the best features of this particular story is the flexibility of the cast: whatever its size, the entire group can take part in it.

Regardless of age, children always respond to the monkeys, and the activity demanded by their antics is conducive to bodily freedom. There is such great opportunity for pantomime in the final scene that the leader might do well to begin with it, as a means of relaxing the group. By the time all have been monkeys, they are better prepared to begin on the story.

In this, and, indeed, in any story selected for dramatization, it is a good idea to work on small portions first rather than to attempt the entire story at once. No matter how well the children may know the material, it is quite another thing to improvise the scenes. Therefore, working on short bits, not necessarily in sequence, makes for more successful playing. In this respect, it is similar to rehearsing a play: the director does not attempt to run through the complete script until he has rehearsed each individual scene.

THE FIR TREE WHO WANTED LEAVES

The German tale of the little fir tree who wanted leaves is a good choice for young children. Although it concerns an individual, it can be done by the group. No dialogue is necessary, but it may be added, if and when the children want to use words. Music to create mood and suggest the changes will help the children play the story.

There was once a little fir tree who grew tired of his needles and wanted leaves like the other trees in the forest. One day, while he was complaining, a voice answered him, asking what kind of leaves he would like. "Oh, green leaves like the other trees," said the little fir. "I want leaves that are green in summer and change to red in the fall."

No sooner had he asked for them, than his needles changed into smooth, bright green leaves. The little fir tree thought he looked very fine indeed. All that morning he moved his branches and admired his appearance. Then, about noon, along came some goats. Seeing the fresh green leaves, they lifted their heads and greedily began to eat them. The poor little tree could do nothing to stop them, and soon all his leaves were gone.

Creative Drama Session, University of Texas at Austin. Courtesy Coleman A. Jennings.

He felt very bad. Finally he said, "I wish I had glass leaves. They would be pretty and no one would want to eat them."

Again, no sooner had he said the words than he found himself covered with sparkling glass. He was greatly pleased. "These leaves are much better than the others."

He moved his branches and watched them sparkle in the sunshine. About noon, however, a storm came up. The wind blew and the leaves hit against each other. They were so brittle that as the storm grew worse, all the glass was broken and fell to the ground.

The little fir was discouraged but not for long. "I know", he said, "I'd like gold leaves. They will sparkle, but the goats will not eat them and they cannot break."

Suddenly he was covered with yellow gold that gleamed in the sunlight. Surely he was the most beautiful tree in the forest! All day long he admired his leaves. Then, as night fell, he saw some robbers approaching. When they saw the little fir tree, they could hardly believe their eyes. "A gold tree," they said, "there's enough gold here to last us the rest of our lives!"

They began picking off the leaves and putting them in sacks on their backs. In no time at all, every leaf was gone. The little tree stood cold and miserable in the forest.

"I wish," he began, "I wish I had my needles back again. They were the best of all."

Quick as a flash his branches were covered with long, dark green needles. And he never wished for leaves again.

The theme of dissatisfaction with one's lot runs through folklore, and it is understood by quite young children. There are many ways in which this particular story can be handled. If the group is small, it can be played by individuals. Better, however, is group playing with some children being the leaves, others the goats, the wind, and the robbers. In this way the imagination is stretched as the players experiment with different ways to show how leaves, glass, and gold might look and move.

The story lends itself to movement as well as to improvisation and offers rich possibilities for discussion and expressive playing.

Fables are popular with some groups, though the obvious moral does not appeal to others. One advantage of a fable is its brevity. There is action as well as a quick and satisfying ending. There is little opportunity for character development, however, though some groups will fill in the plot with delightful and imaginative dialogue. The following is one fable that boys particularly enjoy.

There was once a shepherd lad who went out to the fields each day with his flock. One day, growing tired of his lonely life, he decided to create some excitement. And so, when he was a distance from the village, he cried, "Wolf! Wolf!" The townsfolk, hearing his cries, dropped their chores and ran up the mountainside to help him. When they got there, however, the shepherd boy only laughed, and they realized the trick that had been played on them.

The following morning, the boy did the same thing again, and again the townsfolk ran to his rescue. Discovering that he had fooled them a second time, they returned to their work, angrily vowing that they would not be taken in by this trick again. On the third morning, when the boy was high up on the mountain, he heard a disturbance among the sheep. Seeing a wolf attacking them, he called out in terror. "Wolf! Wolf!" No one came. Again he called, "Wolf! Wolf! A wolf is attacking my sheep!"

The townsfolk heard his cries, but thinking it to be only a joke, did not go to his aid. The shepherd lad learned a lesson that day: if one cries "Wolf!" too often, no one comes when there really is danger.

The leader will not want to spend a great deal of time on this story since there is only one major character. On the other hand, the townsfolk offer opportunities for creating a variety of persons. Who are they? What is each doing when he hears the boy's cries, and what is his reaction when he discovers the trick? Who starts up the mountainside first? How would an old man feel if he climbed up a steep hillside for nothing? How does each one respond the second day? What does each say to his neighbor on the third morning? Such questions as these help the group create individual characters of the crowd.

Because the story is so short, every child can have a chance to try the part of the shepherd. What is he like? How do we know he is lonely and restless? Where are his sheep? How does he hit on the trick he plays? How does he feel when he sees the wolf? What does he do when the people fail to come to his rescue? Does he learn a lesson?

If there is a stage in the room, it may be used as the mountain where the sheep are grazing. If there is no stage, the boy can be at one end of the room so as to suggest the distance between him and the village. There is excitement in this story, and the kind of action that appeals to younger children. The lesson, incidentally, is one that all are able to understand and appreciate.

The Tortoise and the Hare is another fable that has great appeal, and may be played without much time spent in preparation. Although the characters are animals, children enjoy discovering what they can do to suggest their characteristics and give them reality.

THE TORTOISE AND THE HARE

There was once a Hare who was forever boasting of his great speed. In fact, whenever more than two animals gathered together in the forest, he would appear and then take the opportunity of telling them that he could outstrip the best of them. Stretching his long legs proudly, he would declare, "No one has ever beaten me. When I race at full speed, there is no one who can pass me."

The other animals said nothing, for there was no one who wished to dispute him. One day, the Tortoise, who had been listening quietly, replied, "I accept your challenge. I will race you."

"That is a good joke," laughed the Hare. "I could go to the goalpost and back before you had passed the first marker."

"Save your breath until you've won," said the Tortoise. "I'm willing to race you."

The other animals, who were mighty tired of listening to the Hare's boasts, were only too glad to hear someone speak up, though they secretly wished it had been an animal with a greater chance of winning. Nevertheless, they cheered the little Tortoise on and helped draw up a course. Then they lined up on each side and the Cock called the start of the race: 1—2—3—GO!

The Hare was gone and out of sight in a flash as his white cotton-tail disappeared through the bushes. The Tortoise kept his eyes straight ahead and never varied his pace. Presently, the Hare returned and danced around him, laughing at his slow progress. The Tortoise didn't say a word. Then, to show his scorn for the Tortoise he lay down under a tree. He yawned, shut his eyes, and finally curled up and took his afternoon nap. The Tortoise only smiled and plodded on. After a while, the Hare awoke from his sleep. He opened his eyes just in time to see the Tortoise crawl past the winning post. As fast as he could make his legs go, he could not get there in time to save the race. The Tortoise, slow as he was, had crawled steadily forward while the Hare had spent his time running in circles and taking a nap. "I've learned a lesson today," said the Hare, ashamed of himself for having made so much fun of his opponent. "It's hard work, and not speed, that wins the race."

After the leader has told the fable, there is a good opportunity for total group participation: all can be hares, then tortoises. Younger children particularly enjoy the physical movement of this story. After some preliminary pantomime, it can be played in its entirety, since it is so short. A large room lends itself to the race, which may be run in a wide circle or in repeated circling of the space. Unless the group is very large, all may take turns playing the two parts, with the rest participating as the other animals watching the contest. This is a highly satisfying story for use in a single period, or as a change from a more ambitious undertaking. Discussion brings out the moral, which children of ages eight to ten comprehend easily.

The Sun and the Wind and *The Country Mouse and the City Mouse* are favorites with many children. They also provide excellent opportunities for pantomime, as well as ideas for discussion. A group of fables, incidentally, makes a good program without taxing either teacher or players.

A story that appeals to both boys and girls, and is easy to play in a small area, is the tale of *Darby and Joan*. There are only three characters but the story is so short that, unless a group is large, every boy and girl may have a chance to try one of the parts.

DARBY AND JOAN

Have you ever seen a little house about the size of a birdhouse, with two doors in front marked "Fair" and "Rain"? And have you ever noticed that a little woman stands in the doorway marked "Fair," and a little man in the doorway marked "Rain"? And, depending on the weather, that one is always out while the other is in? Well, this little man and woman are known as Darby and Joan, and the following story is told of how they came to be there.

Many years ago Darby and Joan lived happily in a little cottage together. As time went on, however, they began to quarrel. Regardless of how peaceably the day had begun, before long they were disagreeing and finding fault with one another. And so a spell was put on them: from that day forth, one must be out while the other was in, depending on the weather. Our story begins many years later. The day has been fair but the weather is beginning to change, and Darby is about to come out, allowing Joan to go inside and finish her housework. As they talk together, not seeing each other, they regret the quarreling that led to their punishment.

"How I wish I could see you, Joan. Do you realize it has been ten years since we sat down at the table together?"

"I know, Darby. I'm sure if we could be released from this spell, we should never quarrel again."

"Imagine not seeing one's own wife for ten years. It was too cruel a punishment."

As they are talking together, Darby notices someone approaching the cottage. He calls out, "It's beginning to rain. Won't you stop and rest here for a bit?"

The stranger, who is a Fairy in disguise, comes to the doorway and asks Darby why it is he is standing out in the rain while his wife stays in the house. He explains, and sighs over their misfortune. The Fairy then tells him who she is, and offers to release them from their spell but only on condition that they never quarrel again. They agree joyfully, and the Fairy goes off, but not without warning them that if they do quarrel, they will be put under the spell again, and this time it will be forever.

The old couple can scarcely believe their good fortune as they move their arms and legs stiffly and venture outside together. The rain is clearing, and they decide to have supper in front of the cottage. Darby brings out the table and chairs while Joan gets the food. Scarcely have they sat down to eat, however, when Darby criticizes the way Joan slices the bread. Joan replies with annoyance that if he objects, he can cut it himself. Furthermore, she notices that he is wearing his hat at the table. Before they know it, they are quarreling furiously.

Suddenly, the Fairy appears. The old people are stricken. They beg the Fairy for one more chance to try getting along, but she replies, "It is too late. You knew the condition and should have thought of the consequences."

Darby and Joan feel the spell coming on, and slowly move back into their old positions. The Fairy disappears with the old couple once more back in their doorways marked "Fair" and "Rain."

Children of all ages enjoy this story, and have a grand time with the quarrel. First, playing the puppet-like figures while under a spell is a good pantomime for the entire group. Release from the spell gives practice in making the transition from a stiff, controlled stance to free movement. After all have tried it in pantomime, they will be ready to add dialogue. *Darby and Joan* is a delightful little story that calls for strong feeling and changes of mood.

THE BAT'S CHOICE
(A TALE FROM INDIA)

This legend comes from India and offers various possibilities for creative playing.

In India they tell why the bat hides by day and comes out only at night. Many, many years ago there was a war between the birds and the animals. The bat, who had wings like a bird but a body like an animal, watched them fight but could not make up his mind which side to join. Finally, he decided he would go to the winning side. That appeared to be the animals, so he went over to them, declaring his everlasting loyalty.

Then suddenly things changed. With the help of the eagle, the birds began to overcome the animals. Now the bat wondered whether he had made a mistake; perhaps he would be better off with the birds. Until he could be sure, however, he hid in a tree and watched. When peace was finally reached, the bat found himself unpopular with both sides. And so it is to this day that he hides in a tree by day and comes out at night, when the birds and most of the animals are asleep.

This simple legend lends itself equally well to dance, mime, or dramatization. The birds and animals suggest movement, whereas the plot is so simple that it can be easily told without words. There is plenty of action to make it interesting. If the group prefers to use dialogue, however, the story can be improvised. Another way would be to have a narrator tell it, while the group pantomimes the action. In a story of this kind, any number can play. It is included to show the possibilities in a simple tale with a strong conflict and minimal characterization.

The legend of *The Mirror* comes from the Japanese. It is a delightful story for creative playing and is simple enough for quite young or inexperienced actors. It can be used in connection with a unit on Japan or played for the opportunities it offers for characterization and dialogue. The humor of the situation is particularly appealing to children.

THE MIRROR

A grand lady is traveling with her maid in a carriage down a country road. Along the way the carriage breaks down, and the coachman says it will take him some time to repair it; therefore he suggests that the travelers may want to get out and enjoy the countryside. The two women do so. After walking about for a few minutes, the lady sits down on a rock so that her maid can comb her hair. She looks at herself in a small mirror, which the maid carries in her bag. Just then the coachman tells them that he has finished the repair and that they can continue the journey. They forget, however, to pick up the mirror, and it is left behind on the rock.

In a little while two young women come by. They soon discover the mirror, which neither of them has ever seen before, and they think it is the picture of a pretty young girl. They wonder if either of their husbands could have left it here. At this moment the husband of the first young woman comes down the road and his wife shows him the mirror. He picks it up and looks at it, but he sees the face of a young man. He accuses his wife of being unfaithful to him. She, in turn, becomes angry.

Other persons come along, and each is asked what he or she sees in the mirror. Each one insists that it is a *man* or a *woman*, depending, of course, upon who is looking into it. The argument grows more and more heated as it cannot be resolved.

Finally, a priest comes along, and the people rush to ask him to settle the argument. He looks into the mirror long and hard; then he says he sees the face of a very old holy man. As they stand there, perplexed at this reply, the lady's maid returns, asking if anyone has seen a mirror.

One of the advantages of this kind of story is that it offers an opportunity for any number of players and no parts are, or need be, any larger than another. Children think of different kinds of people who might be walking down the road and then create them. Who are they? Why are they there? What work do they do? How old are they?

The situation builds in intensity and humor until it is finally resolved. There is also a possibility, imbedded in the story, for discussion of *appearance* and what a mirror tells us. Older players may find the legend a springboard to an original improvisation on mirrors and reflections. What *does* a glass reveal? Is it a truthful image? What is the relationship between surface and inner beauty? Is the latter seen in one's face?

THE PEASANT WHO DINED WITH A LORD
(A UKRANIAN FOLK TALE)

Once in a small Ukranian village there was a rich lord who would have nothing to do with the common folk. As a matter of fact, he was so proud and so greedy that he had little to do with anyone, save his servants. He had no family, and this gave rise to curiosity on the part of the villagers. Whenever a group of them gathered, their conversation was apt to be about the great lord: who had seen him pass by in his carriage, what he looked like, what clothing he wore. Some, who had never seen him, wondered what his servants had bought in the market that day.

One afternoon a poor peasant, overhearing one of these conversations, said laughingly, "Why spend time asking questions? You can find out by simply climbing over the wall and looking into the kitchen."

"When have you done that?" demanded one of the old men, who had dwelt in the village longer than any of the rest of them.

"Yes," said the others, "have you been inside those gates? Has the master asked you to dinner?"

The group laughed uproariously at the young peasant in his ragged clothes, but he answered impudently, "I could dine with him before the week is out, if I wished."

"Dine with a lord? You?" said one of them; then they all laughed again. "Why, if you so much as put one foot inside the courtyard in those clothes, he would have you thrown off the place!"

"Will you make a bargain with me?" asked the young peasant.

All nodded vigorously in agreement.

"Very well. If I dine with him, then will you each give me a sack of your best wheat and a bullock? If I do not dine with him, I will be your servant and do everything that you ask for one month."

All agreed to the bargain, certain that they would get the better of it. Whereupon the young man walked boldly into the courtyard of the great lord. As had been predicted, he was met at the gate by two servants, who started to chase him out. "Wait a minute," said the peasant. "I have good news for your master, but I can tell it only to him."

The lord, being told of the promised message, was curious about it, and asked that the bearer of good news be shown into the house. The peasant said that what he had to say must be said in private, so the lord ordered his servants to leave. "Now, what is it that is meant for my ears alone?"

"What," whispered the young man, looking cautiously about, "is the cost of a piece of gold the size of a horse's head?"

The lord could not believe his ears and asked that the question be repeated. He was sure that the peasant must have found a great treasure. He tried to discover why such a poor man would want to know the value of so much gold. But the peasant, who was far more clever than he appeared, simply said that if the lord did not wish to tell him, he would be on his way and find someone else who would. The lord, afraid that a great treasure was about to slip out of reach, said, "Why not stay and have dinner with me? We can talk while we eat."

He called his servants and ordered them to bring bread, fruit, meat, and cheese as quickly as possible. Then the two sat down at the table together. When they had eaten their fill, the lord said, "And now, tell me where is your gold the size of a horse's head?"

"I have no gold," replied the young man.

"You have no gold?" the lord repeated after him. "Then why did you ask what it was worth?"

"I just wanted to know, my lord. And it was a kind of bet."

The lord was very angry when he heard this, and he ordered the peasant out of the house.

"I am not as stupid as you think me," said the young man, courteously. "I have had a very good dinner and I have won a bet besides. Now I must go and claim my sacks of wheat and my bullocks."

And bowing low, the clever peasant left, chuckling all the while at the way he had outwitted both the villagers and the lord.

Folk tales telling of cleverness, especially on the part of ones who are young and poor, are popular with most people. Children love the double trick played in this story and are always eager to take turns being the peasant. Although there are only two major roles as the story is told, there is no reason why the villagers cannot be fleshed out, giving each of them his own motives and personal qualities.

The story can be played just as it is, or additional scenes can be added. It can lead to deeper character analysis or a study of the kind of society that is represented by the master and the peasants. Children are quick to detect greed, vanity, arrogance, and scorn, and they like to participate in a discussion of what they are and how they are found in our lives today. The humor amuses them because it functions on two levels.

JACK AND THE HAINTED HOUSE
R. REX STEPHENSON

Most children love ghost stories. The following tale from the Blue Ridge Mountains is simple in structure, yet it has all the elements of a good ghost story for creative playing: a hero with whom children can identify, a scary situation which is resolved in the end, and strong dramatic action. It is told here in the dialect of the region.

This is a story about a boy named Jack. Now Jack is a boy who lives way up in the Blue Ridge Mountains of Virginia. Old Jack, why, he is always getting himself into a fix. This tale is called *Jack and the Hainted House*. "Hainted" is what mountain folks say when they mean haunted. So this tale is gonna find Jack meetin' some ghosts and the like.

Well, one day Jack was walkin' in the woods and it commenced to get dark. Jack was lookin' for a good place to spend the night. Finally he came upon this house with a light in the window and he went up and knocked on the door.

When the door opened, an old man stepped out carryin' a candle. He had about the wildest bunch of hair that Jack had ever seen on anybody's head.

"What can I do for ya, boy?" the old man asked.

"I'm lookin' for a place to spend the night and maybe get something to eat," answered Jack.

"Afraid I have no room here. Too crowded," the old man said, all the time studyin' Jack real careful with his candle.

"I'm awful hungry, too," Jack said.

"Well, I have a goose that I'll give ya. But you'll have to cook hit. Now then, a place to sleep. I got a little house over there you can stay in . . . if'n you want to." With that the old man handed Jack the goose and slammed the door in his face.

Jack took that goose and moved purty slow to the house. When he got there, Jack opened the door and went inside. But before he knew what was happenin' that door shut fast and he was trapped. Try as he would, Jack couldn't get that door open.

Well, all that work tryin' to get that door opened left Jack plumb tuckered out, so he looked around for a place to sleep. He spied a bed over in the corner, picked up a quilt, spread it over himself, and before a cat could of blinked twice, he was fast asleep.

Jack was just beginnin' to dream about bein' home and eatin' ash cakes and sorghum, when he felt this tuggin'-pull on that quilt. Well, the harder Jack pulled, the harder that tuggin'-pull was from the other end. Finally old Jack gave up and tore that quilt half-in-two and said, "I don't know who you are or what you are, but I guess I'll have to give ye half of this quilt if'n I'm gonna get any sleep tonight."

After Jack tore that quilt half-in-two, he went right back to sleep, but it wasn't long before he felt that tuggin'-pull on the quilt again. Jack pulled, but the other thing pulled harder and finally Jack fell on the floor. So Jack just gave that quilt to whatever it was and went someplace else to sleep.

Well, it wasn't long before Jack was fast asleep again, dreamin' of his maw's ash cakes and sorghum, when he heard these strange sounds. When Jack looked up, he saw these seven witches comin' in the room! Well, they surrounded Jack, but when they went to grab him, Jack jumped out of the way and all them witches bumped into one another. Well, old Jack, he jumped up and started yellin', "Get out of here, 'fore I beat the Devil out of ye!"

Well, to old Jack's surprise, those witches left. Jack went over to another corner of the room and decided he'd stay awake, to see if there was any other strange critters in that hainted house.

Hit wasn't long till these seven witches returned, not only makin' those scary sounds but carryin' a dead body. The witches left the body and disappeared again.

Well, Jack remembered something he grandpaw had told him. If you speak to a haint using the Lord's name, hit will talk back to you.

So Jack walked over to that haint and said, "What in the Lord's name are you doin' here?" That haint told Jack that he had been killed in this house many years ago by a robber, who was after his gold. The haint told Jack to go find the gold, which was hid in the fireplace, and to give one-third each to the haint's two sons, and, for doin' that, Jack could keep one-third for himself.

Well, Jack did just what that haint said, and you know Jack took the money and bought him a little piece of ground up on the mountain, and today he's got seven sons, jist as ornery as he was. And that's the story of Jack and the Hainted House.

The leader might begin by having all the children be witches. How do witches move, speak, carry the body, disappear? What makes them scary? Many children will want to try the parts of Jack, the old man, and the haint. When all have had a chance to try their favorite parts, the group will be thoroughly familiar with the story. The mountain dialect provides a special quality of authenticity and distinguishes it from other ghost stories that may be more familiar. Older children will appreciate the humor.

SUMMARY

The preceding stories were selected for inclusion because of their simplicity and successful use with beginning groups of all ages. Though children's stories, each one has been used with both children and adults, and each age brings its own insights, meanings, and humor. There are many excellent stories just as suitable for beginning creative playing, and the interested leader will have no difficulty finding them. Tastes and interests of the group will guide the selection, though one of the values in creative drama is the opportunity it offers for introducing new material and good literature. One thing the leader will discover is that no two groups ever handle a story in quite the same way; if he is able to present it without a preconceived plan as to how how it should be done, he will find that every group brings original ideas to its playing.

The procedures suggested are essentially the same, regardless of age level:

1. presentation of the story
2. organization of the material
3. improvisation
4. evaluation
5. replaying

Evaluation is an important aspect of creative dramatics and leads into the replaying, which should acquire new depth and richer detail. Changing parts with each playing may not always make for a better performance, but it does give each participant a chance to play the part of his choice at least once. When the leader feels that the group has gone as far as it can with the story, he may suggest that the group cast it for final playing. This usually makes for a successful conclusion: the group has created something of its own, and has found the last playing to be the most rewarding.

The older the participants, the more preliminary planning the leader can expect. Children, on the other hand, tend to move quickly into improvisation. Their dialogue will be brief, and the scenes shorter than planned, but their attack is direct. Children, less conditioned to the conventions of the pro-scenium stage, are likewise freer in their use of space, planning scenes in various parts of the room simultaneously. When the class is held in a room with a stage at one end, they are likely to use it as a particular place—perhaps a mountain top or a distant land—rather than considering it as the central playing area. For every age group there are fewer inhibitions if a large room, instead of a stage, is used. Playing in the round reduces self-consciousness and is conducive to freer movement, since the scattered observers do not seem so much like an audience.

When the group has shown that it can handle the problems of simple fables and stories, it is ready to move on to more demanding material. In the next chapter, longer stories are included, illustrating the possibilities offered for characterization and multiple-scene planning.

8

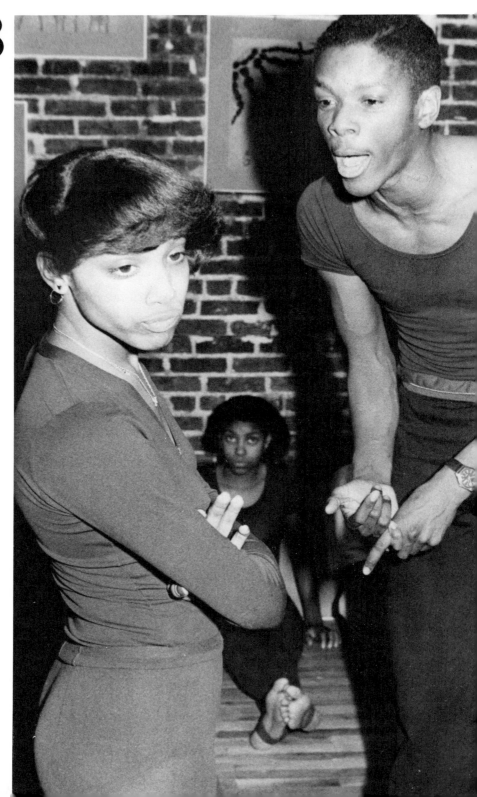

BUILDING PLAYS FROM LONGER STORIES

In this chapter several longer stories are included, with descriptions of some of the ways in which groups have used them. Again, let it be emphasized that there is no right way to dramatize the material. There are as many ways as there are groups, and the illustrations given here merely describe what some groups have done with them. Not only are the plots of these stories more detailed, but the characters are complex, and therefore require more experience to develop than those in the preceding chapter. The stories have been chosen for the possibilities they offer to the group ready to undertake them.

PROMETHEUS

Greek mythology is a rich and generally untapped source of material that can be successfully dramatized. One myth, which has been used many times with success, is the story of Prometheus, who stole fire from the

129

The Harlem Children's Theatre, New York. Courtesy Aduke Aremu games. Photograph by David Thomas.

gods. Basic human emotions and a dramatic story make it particularly appealing to children from seven to twelve. The idea of a formless earth stirs their imagination and provides an unusual opportunity for creativity. The story must be told carefully, and in considerable detail, since not all children will be familiar with it. Although Greek myths are readily available, a brief synopsis of Prometheus is given here, with suggestions as to ways in which the leader may handle it.

The Greek gods and goddesses were believed to have dwelt on Mount Olympus, high above the earth. Ruling over them was the mighty Zeus. Among the young gods, most in favor with Zeus for his bravery in helping defeat the Titans, was Prometheus. One day Zeus and Athena, Goddess of Wisdom, were walking in the garden. They caught sight of Prometheus in the distance, looking down toward the earth. Zeus called to him and asked him what interested him, for he had often seen the young god staring down at the forests and mountains below.

Prometheus replied that he was troubled because the earth was so empty and silent, with no man moving about its surface. Zeus smiled, and said that for some time he had been considering a reward for the young god. "Prometheus," he suggested, "perhaps you would like to descend to the earth and fashion men out of soil." Prometheus was overjoyed.

"You are wise and kind," added Athena. "When you create man, remember to give him a strong body, a keen mind, and a tender heart. Let him also see that there is a need for beauty as well as for the necessities of life."

"You may give man any gifts you wish except the gift of fire," continued Zeus. "That alone belongs to the gods and must remain on Olympus. When you have fashioned your men and are satisfied with your work, I will come down to earth and blow the breath of life into their bodies."

Prometheus was eager to begin, and went off swiftly. Working with power and skill, he modeled his first man upright and powerful, and called him "Man, the Builder." Then he took more soil and made a second man, who was likewise tall and strong. Putting a few grains of corn in his hand, he named him "Man, the Sower and Reaper." The third man he pronounced "Man, the Hunter," and to him he gave a stone. The fourth he called "Man, the Musician." Finally, he finished his fifth man and proclaimed him "Man, the Thinker."

Scarcely had he stepped back to admire his efforts when the deep voice of Zeus was heard from Olympus. "We are pleased with your men, Prometheus. I shall now come down to blow life into them."

Miraculously, each statue came to life and breathed, and moved, and walked. As the days passed, Prometheus cared for his men and worked with them, teaching them to do the special jobs for which they had been created. The men learned quickly and worked happily. One day, however, the seasons changed. The warm air was replaced by cold winds and snowy weather. The men were cold, and Prometheus was deeply disturbed as he watched them huddling together, trying to keep warm. Finally, he could bear it no longer. He knew he must give them fire.

When he called to Athena for help, she asked, "Do you care so much about your men, Prometheus?"

Prometheus declared that he did.

"Enough to risk the wrath of Zeus!" continued Athena. "He will surely punish you. The one thing he has forbidden them is fire."

"I have made my men, and I must help them, even though I suffer for it," replied Prometheus.

"Very well, then," said Athena. "I will help you find the fire to give them."

As swiftly as he had gone down to earth, Prometheus returned to Olympus to get the fire that he was determined his men must have. Then he called the five together and told them not to be frightened, but to learn to use their new gift. Just as he had taught them other things, he taught them how to use a fire for warmth, and for the cooking of food. He warned them never to let the fire go out. The men were fascinated with the many possibilities of fire, and were soon warm and comfortable again.

It was not long, however, before Zeus learned what had happened. Angrily he told Prometheus that he had disobeyed, and must be punished for his act.

"I am ready to accept my punishment, great Zeus," Prometheus replied, "for I cannot let my men suffer from the wind and cold."

"A gift that has been given cannot be recalled," continued the god. "Men now possess fire, but you must pay the price. I shall have you bound by chains to yonder mountain. There you must remain forever, and serve as an example to those who dare to disobey my laws."

So saying, Zeus sent his messenger, Hephaestus, down to seize Prometheus and put him in chains. The men were grieved when they saw the dreadful thing that had happened to their creator and teacher, but their hearts were filled with gratitude for his great gift to mankind.

The discussion preceding the story can take many directions. It may begin with a consideration of human qualities and feelings. It may, on the other hand, begin with man's occupations, and some pantomime suggesting them. It may begin with an analysis of the characters in the story and their conflicts. Eventually, in whatever way the story is introduced, there must be a focus on the characters, their behavior, and the consequences of Prometheus' act.

As in the other stories, the myth will be broken down into scenes before it is acted. Work in pantomime can easily be done with the whole group, for there is rich opportunity here. Together, the children can do the following actions: build a hut, hunt for food, plant a field, make a musical instrument (drum or pipe) and discover how to play it, suggest the beginning of man's thought process. Each activity gives scope for imaginative pantomime. Music may be helpful in stimulating movement, though it is not necessary. Children love playing the statues who come to life and learn to do the things for which they were intended. One whole period may easily be given over to these pantomime activities.

When the players are ready to begin on the story, they may wish to take turns playing gods and men. If playing in a large room, the children may conceive of one end of it as Olympus and the other as the earth. Or, if there is a platform, they may decide to locate Olympus on a higher level. The plot calls for at least three scenes, though some groups may see it in five or six. More than one group has played it with use of a simultaneous setting, with Zeus and Athena observing and commenting, while Prometheus works. When this approach is used, the scenes may move back and forth without a break, or scene division.

Prometheus is a story strong enough to hold the interest for three or four class sessions, with constructive discussion preceding and following each playing. If the group enjoys the story, other myths may be introduced, for there are many with fine dramatic action, and values that children comprehend. Like the other stories in this chapter, *Prometheus* gains depth and detail with each new playing. The young god's sense of responsibility and compassion for his men begins to emerge, adding another dimension to the character. The conflict between the law of Zeus, and Prometheus' moral courage as he begins to feel for his men, makes for powerful drama. The final playing can be most rewarding, as theme, story, character, and action are unified. The group that has become really involved in Prometheus' dilemma will have had a rich experience. This is a story better suited to an older group, though even seven- and eight-year-olds can understand and play a simplified version.

BLUE BONNETS

This Indian legend, telling how the first blue bonnet flowers appeared in the earth, is a story that appeals to children of middle and upper grades. Many Indian legends are excellent for improvisation, but this one has a special appeal since it is the story of a child and her sacrifice.

Yellow Star is a little Indian girl, who lives with her father and mother in a village belonging to the Comanche tribe. As the story begins, the Chief calls his people together. He describes the trouble that has come to their village after many weeks without rain. The long drought has caused the brooks to dry up; vegetation is dying, and animals have left the parched plains in search of food. The people sit quietly in a circle around the campfire as they listen to their leader. Then they beat the drums and dance, praying to the Great Spirit for rain. At first, nothing happens. Then, suddenly, they hear the voice of the Great Spirit far in the distance. They stop, put down the drums, and listen: "You are being punished for your selfishness and greed. You have lived in a land of plenty for many years, but your people have not shared with their brothers."

The Chief begs for mercy, but the Great Spirit replies, "I will forgive your tribe and send you the water you need only when one among you sacrifices on the campfire that which is dearest to his heart."

Excitedly, the braves talk together. They suggest that one give his horse, another his jewelry, and that still another offer his beautiful young squaw to the Great Spirit. No one, however, is willing to make a sacrifice for the sake of his brothers, and so they move from the campfire and start slowly off toward their homes. The Chief calls them. "Come to this place again in the morning. By that time one among you may have found the gift that will bring us all forgiveness."

The people slowly disappear, each hoping that someone will think of a way to save them. Only little Yellow Star remains. In her arms she carries her fawn-skin doll with its bonnet of blue jay feathers. The doll is her dearest possession. She realizes that she must throw it into the fire to please the Great Spirit, but it is not easy to part with her only toy. Finally, she reaches her decision, as night falls on the village, and she tells the Great Spirit that she is ready to give that which is dearest to her heart. She watches the doll burn slowly, then, seeing the blue feather bonnet lying in the ashes, she picks it up and throws it into the flames. To her amazement, the feathers do not burn, but become small blue flowers. Yellow Star knows, then, that the Great Spirit has accepted her gift, and with a light heart she runs home.

The next morning, all the Indians gather together as their Chief has commanded, but where only last night there was a campfire, there is now a huge bed of blue flowers. The people are mystified, for they cannot understand how flowers could have sprung up in the hard, dry earth.

Yellow Star's mother tells the Chief about the doll. "Surely," she says, "it must be a sign. Hundreds of flowers now grow on ground that was trampled and dry."

The people, however, are unwilling to believe her story, for why should the Great Spirit be satisfied with so small a gift as a child's fawn-skin doll? At that moment, there is a roll of thunder in the distance. The Chief knows now that the Great Spirit has accepted Yellow Star's offering. Again, he asks his people to beat their drums and give thanks that they have at last been forgiven. The first raindrops fall.

This charming legend gives an opportunity for total group participation. Since movement is an important element, a good beginning can be made with a dance around the campfire. The use of a drum aids enormously in building rhythms, as the Indians move and dance and pray. The leader can, of course, begin with the story, but before dialogue is attempted, practice in rhythmic movement helps the players to become involved.

Discussion of the story and its theme should precede the playing, inasmuch as this will deepen the understanding of a people different in custom, yet like us in their human strengths and weaknesses. When the group is ready to begin, it is again suggested that short scenes, rather than the whole story, be played first. For example, the opening scene, in which the Chief calls his people together and explains the seriousness of their situation, is quite enough for one sequence. Yellow Star's sacrifice is another. The players may conceive of the story as taking place in one act, with a break to indicate passage of time, or they may see it as a play in two or three scenes. Because it is a story in which any number may participate, playing it in the round is desirable, if possible. Players and observers are one, and are, therefore, involved to an unusual degree.

The part of Yellow Star is a favorite, but the Chief, the mother, and the selfish braves and squaws can all be built into characters who are believable and interesting. If this story finds favor, the leader may wish to bring other Indian legends to class. Most of them require little more than space for playing, since they are concerned with human beings in conflict with nature, and human weaknesses familiar to all.

A LEGEND OF SPRING

Another Indian legend that has proved extremely successful for creative playing is *A Legend of Spring*. It is simple in plot but provides a wonderful opportunity for group pantomime and movement. Players of all ages find it appealing and develop it in proportion to their experience and the time that is given them.

The Indians of the Great Plains had suffered through a long winter, but this year no sign of spring had appeared. Neither sun nor wind nor warm rains had come to awaken the seeds or bring the wild animals out of their winter hiding. One day, the Chief of the tribe called all the braves and squaws together. He explained to them that unless food were found soon, they would have to abandon their village and seek a home elsewhere. There was silence. The people looked up at the cold, gray sky, and down at the hard frozen earth. They knew the Chief was right, yet no one wanted to leave the pleasant valley in which they had dwelt for so many years. Finally White Cloud, youngest and strongest of the braves, spoke out. "I will go into the forest in search of food. With my strong bow and arrows, surely I can find food to bring back to my people."

"I will go with you," cried a second, then a third and a fourth. Others rose from the campfire, where they had been sitting, and joined him. The old Chief smiled. "Go," he said. "Perhaps if you hunt deep enough in the forest you will find the deer and rabbits to provide food until the spring comes to our land. While you are absent, we shall pray to the Great Spirit to make the sun shine again and the clouds empty warm rain on our fields."

The young men ran out as the drums beat a farewell. Then the old Chief called to the Great Spirit for help. The people danced around the fire, asking for sun, rain, and wind for their planting, and game for their hunters. When they finally dropped to their knees, exhausted, there was a rustle in the bushes. Looking up, they beheld a large golden bird flying toward the clearing. Scarcely had it appeared when White Cloud and his band of hunters broke through the underbrush. Two or three of the men had already raised their bows when White Cloud spoke.

"Do not shoot the golden bird. Perhaps it has come from the Great Spirit. It may be a sign for us if we wait to see what it wants. Hold your arrows. Do not shoot!"

The braves put down their bows and waited. Then the golden bird, seeing that the people meant her no harm, glided gracefully into their midst. Suddenly, she was transformed into a lovely young maiden with a golden bow and arrow.

"I have come from the Great Spirit," she said. "Listen to me carefully. Here is an arrow which one of you must shoot straight into the dark cloud overhead. If the cloud is pierced, the rains will begin, and winter will leave your valley. If he who shoots the arrow does not succeed, you must prepare to leave your homes, for spring will not come this year."

So saying, she handed the bow to the Chief, asking him to select the brave who could shoot the straightest arrow. "You choose, golden maiden," he said. "It is your arrow. You choose the one who will send it from the bow."

Slowly the maiden circled the campfire, first looking at one, then another. Finally she stopped before White Cloud and handed him the golden bow and arrow. He took it from her silently, aimed at the cloud and released it. Up and up it went until it was lost from sight. Then, suddenly, a crack appeared in the sky. The sun came out and the warm spring rain began to fall. The drum beat joyously as the people danced again, this time in thanks to the Great Spirit, who had answered their prayers.

Like the other Indian legend, this one is best begun with movement. Pantomime and dance, expressing the people's need for rain, wind, and sun, help the group get into the story. Hunting, fishing, planting, eating, and moving camp are activities that may also be expressed in pantomime by each member of the group. If a sufficiently long time is spent on movement and pantomime, many ideas will come that can later be incorporated into the story. Children love to think of as many ways as possible to show how the Indians lived, and of how they expressed their needs to the Great Spirit. Actually, the whole story can be played without words, although most groups will want to invent some dialogue. A drum is a valuable property for the leader at first, but he will want to pass it along to one of the participants later. Some groups see the story in a single scene; others may wish to break it into several. However it is handled, *A Legend of Spring* is a strong story for creative playing. A drum and plenty of space in which to move freely are the only requirements.

THE COINS OF LIN FOO

The following legend, which comes from the Chinese, is particularly good for dramatization. Younger groups will enjoy playing the story; older groups may wish to try it in the Chinese manner. It is included because of its flexibility, its many good characters, and its engrossing story.

There was once in a small village in the State of Tsin a lad named Lin Foo, who lived with his widowed mother, Wing Soong. After the father's death hard times had come upon them and they had been forced to leave their home and sell their plot of land. Wing Soong, in order to earn a living for herself and her son, made fritters each week, which Lin Foo took to the market to sell. How his mother wished that she might someday earn enough money to educate Lin Foo, for he was as bright as he was industrious!

On this particular morning, when Wing Soong handed him the basket of fritters, the boy asked if he might stay longer in the village, for there was to be a fair and he wanted to join his friends and look around. "I should like to see the wares in the booths, the flags, and the little carved dragons and birds."

"Of course," said his mother. "Just mind you keep the money safe and do not stay so long that it grows dark before you reach home. You'd better be off now, for the way is long and already the village will be crowded with the farmers and their carts."

Lin Foo spent a happy and profitable day in the village. First he sold his basket of fritters and put the money in his pocket. Indeed, he had no trouble at all in selling the fritters, for the humble Wing Soong was known throughout the village for her fine cooking and fair bargains. The lad went from booth to booth, finally deciding that the safest place for his money was under a stone near the entrance to the fairgrounds. If he did this, he thought to himself, he could move among the crowds to his heart's content, with no fear of the coins slipping out of his pocket and rolling away in the dust. Carefully he placed the money under the stone and went off to join some village boys he knew. Finally, it was time to start for home. He bade his friends farewell and went to the stone under which he had hidden his money. But to his dismay, when he lifted it up, there was nothing there. Lin Foo was sure that someone must have stolen it. Disconsolate, he sat down at the edge of the road, wondering what he would tell his mother and what they would do without money for the coming week. While he was sitting there An Li, the magistrate, came along; seeing the boy, he asked what was troubling him.

"Oh, master, I am a poor boy, whose mother makes fritters to sell on market day. She entrusted me to bring home the money, which I hid under this stone for safekeeping. When I came back just now to get it, I found it had been taken. And so I have neither money nor fritters to take home with me."

"Have you a father, my boy?" asked the magistrate.

The lad replied that he had not, and that he lived alone with his mother, Wing Soong. He told the kindly man that all the money they had was what he got for the fritters. The magistrate questioned him further. "Did you put the money well out of sight?"

"Oh, yes, honored sir. No one could possibly have seen it."

"Is this the stone?"

The boy nodded his head.

Then An Li said, "I shall arrest this stone. You, boy, go on home. But return with your mother tomorrow morning at ten o'clock. I shall try to get your money back for you."

Lin Foo went home. After he had gone, the magistrate had his attendants summon all the villagers who were at the fair that day and order them to be present the next morning for the trial of the stone. He requested that the magistrate's table and chair, two stout bamboo sticks, and a large jar full of water be brought to the spot for the trial.

The following day, Lin Foo and his mother set out for the village. A crowd was already there by the time they arrived. Many of the people thought that An Li lost his wits from too much study of the law. Some were willing to wait to see what the wise man had in mind. At length An Li appeared with his attendants. He asked if the boy, Lin Foo, were present. Lin Foo stepped forward. Then he asked if the boy's mother were there also. Wing Soong bowed humbly. Finally, he asked if this were the stone that had stolen the coins. When the boy, mystified, replied that it was, An Li order his attendants to strike the stone fifty times with the bamboo sticks. Many people laughed and some tapped their heads in ridicule. Angrily, An Li shouted, "Silence! You are showing contempt for this court. Each one of you shall be fined twenty li, which you will toss into this jar."

Soberly the people filed past the jar in a circle and dropped in their coins. As the last man contributed his coin, the magistrate jumped up and shouted, "Arrest this man! He is the thief."

There was a murmur of excitement and bewilderment in the crowd. They asked each other how the magistrate could know that this man was the thief or if, indeed, he was. Finally, An Li picked up the jar, which he showed to the crowd.

"Do you see here? When this man dropped his coin, these streaks of grease appeared on the surface of the water. Only that coin could have come from the basket that carried the fritters." Then he turned to the thief. "Where is the rest of the money?"

The thief pulled it unwillingly from his pocket. "Here it is, Your Honor."

An Li asked that the money be put in the jar with the rest, and then he announced that the court was dismissed. The villagers began to leave but not without expressing their amazement and respect for the magistrate's wisdom. When they had all gone, An Li handed the jar to Wing Soong. "There you are, my good woman. Your money is restored to you. I hope your son has learned his lesson—never to leave things of value foolishly in such a spot as this, thus tempting the dishonest folk who are watching to steal them."

Wing soong took the coins gratefully. She thanked the wise magistrate for what he had done and for giving her twice the money the fritters had brought.

If the group is inexperienced, it will be wise to play the story just as it is, with no attempt made at doing it in the Chinese manner. Any number of children can take part, for although there are only a few main characters, there is great opportunity to add any number of villagers, farmers, and merchants at the fair. This will give everyone in the class a chance to work on pantomime and characterization and will also help to set the mood. The magistrate's trick to discover the thief is enjoyed by children of every age, and a trial scene always makes for good drama.

Older and more experienced groups may want to play the story in the style of the Chinese theatre, adding to the cast a narrator and a property man. A study of the Chinese theatre should precede any attempt at dramatization. This legend ties in well with a unit on China, should a class be studying it in social studies. If the children want to share their work with another class, it is suggested that simple properties and possibly a panel or backdrop would be fun to make and would also enhance the presentation.

The following story can be enjoyed for its simple story line, played in connection with a music theory class, or used as a springboard to another activity or project.

THE MAGIC STONES[1]
AVIVA LAYTON

(Arranged for creative playing by Nellie McCaslin)

A long time ago, in a little village which has long since disappeared, there lived a boy named David.

"He's an odd one," the villagers said. "Always mooning and humming to himself. Never know what the lad is thinking."

And it was true. Often David would leave the village and go into the hills where he gathered wild flowers. He listened to bird calls. Sometimes he just lay on his back looking at the sky.

One evening when David was returning from one of his trips to the hills, he heard a great commotion in the village square. All the villagers were gathered in a circle around something that was making the most peculiar wailing sounds David had ever heard. Quickly David

---

1. Aviva Layton, *The Magic Stones* (Toronto: Magook Publishers Ltd., 1977).

pushed his way through the crowd. There to his surprise he saw that the wails were coming from five little black stones lying on the ground. David stared at them, fascinated. As he listened to their strange wails he had a feeling that they were trying to say something important to him.

Meanwhile, the village was in an uproar. What were the stones? What did the wailing mean? Finally the elders decided to call a meeting.

"Silence, good people," commanded the eldest of the elders. "It is obvious that evil spirits are at work. We must rid our village of these stones as soon as possible."

He looked at the crowd. "Who will volunteer to put the stones in a sack, carry them to the river and throw them in, so that they never disturb us again?"

No one spoke. Everyone was afraid. Then a small voice piped up from the back. "Must the stones be thrown away? I have a strange feeling that they have something wonderful to tell, if only we can find some way to stop their wailing."

There were angry mumurs from the crowd. A woman called out, "That's just what David would say. Everyone knows that he's an idle, good-for-nothing boy, wandering around all day instead of doing honest work."

"I wouldn't be surprised if he were in league with the evil spirits who have brought these wailing stones to us," said a man.

The crowd grew louder and louder and angrier and angrier. Then the eldest elder had an idea. He held up his hand for silence. "David," he said, "since you are the only one who wants the stones, I appoint you to take them away. I will give you a choice. You can throw them in the river. Or you can keep them. But if you decide to keep them, you must never return to the village."

David did not hesitate a moment. Running to where the stones were lying, he scooped them into a sack.

"I shall ask the wisest man in all the land to find out what is troubling you," he said to the stones. "I am sure you are trying to tell us something wonderful."

The first wise man whom David visited was a hermit who lived on the top of a mountain. When David explained what he wanted, the hermit told him to leave the sack and return in seven days for his answer. David agreed, and returned when the time was up. But all the hermit would tell him was that he was wasting time. "I have waved my hand over these stones every seventh minute of every seventh hour," he said, "but I can still make no sense out of their wailing."

David thanked the hermit politely and set off again. This time he went to a great scholar. When he had explained what he wanted, the scholar said to him, "You have come to the right person. Just let me have three days in which to consult my books. Then you will have your answer."

At the end of three days David returned. But the scholar could not solve the mystery, for the answer was not in any of his books. So David thanked him and continued on his way. At last he came to the palace of the king. Now the king kept a court jester who was said to be wiser than all the wise men put together. When the king heard David's story, he clapped his hands and commanded that the jester be brought before him.

"Wise jester," said David, "I have brought these wailing stones to you so that you may tell me what they are trying to say."

"A jester, wise?" said the jester. "That's the best joke of all!" Then he turned to the king. "I am a fool, but if you command it, I shall listen to this terrible noise and see if I can tell you what it means."

"Of course, I command it," said the king.

The jester cocked his head to one side and listened. Then he jumped up and said, "They are wailing because *I* should be king and *you* should be jester!"

"Silence," thundered the king. Then he turned to David. "You will never find your answer here, so be off with you."

Poor David. There was nowhere else to go. In despair he wandered into a field to look for a place to rest. There he found a wooden fence with five wooden rails. He leaned against it wearily.

"The villagers were right," he said, looking at the stones. "I should have thrown them into the river a long time ago.

Idly, he took the stones out of the sack and set them on the wooden rails. He put the second stone above the first, the third above the second, and so on. Suddenly David heard a new sound. It was the sweetest sound he had ever heard. But where was it coming from? Could it be from the stones?

All the rest of the day David stood by the fence, arranging and rearranging the little black stones. He found that he could make many kinds of singing sounds by putting the stones in different places.

"I was right about you all along," he said. "You do have something wonderful to say. But I must not keep you to myself. The whole world must hear you singing."

David put the stones back in the sack. Now they were quiet, because their secret had been unlocked. Once again David set out, but this time it was to his own village. When the villagers heard the beautiful sounds that came from the singing stones, David became a hero.

The eldest elder boasted that he was the one who had appointed David the keeper of the stones. And the villagers whispered that they had known all along that David would do something great and special. As news of the singing stones spread, people came from the far corners of the world to hear the wonderful sounds. There was only one thing they wanted to do. They could try to make something that would have the same sounds. Many different people from many different countries set to work. One young man drew a bow across a tight string and said, "This is the exact sound."

Another blew through a reed and he said, "No, *this* is the exact sound."

Still another tapped a piece of tightly stretched skin with a little hammer and said, "Both of you are wrong. This is the exact sound."

"Let us consult David," the first young man replied. "He will decide which one of us has captured the exact sound of the singing stones."

David listened carefully. But instead of choosing one, he said, "Each of you has made the sound in your own special way. You should all play together."

And so they did.

This simple tale of a dreamer and his discovery of musical sounds and notes offers a rich opportunity for characterization and conflict. There can be as many or as few characters as desired, which makes it good material for classroom use. *The Magic Stones* also brings up questions regarding superstition, self-confidence, and social attitudes toward the person who dares to be different from the rest of the crowd. Obviously, this can lead to much more than a superficial discussion.

The arrangement of stones on the fence suggest notes and staff and might be a way of showing how music is written and read. This story can be simplified or expanded according to the age and interest of the children.

Stories and legends of the Bahamas are almost unknown in this country. Yet, like all places where people have lived, worked, played, and worshipped, a rich store of folklore exists. It waits only to be discovered. The following tale from the Bahamas makes wonderful material for creative playing.

THE OLD MAN AND THE GOOMBAY CAT
KITTY KIRBY

Cat Island was home to William T. His father and grandfather were born there. William's father had sold fish by day and had given organ lessons to the island children by night. He had been a "church-going" man. And, like his father, William T. was also a fisherman and gave organ lessons; but now he was getting old and could no longer see the notes.

His wife was dead, and his two sons and daughter had left the island. His only companion was a parrot named Penny. Penny had flown into the old wooden house one day after a tropical storm had swept over the island. She had just flown through the window and adopted old William T. Many afternoons the children would stop by the old man's house to say hello to Penny. The children called William T. Cousin Will-Yum, and loved to listen to stories of his boyhood. They would sit on the old wooden porch and listen attentively as William T. swung in his wornout hammock and drew in long breaths of smoke from his pipe. Then he would begin:

"When I was about sixteen, I was one of the best sea divers on the island. My father used to take me out in his small boat to the coral reefs. There we would dive down into the clear, blue-green water into a sea-garden. It was still—so still—we would swim through coral caves with plants all around us. There were hornlike plants and sea fans that looked like feathers. Pink plumeworms with spindly flower petals danced like angels. And bright, jewel-like fish were swimming all around us: red parrot fish, blue parrot fish, and silvery grunts."

As he spoke little girls' eyes would shine brightly as they listened, but the boys would be fidgety and impatient.

"Tell us about the sea monsters and how you set yourself loose from the water octopus," the little boys would beg.

Penny knew these stories well, and would interrupt William T. each time he spoke of the sea fans, the grunts, and the parrot fish. Still, the children would never leave until the old man had finished his stories. Then, after picking some tamarinds from the century-old tamarind tree which shaded the old man's hut, the children would say good-bye to Cousin Will-Yum and Penny and leave.

William T. never needed a clock to wake him up in the mornings because every morning when the rooster crowed he knew it was time to get up and go fishing.

"Breakfast, Will-Yum Tee. Breakfast!" Penny squawked.

"Come, come, Penny. Give me some time to get hold of myself," answered the old man.

William T. fed Penny and fixed himself a bowl of hominy grits. Penny not only ate her own food, but she helped William T. with his, too.

"Such a glutton," said William T.

"Glutton, glutton!" repeated the parrot. "Yes, you are, but I don't know what I would do without you," said the old man as he put Penny back into her cage.

"Fish biting good today, Will-Yum Tee? Fish biting good today?" chattered Penny.

"Hope so, Penny. You know tomorrow is Goombay Day!" said the old man as he gathered up his fishing pots and said good-bye to the bird.

William T. started down the hilly steps and narrow lanes towards the fishing cove. He hoped that today would bring a good catch. He hadn't had much luck lately. Walking along, he passed barefoot boys and girls on their way to school. They reminded him of when he was a boy. Their faces broke into a smile when they saw him.

"Good morning, Cousin Will-Yum," said the children.

"Morn-in', children. Have a good lesson today and mind the teacher!" answered the old man.

The children giggled. William T. waved good-bye and continued on his way. He walked along the busy waterfront until he came to the edge of Rock Cove. Then he sat down on the warm, pink sand and took his shoes off because he had to wade a little before reaching his rock in the deep water.

"Fish biting good today, mon?" asked William T. as he climbed onto the rock.

"Hope so," answered the other old fishermen.

William T. sat down and began to bait his fishing-pot with pieces of conch.

"Mon, you still using that old fish-pot trap?" teased one of the fishermen.

"Never mind. 'Tis good enough," answered William T.

William T.'s father was known to have made the best triangle fishing-pot traps on the island. The method had been handed down to him from *his* father and he, in time, had taught it to William T. The old man was very proud of the fishing-pot trap and felt it was still good enough to use today. He was just about to lower his pot into the water when the cry of an animal brought him to his feet. The tormented cry grew louder. Leaving his pot behind, William T. went to see what was wrong. He walked to a nearby rock that jutted out into the water. Not too far from there he saw newcomers. They were teenage boys and they were having lots of fun throwing rocks and pebbles at a scrawny, old, black cat.

"Stop it! Can't you see you are hurting a poor, helpless animal?" shouted William T.

"Go 'way, you silly old man!" said the boys as they continued to torment the cat. "This is a fisherman's rock. You can't even bait a catch. You are too old!"

Shoving one of the boys aside with his elbow, William T. butted the other two with his head. The youths were so amazed at the strength of the old man they quickly ran to the other side of the rock. William T. looked down at the cat as it let out a mournful "meo-o-ow."

"They won't hurt you anymore," said the old man as he picked up the cat, and together they went back to his fishing spot.

The old man sat down and dropped his pot into the water. Then he and his newly found friend waited. The fish were not biting, and the old man had grown tired, so he pulled in his pot. The cat jumped into the wet pot and rolled over and over in it.

"Mon, you look like one big cat-ball!" said William T. laughingly. He laughed so loudly that all the other fishermen stopped to see what had happened.

"You catching cat instead of fish?" they teased jovially.

"Haven't seen a cat in a long time on the island," said another fisherman. "How did he get on the rock?"

"Don't know," answered William T. Then, looking at the cat, he kept on laughing as he watched it roll out of the pot.

With his head turning and his tail swishing, the cat pranced lightly over to one of the fisherman's baskets and with one swipe of his paw hooked a small porgy and ran back to William T.

"Tut, tut. That was not nice," said the old man, watching the cat devour its delicious dish. After finishing his meal the cat licked his whiskers and strolled over to William T. Settling himself on the old man's lap, the cat purred and purred and soon fell asleep.

Once more the old man lowered his pot into the water and hooked the ends to the edge of a rock alongside him. He sat there gazing out at the ocean at the hundreds of fishing boats looming over the waters. William T. thought to himself:

"Mon, what big boats! And listen to the sound of those engines and young fishermen singing. Not like the little boats that me and my father used. They even got machines to help catch fish. Look at that haul of Nassau groupers, jack-runners, margaret-fish, and the largest fresh conch that I've ever seen! You've got to be young and strong to carry all that load on your back. Big Goombay Day for them . . . and all that is left for us old fishermen are little fish that got away from the big nets."

He looked further up the rock and saw more newcomers.

"I wonder how long it will be before they take over this rock?" he thought. "My father and grandfather fished here, so in a way I inherited this rock." Then he thought of the young boys telling him he was too old for fishing.

At that moment the cat stirred on the old man's lap. William T. stroked the furry body. Somehow he felt calmer, and as he gazed out into the ocean the ripples of the water made him fell drowsy, and he drifted off to sleep.

Many hours passed. The old man was awakened by the tapping of the cat's paw on his arm. He looked around and saw that everyone had gone.

"I'm glad you woke me," said William T.

The cat pushed the fishing-pot with his two large paws and swung the handle from side to side.

"All right, all right! I'll hurry!" said the old man as he pulled in his meager catch. Showing them to the cat, he said, "I did not catch much fish, but you were good company." The cat blinked his eyes and purred.

With the catch over his shoulder and the cat under his arm, William T. climbed off the rock and waded in the water until he reached the pink, sandy shore. The cat jumped from the old man's arms.

"Don't get lost again," said William T. as he waved good-bye to the cat.

After walking for some time, William T. felt he was being followed.

"Meo-ow, meo-ow."

William T. turned around, and there, nosing into some seashells and fishbone along the road, was the cat!

"You are following me. I'd like to take you home, but I'm a poor fisherman and already have a bird that I can barely feed."

"Meo-o-ow," replied the cat mournfully.

As William T. started to leave, he thought he saw teardrops falling from the cat's eyes, but then he thought of Penny. He was late with her supper. So he hurried on his way.

The sun, shining like a large copper ball, was dropping lower and lower behind the fertile green hills. Tourists riding in bright blue surreys, pulled by horses wearing straw hats, nodded their heads in greeting to the old man as he hurried along. The soft night winds rustled the palm leaves of the coconut trees that stood tall and majestic all over the island. The air was also warm and fragrant with the smell of thousands of hibiscus plants. And lamplighters, flickering in and out of trees, lit up the night with their twinkling lights.

The old man trudged up the rocky steps until he reached his house on the top of the hill. From the porch came the sound of Penny.

"Will-Yum Tee, Penny wants supper! You're late! You're late!" squawked the parrot.

"Just now, Penny. I'm coming," said William T. But the parrot just kept on talking.

"Will-Yum Tee! Will-Yum Tee . . .!"

William T. opened the door, found his oil lamp, and lit it. He then washed his hands and mixed some dilly seeds and pumpkin seeds together. Then he went outside to feed Penny, who was still being talkative. While the old man was feeding Penny, the cat was making his way soft-footed around the side of the house. The cat leaped through an open window and landed silently on the cracked, wooden floor. William T. said good-night to Penny and went inside to prepare his supper.

"MEO-O-OW!"

"My goodness, you followed me. And how did you get in here?" asked the old man.

The cat nodded his head up and down, swished his tail, and turned around. Then before William T. knew what was happening, the cat tore across the kitchen of the two-room house and stopped suddenly in front of the table. Looking up at the bowl of coconut milk, he meowed and meowed.

"So you are still hungry? I will share some of my supper with you," said the old man. He gave the cat some coconut milk, mixed some okra and rice with his meager catch of fish, and went outside to cook it on his coal stove. Finally, William T. and the cat sat down to eat their supper.

After the old man and his little friend had finished eating, the cat stretched his two front paws, brushed his whiskers, blinked a cat blink, and yawned. Then he strolled across the room and curled up in an old, wornout chair. Staring straight at the old man, the pupils of his eyes grew large and bright. His mouth widened into a large grin. The fisherman noticed a strange look on the cat's face. Suddenly the wooden walls began to creak and the sound of bells and drums echoed throughout the room.

"Who's there? Who's there, mon?" he gasped.

William T. tried to get up, but he could not move. There rising up in front of him was an enormous cat of black, shimmering fur. His brillant eyes, almost blinding the old man, were as green as the ocean. Around his neck he wore a necklace of coral seashells. His silvery whiskers sparkled as he smiled and swayed from side to side to the rhythm of the Goombay. The old man was dumbfounded and his mouth dropped open when the magnificent cat began to sing:

Goombay fish is very nice.

Eat it once, you eat it twice.

Mix it with some okra and rice.

Goombay fish is very nice.

Finally the fisherman found his voice. "A Goombay Cat!" he cried. "A Goombay Cat! Gracious! Heavens, am I dreaming?"

The singing and music stopped as suddenly as it had begun. William T. rubbed his eyes and looked again at the worn-out chair. There, staring, and smiling, was the scrawny cat. Shaking nervously, William T. got up and went outside to see if Penny had heard the singing and music too, but the parrot was sleeping soundly.

"My mind must be playing tricks," said William T. to himself as he went back into the house. Gazing curiously at the cat, he patted the animal several times and found him a place to sleep. Then he went off to bed muttering to himself.

"I, I, I, must be get-ting old . . . very old."

The next morning William T. was awakened by a light weight on his chest and a tickling on his cheeks. It was the cat sitting there and blinking at him.

"Morn-in'," chuckled the old man as he rubbed his rugged cheeks. "Your whiskers tickled me."

The cat leaped forward, leaped up in the air, turned three somersaults, and landed with a bounce on the old wooden floor.

"Mon, what a cat! You're sure feeling good this morning."

Looking at the cat and studying him for a moment, he remembered last night. Should he tell his friends about what happened? Would they believe him if he told them about the cat? Or might they say: Cousin Will-Yum is getting old . . . very old. Then he thought to himself—how did the cat get on the rock? And why was this island named Cat Island? Did some strange cats live here long ago? He decided to keep all this to himself, but someday he would tell the story to the children.

Bracing his back, he sat up on the edge of the bed. As he went to put on his shoes the cat pounced at them, pulling at the shoestrings.

"Don't tan-ta-lize me, mon. Let me put my shoes on in peace. I gotta hurry 'cause today is Goombay Day!"

But the cat would not let go.

"Don't vex me," said the old man impatiently. Just then a squawk came from the porch.

"Will-Yum Tee! Will-Yum Tee! Don't forget my breakfast! You're late! You're late!" screeched Penny.

The cat let go of the shoestrings and perked his ears towards the sound. Before William T. could stop him, the cat ran to a hole in the screen door and eased himself through the opening onto the porch.

Suddenly the cat caught sight of the beautiful red bird with her flowing tail of brilliant green and yellow feathers. His eyes grew wide and bright as he meo-o-owed loudly. Seeing the cat, Penny flapped her wings furiously as she scuttled wildly around in her cage. Her ruby-red eyes glared in panic.

"Will-Yum Tee! Will-Yum Tee! Hurry! Hurry!"

Thinking something horrible had happened to Penny, William T. rushed outside; by now he was out of breath. He calmed down when he saw the cat just sitting there watching the wild performance of the bird.

"Come, come, Penny. He won't hurt you. He wants to be your friend."

Penny looked at William T. and then at the cat. With her beak held high, she moved to the corner of the cage.

"Come, Penny," he pleaded as he opened the cage door. Penny hesitated, then flew onto William T.'s shoulder, keeping an eye on the cat.

William T. was very happy and chuckled to himself as he went inside to prepare breakfast for his two friends. After breakfast was over, Penny quickly flew into her cage. She was very quiet. The cat followed William T. and watched him as he locked the cage door.

"Good-bye Penny. I'll bring you some sweet benny-cake for Goombay."

The cat looked up at Penny and winked his eye, but Penny only flapped her wings. The old man gathered his fishing-pot trap and threw it over his shoulder. He put his last piece of conch, which he had to use as bait, into his pocket; then he and the cat started on their way to Rock Cove.

William T. had seen many a Goombay morning, but somehow there was a strange and happy feeling about this one. The sky was so blue and wide it seemed to run right into the blue-green water. You could not tell where the sky began and the ocean ended. He was so happy that he began to whistle an old familiar tune. Looking down at his little friend, who was strutting gracefully to the rhythm of the tune, he began to sing:

> Got-ta catch fish, before big boats come.
> Got-ta get it done, before the mid-day sun.
> Got-ta catch fish to sell to ev-ry one,
> Got-ta catch fish, before the big boats come.

As he was singing he looked up at the sky. Not a cloud was in sight, and the sky was bluer than he had ever seen it. He could feel the heat from the blazing sun burning through the soles of his shoes. The sweat was running down his face. The old man and his friend stopped to rest a while under a shady silk-corton tree.

"Good morn-in', Cous-in Will-Yum," said a group of women with shiny faces. They were carrying baskets on their heads filled to the brim with fruits: soursops, saperdilles, spanish limes, casavas, tamarinds, and sea grapes.

"You are early, Cous-in Hilda, Rebecca, and Cous-in Eunice," said the old man.

"Yes 'cause it's Goombay Day!" answered the women, swinging their brightly colored, well-starched dresses. Everyone was moving so fast no one noticed Cous-in Will-Yum's new friend.

"Come, come, let us hurry," said the old man to the cat as they moved along with the crowd. Nearing the waterfront, he and the cat stopped at the Open-Straw Market.

"Big boat in today for Goombay, Cous-in Will-Yum," hollered Auntie Hattie B. from her booth in the Open-Straw Market.

"Yes, child. I seen them big tourist ocean liners down by the Prince Charles stop. Lots of money mak-in' to you."

"We'll set up a table for you right by Cous-in Eunice on the waterfront," she said.

"Where did you get the cat?" asked Cous-in Hilda, noticing the cat for the first time.

"Found him yesterday on top of the rock," answered William T.

Leaving the Open-Straw Market, William T. passed brightly decorated straw booths running along the waterfront. The sun illuminated the blue-green water till it sparkled a jade green. Multicolored seashell beads, big straw pocketbooks, gaily colored straw dolls, and straw hats bedecked with seashells lined the booths.

Suddenly the smell of smothered conch and pigeon peas and rice filled the air. William T. knew he was near the market range with its many booths full of steaming vegetables, sweet fruits, and dazzling pink and white conch shells. Cousin Charlie had his booth here.

Cousin Charlie was busy cooking conch smothered in tomato sauce, and pigeon peas, and rice for the festival. The succulent dish bubbled in a big, cast-iron skillet on an open fire.

The cat ran up to Cousin Charlie's stand, looked up, and meowed and meowed. He licked his tongue and kept his eyes on the smothered conch.

"Mon, where did you find the cat?" asked Cousin Charlie. "Why, I haven't seen one for a long time on this island."

"He found *me*!" laughed William T.

Cousin Charlie fixed a plate of smothered conch and rice and gave it to the old man and the cat.

"Thank you. We will have a good lunch today," said William T. as he and his little friend pushed their way through the Market Range and headed for the waterfront. When William T. and the cat arrived at the fishing rock, he noticed that the cat's back was arched high, his ears were turned up, and he was switching his tail vigorously in signs of anger. It was then that he looked around only to see the young boys who had taunted the cat yesterday. They were fishing not too far from the old man's spot.

"Come, come. They won't bother you," said William T. as he sat down to bait his fishing trap.

The cat flexed his muscles, his tail stood straight up, and his eyes grew large and bright as he watched the fishing trap being lowered into the blue-green waters. William looked at the cat. He gasped when he saw that once more the cat was changing in size. He began to tremble and broke out in a cold sweat as harmonious sounds of bells and drums swelled across the ocean. At that moment a gigantic wave rose up and the great cat leaped into the oncoming billowing waves.

"Help! Help!" cried William T. "My cat is in the water!"

But the other fisherman were so frightened by the crashing of the water against the rocks that they did not hear his cry.

Suddenly the music stopped and the waters were calm again. William T. noticed the fishing-trap was still in place, but there was a heavy tugging on it. He tried to pull the trap up, but it would not give. Again he cried for help. Hearing his call, his fishing companions came to his rescue. Together they grabbed hold of the fishing-trap and began to pull and pull. All at once out of the water came the trap-pot filled with hundreds of beautiful fish shimmering in the sunlight. And there amidst the miraculous catch nestled the cat.

"My *cat*! My *cat*!" cried William T. But the fishermen were so amazed by the miraculous catch they paid no attention to the cat.

"Mon, look at that catch! Biggest I've ever seen!" shouted one of the fishermen.

"Never seen so many fish in one haul," said another.

Tears of joy ran down William T.'s cheeks as he lifted the wet, shivering body out of the trap and cradled it under his tattered old coat.

"Are you all right, mon?" he whispered. The cat looked up at William T. and purred contentedly.

"Old man, how did you catch all those fish?" asked the teenage boys.

It was then that William T. looked at his fishing trap piled high with goggle-eyed fish: margaret fish, jack-runners, grunts, and Nassau groupers. He was so happy that he could not speak for a moment. He just stood there staring at his catch. Then, remembering the boys' question, he looked down at the cat and said:

"Just luck, mon. Just luck."

"Will you sell us some of your catch?" asked one of the boys.

'No! I will not sell you any of my catch . . . but I will give you some of them." He then shared many of his fish with his companions and the boys. The boys felt ashamed and sorry for the way they had treated the cat and the old man.

"May we help you carry your load off the rock?" asked the boys.

The cat purred; the old man smiled, and said he would like that very much.

News of Cousin William's catch spread all along the waterfront. Auntie Hattie B., Cousins Eunice, Hilda, and Rebecca, and all the women left the Goombay tables to see the great haul of fish. Even Cousin Charlie left the Market Range to see Cousin William's big catch. Children came from all over the island when they heard the news of the old man's catch. Now they danced around him, playing big bass drums and singing a song of the Goombay catch:

> Cous-in Will-Yum caught big catch!
> From the blue-green waters.
> He caught them in his fish-pot trap,
> From the blue-green waters.

While the children sang, the cat swished his tail to the rhythm of the song. William T. was so happy he began to sing too:

> Goombay Cat caught big fish,
> From the island wat-ters
> He caught them with a great big smile,
> From the island wat-ters.

The teenage boys walked tall, their heads held high, as they carried William T.'s catch to his table. William T. strutted proudly before them with the cat riding on his arm. It was a grand sight to see the joyous procession marching to their tables to begin the Goombay festival. Tables were quickly filled with fried chicken, sous, coconut cakes, and other delectable dishes.

"Well, mon," said William T., setting the cat by his table. "It's time for us to fix our table."

The old man was about to pick up his fish-pot when he heard the sound of the Goombay song! It lasted for a brief second, and when

William T. looked down again the cat was gone! Where his little friend had stood was a shiny, coral, seashell necklace. He picked it up slowly and he knew that his little friend was now gone forever.

However, William T. was not sad. The beautiful necklace was left by the Goombay Cat to remind him that miracles still happen and that he wasn't so very old after all.

This tale gives information about the Bahamas in its description of the country, the plants, the foods, and the customs, including the legends told by the people. It could, therefore, be used in connection with a social studies unit on the islands. It could also be played purely for the narrative. William T. is an appealing character, but the others can be more fully developed than they are in this account of his strange experience.

After the children have decided which characters are necessary to the telling and which others may be added, they are ready to decide on the scenes. If playing in a large room, one end can be William T.'s cabin; the other, the fishing area. The middle of the room might be the village square. If the space is small, the scenes can follow in sequence. The procession at the end can be handled in a variety of ways. One group had it move around the playing space in a large circle; another had it weave in and out, suggesting that it was going into different parts of the village. Carefully selected music will suggest movement and a mood.

All can try playing William T. —showing how he moves, walks, sits, runs, handles his fishing pots, and rescues the cat. When the class is thoroughly familiar with the story, it will want to go on to the enactment of scenes. Again, by allowing small groups to play bits of the story, each will have an opportunity to contribute dialogue, characterization, and movement. Some groups can be villagers, creating individual characters and showing their love for William T. An experienced group might want to create earlier scenes in William T.'s life, showing what he was like when he was a boy. Groups handle the cat differently. One class wanted to have a child play the part, when it became large. Another group used a "prop" cat in the scenes where it was small, but had a large boy play him when it grew to enormous proportions. Still another imagined it throughout, using offstage sounds when the cat and the parrot spoke. This last was probably the most satisfactory solution, but it's good to let the class wrestle with the problem and come up with its own solution.

Some children chant the songs, but one group composed its own music to "Goombay fish is very nice." Superstition and the supernatural intrigue most children, so this aspect of the story usually has particular appeal. There is a rich opportunity here for learning and creative playing. The results will be as simple or as detailed as the children are able to make them.

The Clever Lad from Skye comes from the Hebrides, and, like many folk tales, tells about the poor boy who outwits a rich lord. Tormod's adventures offer a number of good roles but, in addition, allow for participation on the part of the entire class, if desired. Servants and townsfolk are called for, as well as sound effects.

THE CLEVER LAD FROM SKYE

Tormod MacLeod was a lad belonging to the class of MacLeods who lived on the Isle of Skye. His father had little money and many mouths to feed, so Tormod decided to seek his fortune on the mainland. He wandered from one town to another until he arrived in Glasgow, and there he found a job with a blacksmith who needed an apprentice. Tormod did well and his master was pleased. In fact, Tormod was so clever and quick that the blacksmith blessed the day he had hired him.

Now there was a man in Glasgow who had a fine horse that he often brought into the smithy to have shod. While Tormod was shoeing it one of these times, the lad said, "That's a fine horse you have there."

"Aye, he is," replied the gentleman.

"What will you take for him?" asked Tormod.

"He's not for sale," the gentleman said. "I'll not part with him for any money."

"Aren't you afraid he will be stolen?" asked Tormod.

The gentleman laughed and said that this could not be done. "Why, I have four stable boys taking care of him and all kinds of bells to sound an alarm, if anyone tried to take him away."

Now Tormod, who was as bold as he was clever, said, "I could steal him, if I wanted to—right out from under the noses of your guards."

The gentleman was very angry at this and said, "If you can do that, you can keep him and one hundred pounds besides!"

Tormod thought about this for a long time. Then, one day as he passed a pub, an idea came to him. He would buy two big bottles of ale and put them in his pockets. He would spill some of the ale on his clothes to make the guards think he had been drinking. Then he would stagger around and fall down on the straw near the horse's stall. Thinking him asleep, the guards would drink the contents of the two bottles, go to sleep themselves, and Tormod would lead the animal safely out of the stable.

The plan worked just as he planned it. The next morning the gentleman came storming into the smithy's shop, demanding the arrest of the boy who had stolen his horse. But the blacksmith, who had overheard the gentleman's bargain, stepped up and reminded him that he had said if Tormod stole the horse, he could keep it. And that, furthermore, he would give Tormod one hundred pounds. Angrily, the gentleman went out, leaving Tormod the horse and the money.

Tormod's next adventure was even bolder than his first. It was said in the village that the old gentleman planned to marry his daughter to a rich, elderly lord, and that her father had locked her in her room to prevent her from escaping. When the gentleman came to the blacksmith's soon after this, Tormod asked him if the gossip was true. Being assured that it was, the young man asked what would happen if he managed to get the bride out of the house. "If you can do that, my lad," said her father, "you may have her and five hundred pounds besides."

Again, an idea came to Tormod. Why not rescue the young woman from her fate? So he went to the home of the seamstress who was making her wedding gown, paid her well for the use of the woman's own clothing, took a large basket, and approached the gentleman's house for a second time. Meanwhile, Tormod had dressed himself in the seamstress's clothes. When he arrived at the door, he said, in the highest voice he could muster, that he had come for a fitting of the young lady's wedding gown. The servant, believing him to be the seamstress, told him to come on upstairs and that he would unlock the door.

When the servant had left, Tormod removed the seamstress's dress and apron and shawl. The young woman was so startled to see a young man standing before her that she was about to scream. But Tormod said quietly, "Please don't be frightened. I have only come to help you escape. If you do as I say, you will be able to leave this house forever and so free yourself from this marriage."

The young woman realized that the speaker seemed honest and, furthermore, that he offered her a means of escape from her prison. So she accepted his offer of help. Tormod explained that if she got into the basket, he would cover it over again, put on the seamstress's clothing, and call the servant to help him carry this heavy load back downstairs. He would take her to the blacksmith's house, where she was welcome to stay as long as she liked.

Again the plan was successful. The next morning the old gentleman was furious when he discovered the trick that had been played on him. Fuming, he hurried to the blacksmith's shop, declaring that he had been robbed and that his daughter had been kidnapped. But the blacksmith, who had again heard the whole conversation, stepped up and said, "What about the 500 pounds you said you would give to the one who could outwit you?"

Realizing that there was nothing he could do, the old man threw down the gold and declared he would never leave his house again.

Tormod was becoming a very rich man. Moreover, he and the gentleman's daughter had fallen in love, and, in the course of time, were married. Thinking it a pity that his wife and her father never saw each other these days, Tormod invited the old gentleman to visit them. But his father-in-law was still so angry that he said he would not budge until the day he willingly followed the young man out of the house, and that that day would never come.

Tormod thought hard and long about this. Suddenly an idea came to him. He would dress himself in a sheet and go to the gentleman's house that night. He would tell him that the end of the world was at hand and that he had come for him. As before, the scheme worked. The old man was so frightened at being wakened out of a sound sleep by a ghostly stranger that he agreed to go at once. Tormod told him to put on a white garment like his own, covering his body and head, and he would do what he could to save him. Then, taking the old man's hand, he led the white-robed figure out of the house and down to the blacksmith's shop. There Tormod and the smithy made all kinds of noise. With hammers and bells and chains, they suggested purgatory. Tormod asked the old man to repent of his sins. The terrified figure, his eyes still covered, fell to his knees and begged forgiveness, if only his life could be spared. Tormod agreed and pulled the sheet off his head.

Then Tormod explained everything, even calling his wife into the shop. The old man was so overjoyed at finding himself and his daughter alive that he forgot to be angry. Tormod then brought out the horse and all the money he had won and gave it back to its rightful owner. As he explained, he was a fortunate man, with a wife, a wee son, and a good place as the blacksmith's partner. After all, what more would any man want?

This is a longer and more complex story than any of the others, but the fact that it can be handled by scenes puts it within the capabilities of children in middle and upper grades. If the teacher has had any experience with participatory theatre, he will find *The Clever Lad from Skye* a story that can be dramatized in this way. However it is done, the first step is to list the characters, and the second step is to decide on the number of scenes. Then, depending on the age and the experience of the children, planning can proceed.

It is a good idea to spend some time in a discussion of rural life in Scotland a hundred years or more ago. Pantomimes of the following activities might follow: working in the smith's shop, leading the horses around the courtyard, stealing in and out of the gentleman's house, pretending to be the ghost that the gentleman follows. Making the various sounds that are such an important part of the story also challenge the ingenuity. When every child is thoroughly familiar with the details, and the entire class has had a chance to try the different noises, actions, and pantomime, the dramatization can begin. Because of the length of the story, it's wise to play it by scene, using a different Tormod and blacksmith each time. This gives many children an opportunity to play these parts as well as to contribute different ideas about the characters and ways of handling the narrative. This tale, incidentally, is excellent to use in social studies as a part of an integrated project. It reveals the customs and attitudes of a people in a particular time and place.

The Clever Lad from Skye can also lead to a discussion of moral and ethical behavior, human relationships, social codes, and tricks with far-reaching consequences. The denouement is different from most tales of the clever lad in that Tormod returns the horse and the money in an effort to heal the breach and establish a good family relationship. This ending can be compared with other more familiar folk tales, in which the hero destroys his adversary and keeps the goods he has won in a battle of wits.

SUMMARY

Because of the greater plot complications and length, all these stories will demand more time in planning than those in the preceding chapter. There is sufficient content to absorb the interest of the average group for several sessions, depending, of course, on the length of the class periods and the age of the participants. Characters are presented in greater depth, hence much more time must be spent on their development. Most groups like to consider such questions as:

1. What is the character really like?
2. Why does he behave as he does?
3. What do others think of him? Why?
4. If he is not like that, why do they think so?
5. How is he changed, or what has he learned as a result of his actions?

As the participants grow in experience, they will find new ways of telling the story. Some will want to use narrators; others, many scenes; and some may rearrange the sequence of events altogether. As was said in the previous chapter, every group is unique, and the leader learns to expect an endless variety of ways in which the same material can be handled and interpreted. The growing self-confidence of the players releases ideas, which lead to further thinking and experimentation. Each group, regardless of age, becomes more critical of its efforts as, with the help of the leader, it strives for a higher level of accomplishment.

9

THE POSSIBILITIES IN POETRY

Children like poetry. They are sensitive to the rhythm of it, and enjoy the repetition of sounds, words, and phrases. The direct approach of the poet is not unlike their own; hence poetry, unless it has been spoiled for them, has a special appeal. The music and language, as well as the ideas, feelings, and images of poetry reach the younger child particularly, capturing and stimulating his imagination. For this reason, poetry can be used in creative dramatics, often with highly successful results.

Many leaders find poetry a more satisfactory springboard than prose for introducing creative playing to a group. This is probably an individual matter, depending as much on the leader as on the participants. If the leader or teacher enjoys poetry himself, he will find that it provides a rich source of material that can be used at all levels of experience, and with all ages. For children, poetry and play go quite naturally together. "The affinity between poetry and play is not external only; it is also

159

apparent in the structure of creative imagination itself. In the turning of a poetic phrase, the development of a motif, the expression of a mood, there is always a play element at work."[1]

For these reasons, the possibilities in poetry as motivation are considered. What kinds of poems are usable? How can poetry and movement be combined? Has choral speaking any place in creative dramatics? For the answers to these questions, one has only to go to children themselves, as they engage in their play. Many of their games are accompanied by chants, which are a form of choral speaking. In action games, rhythm is basic, while some games are played to verse with the players often making up their own original stanzas. If we listen, we note the enjoyment of repetition, refrain, and the sounds of words. Only very much later does poetry become a literary form to be taken seriously, and when it does, the element of play is, unfortunately, too often lost.

CHORAL SPEAKING

Because poetry lends itself so well to group enjoyment, let us begin with a consideration of choral speaking, its purposes and procedures. Choral reading, or speaking, is simply reading or reciting in unison under the direction of a leader. It is not a new technique, for people have engaged in it for centuries. It antedated the theatre in the presentation of ideas, and became an important element of the Greek drama. Evidences of choral speaking have been found in the religious ceremonies and festivals of primitive peoples, while today it is still used for ritualistic purposes in church services, and on patriotic occasions. In the early twentieth century, however, it was recognized as one of the most effective methods of teaching the language arts and of improving speech habits.

In the past, choral speaking was used as an important means of communication and communion; today it is an art form as well and is employed both ways by the theatre, the church, and the school. When working with older children or adults, the two major purposes of the activity are:

1. Learning (when the purpose is process and, therefore, participant-centered).
2. Performance (when the purpose is program and, therefore, audience-centered).

---

1. J. Huizinga, *Homo Ludens, A Study of the Play Element in Culture* (Boston: Beacon Press, 1955), p. 14.

Often the former leads into the latter, but, like creative drama, it does not necessarily follow that practice must result in performance. Practice has values of its own, whether or not the product is shared.

Values

One of the values of choral speaking is that it can be used successfully regardless of space or class size. While a group of twenty or so is more desirable than one of forty or fifty, the larger number need not be a deterrent.

Many teachers consider the greatest value of choral speaking the opportunity it provides for speech improvement. Pitch, volume, rate, and tone quality are important to the effective interpretation of material. The need for clear diction is apparent when a group is reading aloud, whereas the practicing of speech sounds alone is often a tedious and unrelated exercise. During discussion, even young children will make suggestions as to how a poem should be recited. Vocal expression and the clear enunciation of speech sounds are often acquired more easily and with greater motivation when the group works together on meaning.

A third value, and one shared with creative dramatics, is the opportunity it provides for social cooperation. Choral speaking is a group activity, and by its nature, therefore, directs each individual to a common goal. The child with the strident voice learns to soften his tone, whereas the shy child can work for more volume without feeling self-conscious. Even the speech-handicapped may recite without embarrassment, because he is not speaking alone and, therefore, is not conspicuous.

A fourth value of choral speaking is its suitability to any age level. It may be introduced in the kindergarten, but is equally effective when used in high school or college classes. Not all material is adapted to choral work, but much of it is, and the major criterion is probably that it be enjoyed and recommended by the readers themselves.

Procedures

There are many ways of beginning choral speaking, but with younger children, it will probably spring from their own enjoyment of a poem and their obvious desire to say it aloud or to the accompaniment of action. With older children who have had no experience in group reading, the teacher will not only select the material with care but will give some thought in advance to its interpretation. Discussion of the meaning, and the various ways of reading it so as to bring out the meaning, give the pupils a part in planning it. A second reading will reveal further meaning, as well as difficulties in phrasing and diction.

As the group becomes more experienced, it will offer suggestions as to those lines that may be most effectively taken by the whole group, part of the group, and by individual voices. Although a structured activity, choral speaking offers a real opportunity for creative thinking, as each group works out its own presentation. The teacher leads, indicating when to start, and watches the phrasing, emphases, and pauses suggested by the readers. The amount of time spent on a poem will vary, but it is more important to keep the enthusiasm alive than it is to work for perfection. With practice, the group will grow increasingly sensitive to the demands of different kinds of material, and their results will improve in proportion to their understanding and enjoyment.

Most authorities on choral speaking suggest dividing the group into light and dark voices. This is not quite the same as a division into high and low, or soprano and alto voices, but has to do with quality and resonance as well as pitch. Some leaders, on the other hand, believe that a division in which there are both light and dark in each group makes for more interesting quality. However it is done, some division is necessary for any group of more than ten. Some poems can be read by three groups if the class is very large. These may include middle voices; though, again, it is the material that will suggest the groupings rather than an arbitrary division.

Ways of Reading

UNISON—The whole group reads together. Though the simplest in one sense, this is the most difficult, since using all voices limits variation. Some poems, particularly short ones, are most effective when read or spoken by the entire class.

ANTIPHONAL—This is a division into two groups with each taking certain parts. Many poems are more effective when read in this way. The poem will dictate the way it may be read.

CUMULATIVE—When this technique is used, it is for the purpose of building toward a climax, or certain high points in the poem. As the term suggests, it is the accumulation of voices, either individually or by groups.

SOLO—Often lines or stanzas call for individual reading. This can be an effective technique as well as a way of giving an opportunity for individual participation.

LINE-AROUND—This is solo work, in which each line is taken by a different reader. Children enjoy this, and are alert to the lines they have been assigned.

As the group progresses and attempts longer and more difficult material, it may suggest using several or all of these techniques in one poem. The results can be remarkably effective, encouraging attentiveness and self-discipline, as well as imaginative planning. Occasionally, sound effects can be added. Music, bells, drums, and vocal sounds, produced by the readers themselves, provide an opportunity for further inventiveness.

Because our primary concern is creative drama, only those poems that suggest movement or pantomime are included here. The following have been used successfully with groups, combining choral speaking and activities suggested by the content or sounds. The first, "Happy New Year," is an old rhyme, suggesting the simplest kind of movement as a beginning:

> Happy New Year! Happy New Year!
> I've come to wish you a Happy New Year.
> I've got a little pocket and it is very thin.
> Please give me a penny to put some money in.
> If you haven't got a penny, a halfpenny will do.
> If you haven't got a halfpenny, well—
> God bless you!

In England, children went caroling from house to house on New Year's Day. Their neighbors gave them money, much as we give candy and apples for trick-or-treat on Hallowe'en. Whether they received a contribution or not, they sang or spoke, and this old rhyme has been handed down. The group can say the verse together, with one child acting the part of the caroler; or half of the group can speak, with the other half playing the carolers. Perhaps the entire group will want to speak and move. There are various possibilities in even as short a rhyme as this.

A very simple verse, but one that offers an unusual opportunity for imaginative movement, is "Jump or Jiggle." Not only children but adult students as well get into the spirit of it, and have a good time thinking of movements that characterize the animals mentioned.

JUMP OR JIGGLE

EVELYN BEYER

> Frogs jump.
> Caterpillars hump.
> Worms wiggle.
> Bugs jiggle.

Rabbits hop.
Horses clop.
Snakes slide.
Sea gulls glide.
Mice creep.
Deer leap.
Puppies bounce.
Lions stalk—
But
I walk.

The next verse suggests the use of sound effects rather than action. Part of the group might say the first and third lines, with the others taking the second and fourth. Or, if two clocks are suggested, a solo voice might take the first and third, with the total group taking the other lines. Even so simple a poem as this provides some opportunity for inventiveness.

Slowly ticks the big clock:
  Tick-tock; tick-tock!
But cuckoo clock ticks a double quick:
  Tick-a-tock-a, tick-a-tock-a,
  Tick-a-tock-a, tick!

MERRY-GO-ROUND
DOROTHY BARUCH

I climbed up on the merry-go-round,
And it went round and round.
I climbed up on a big brown horse,
And it went up and down.

Around and round and up and down.
Around and round and up and down.

I sat high up on a big brown horse,
And rode around on the merry-go-round,
And rode around on the merry-go-round.
I rode around on the merry-go-round
Around
And round

And
Round.

This poem is fun for children of all ages because of the action, which requires some coordination. As with the others, half of the group can read it while the other half acts the merry-go-round; or, if the group is small, everyone can do the action while repeating the lines. It is probably more satisfactory handled the first way, with variety achieved by having individual voices take the lines beginning with "I." Sometimes children like to imagine the merry-go-round running down until it comes to a stop.

ECHO
AUTHOR UNKNOWN

I sometimes wonder where he lives,
This Echo that I never see.
I heard his voice now in the hedge,
Then down behind the willow tree.

And when I call, "Oh, please come out,"
"Come out," he always quick replies.
"Hello, hello," again I say;
"Hello, hello," he softly cries.

He must be jolly, Echo must,
For when I laugh, "Ho, ho, ho, ho,"
He answers me with "Ho, ho, ho."

I think perhaps he'd like to play;
I know some splendid things to do.
He must be lonely hiding there;
I wouldn't like it. Now, would you?

Echoes are fascinating, and this poem is one that may prompt a group to make up an original story about echoes. It lends itself so well to choral reading that it is suggested the class try it this way first, then discuss whether something else might be done with it. The lines in which the Echo speaks are good solo lines that stimulate speculation as to who the Echo is, what he is like, where he is hiding, and whether or not he is ever discovered. Some groups have made up delightful stories about him after reading the poem together first.

Although choral speaking is an effective way to begin pantomime, it is not the only way of using poetry. Often a poem can be introduced by the leader, either before or after improvisation. It may serve as a springboard to action in which the whole class participates but does not necessarily repeat or read the verse. One short poem that has proved highly successful with many groups of all ages is "Hallowe'en."

HALLOWE'EN
GERALDINE BRAIN SIKS

Sh! Hst!
Hsst! Shssssh!
It's Hallowe'en.
Eerie creatures now are seen.
Black, bent witches fly
Like ugly shadows through the sky.
White, stiff ghosts do float
Silently, like mystery smoke.

Lighted pumpkins glow
With crooked eyes and grins to show
It's Hallowe'en
Hssst! Shssh!
Sh! Hst!

The period might start off with a discussion of what we think of when we hear the word Hallowe'en. Most groups suggest pumpkins, witches, orange and black, elves, broomsticks, cats, night, ghosts, trick-or-treat, and masks. Some pantomime to music can be introduced here, with the whole class becoming witches, cats, or ghosts. After they are thoroughly in the spirit of Hallowe'en, the poem can be read. When the group is small, all may be eerie creatures, witches, and ghosts. When the group is large, it can be divided into several parts, with each one choosing one idea to pantomime. Pumpkins have been suggested in a variety of ways: rolling about on the floor in rounded shapes, squatting with big smiles, and moving in circles to music. Music is helpful, though not necessary. This poem never fails to arouse a response, and on one occasion led to an informal program of Hallowe'en poems and improvisations.

The next poem is one that has been most successful with both children and adults. The universality of its theme appeals to everyone, and stimulates

an imaginative response at any time of the year. It was the basis for a delightful improvisation by a group of Puerto Rican teachers, who understood and
enjoyed it, then improvised it with Spanish dialogue.

SING A SONG OF SEASONS
ALICE ELLISON

It's spring.
Such a hippity, happity, hoppity
First spring day.
Let's play! Let's play! Let's play!

It's summer!
Such a swingy, swazy lazy
First hot day.
Let's play! Let's play! Let's play!

It's fall!
Such a brisky, frisky, crispy
First fall day.
Let's play! Let's play! Let's play!

It's winter!
Such a blowy, snowy joy
First winter day.
Let's play! Let's play! Let's play!

Before reading the poem, there can be pantomimes of simple sports and
games. Flying kites, skating, tossing a ball, jumping rope, and playing tennis
are familiar activities that serve to get the group moving and break down the
barriers of self-consciousness. After perhaps fifteen minutes of this kind of
activity, the teacher is ready to read the poem. Discussion as to games and
sports appropriate to each season directs the thinking, and often brings some
unexpected suggestions. After everyone has had a chance to offer ideas, the
teacher can ask how the poem might be played.

If the class is separated into four groups, each group can take a season,
showing various games and sports belonging to it. Some groups create situations for each, such as going to the beach in summer, with sunbathing, swimming, picnicking, and the like. More than one group has created a scene with
characters for each season, using the poem only as a springboard for an

original situation. It is urged that this be done in the round, rather than on a stage or in the front of a room, so as to allow for as much movement as possible, and easy passage into the center without breaking the mood.

IMAGININGS
J. PAGET-FREDERICKS

Imagine!
A little red door that leads under a hill
Beneath roots and bright stones and pebbly rill.

Imagine!
A quaint little knocker and shoe scraper, too—
A curious carved key
Is waiting for you.

Imagine!
Tiptoe on doormat, you're turning the key.
The red door would open
And there you'd be.

Imagine!
Shut the door tightly, so no one could see.
And no one would know then
Where you would be.
Imagine, if you can.

A poem such as "Imaginings" lends itself to all kinds of improvisation. Every age will find an answer to the question: What lies behind the little red door? It is a good idea for the teacher to read the poem aloud two or three times before asking what the group sees in it. If the class is not too large, every child may be given a chance to describe what he sees. Younger children find buried treasure, a forbidden city, thieves, a ghost town. Some may describe a place they know, with friends or neighbors inhabiting it. This particular poem is a wonderful springboard for the imagination, since it leads the listener to the threshold, and then leaves him free to follow his own ideas.

Some groups have been stimulated to plan an original play, involving several characters. If many good suggestions come out of the discussion, the leader may want to break the class into small groups of three or four, who will, in turn, dramatize their ideas. Occasionally, if a group is very small, or if the teacher wants to plan an individual lesson, each child may pantomime what he sees and does behind the red door. The poem can hold a group for two or three sessions, depending on their readiness to use the material, and the interest it stimulates.

SOME ONE
WALTER DE LA MARE

Some one came knocking
　At my wee, small door;
Some one came knocking,
　I'm sure — sure — sure;
I listened, I opened,
　I looked to left and right,
But nought there was a-stirring
　In the still dark night;
Only the busy beetle
　Tap-tapping in the wall,
Only from the forest
　The screech owl's call
Only the cricket whistling
　While the dewdrops fall,
So I know not who came knocking
　At all, at all, at all.

"Some One" has the same power to evoke an imaginative response. Though the poem is short, it creates an atmosphere of mystery and wonder. Who can be knocking? How large is the "wee, small door"? Who am "I"? Do I ever find out who my mysterious visitor was? How do I react? Groups of all ages enjoy imagining this situation, and the teacher may expect a variety of responses and interpretations. Some children have insisted that the door can be no more than a few inches high, which, of course, leads into the question of whose house it is. Fairies, elves, friendly insects, and mice have all been suggested. Other children have seen it as a cottage door—small compared to the doors of city buildings. Visitors, in this case, vary from mysterious strangers with magic powers to actual persons — frightened, and faint with weariness. Indians have been suggested, investigating an early settler's cabin. Because the poet does not say who knocked, the reader is entirely free to create his own situation, and some delightful stories have been inspired as a result.

SEA SHELL

AMY LOWELL

Sea Shell, Sea Shell,
  Sing me a song, O pleasé
A song of ships, and sailor men,
  And parrots, and tropical trees.

Of islands lost in the Spanish Main
Which no man ever may find again,
Of fishes and coral under the waves,
And sea-horses stabled in great green caves.

Sea Shell, Sea Shell,
Sing of the things you know so well.

Although "Sea Shell" offers vivid imagery, it leaves the imagination free to roam tropical isles, and savor adventure. Every child responds to the singing of a shell, and most will go on to ideas of their own. Perhaps having the group tell their own stories is a good beginning. What did you hear? Where did you find the shell? What is it like? What did it sing when you listened? Tell us its story.

Having a collection of shells adds to the interest as the children feel and examine them. Elaborate plays set on unknown shores have resulted, with the children responding to the thoughts of sailors, pirates, and treasures buried in the sand.

The poems of Robert Louis Stevenson have long appealed to children, and both their content and the suggestions for action make them especially appropriate for creative drama. The two poems that follow can be used with quite young children, who may already be familiar with them.

MY SHADOW

ROBERT LOUIS STEVENSON

I have a little shadow that goes in and out with me,
And what can be the use of him is more than I can see.
He is very, very like me from the heels up to the head;
And I see him jump before me, when I jump into my bed.

The funniest thing about him is the way he likes to grow—
Not at all like proper children, which is always very slow;
For he sometimes shoots up taller like an India-rubber ball,
And he sometimes gets so little that there's none of him at all.

He hasn't got a notion of how children ought to play,
And can only make a fool of me in every sort of way.
He stays so close beside me, he's a coward, you can see;
I'd think shame to stick to nursie as that shadows sticks to me!

One morning, very early, before the sun was up,
I rose and found the shining dew on every buttercup;
But my lazy little shadow, like an arrant sleepy-head,
Had stayed at home behind me and was fast asleep in bed.

The idea of a shadow offers all kinds of possibilities. The group might try this one altogether—half being children; half, shadows. This could also lead into original stories, with use of shadows as a theme. It could also stimulate the writing of original verse.

THE WIND
ROBERT LOUIS STEVENSON

I saw you toss the kites on high
And blow the birds about the sky;
And all around I heard you pass,
Like ladies' skirts across the grass—
    O wind a-blowing all day long,
    O wind, that sings so loud a song.

I saw the different things you did,
But always you yourself you hid.
I felt you push, I heard you call,
I could not see yourself at all—
    O wind a-blowing all day long,
    O wind, that sings so loud a song.

O you that are so strong and cold,
O blower, are you young or old?
Are you a beast of field and tree
Or just a stranger child than me?

O wind a-blowing all day long,
O wind, that sings so loud a song.

Like the preceding verse, "The Wind" offers a wonderful opportunity for strong movement. The group can divide up in many ways, being everything that is mentioned: the wind, the birds, the kites, the skirts, and other things that the children may suggest. Wind is a good topic for discussion, often developing original stories as well as the search for other stories such as Aesop's fable about *The Sun and the Wind.* A whole unit could be developed on the subject or on the natural elements.

Most children at one time or another have made a mobile. Perhaps there is one in the classroom. The following poem describes a mobile, suggesting how it moves and seems to be alive. How can it be used as a springboard to suggest movement and dramatic action? See what it suggests to the class.

MOBILE
DAVID MCCORD

Our little mobile hangs and swings
And likes a draft and drafty things:

Half-open doors; wide-window breeze,
All people when they cough or sneeze;

Hot dishes giving off their heat;
Big barking dogs, small running feet.

Our mobile's red and made to look
Like fish about to bite a hook:

Six fishes with a hook in front
Of each. They range in size—the runt,

Or baby, up to papa fish,
With hooks to watch and make them wish

That they could reach the nice blue worms
A-dangle there with swirly squirms;

Six fishy mouths all open wide,
Six sets of teeth all sharp inside,

Six fishy holes where eyes should be,
Six fish to swim on airy sea.

I'm eating breakfast now and they are watching me.
And I must say

That every time I take a bite
I see and feel their sorry plight.

Birds, fish, and sailboats are often used as subjects for mobiles. This is because they all move, dip, turn, and swirl as the air circulates around them. There is almost a magic in the way a mobile moves, even when there appears to be no breeze stirring. Without using words, have the class be a mobile:

moving as separate parts of the mobile
putting the parts together in a formation
moving without touching the other parts of the mobile

Now break the class into small groups, each suggesting in movement the images described in the verse. Try adding the images to the moving mobile.

This may lead to the making of a mobile or the creating of a verse. Or it may lead to an entirely different way of suggesting a mobile. See what it makes the class feel, see, do.

Langston Hughes's poetry is rich in images and rhythms. This particular short work suggests strong movement which older children enjoy using to create the different rivers.

THE NEGRO SPEAKS OF RIVERS
LANGSTON HUGHES

I've known rivers:
I've known rivers ancient as the world and older than
    the flow of human blood in human veins.
My soul has grown deep like the rivers.
I bathed in the Euphrates when dawns were young.
I built my hut near the Congo and it lulled me to
    sleep.
I looked upon the Nile and raised the pyramids above
    it.
I heard the singing of the Mississippi when Abe Lincoln

went down to New Orleans, and I've seen its muddy
bosom turn all golden in the sunset.

I've known rivers:
Ancient, dusky rivers.
My soul has grown deep like the rivers.

After some discussion of the places and the different kinds of rivers
described in the poem, the children will be ready to use it as a springboard.
Strong movement and use of the whole body are called for; perhaps large
groups, moving together, can suggest the vast bodies of water better than one
or two persons. What else is there besides the waters? Are there any people?
Does anything happen? What does the last line mean? How can this be expressed?

THE OLD WIFE AND THE GHOST
JAMES REEVES

There was an old wife and she lived all alone
In a cottage not far from Hitchin:
And one bright night, by the full moon light,
Comes a ghost right into her kitchen.

About that kitchen neat and clean
The ghost goes pottering round.
But the poor old wife is deaf as a boot
And so hears never a sound.

The ghost blows up the kitchen fire,
As bold as bold can be;
He helps himself from the larder shelf,
But never a sound hears she.

He blows on his hands to make them warm,
And whistles aloud "Whee-hee!"
But still as a sack the old soul lies
And never a sound hears she.

From corner to corner he runs about,
And into the cupboard he peeps;
He rattles the door and bumps on the floor,
But still the old wife sleeps.

Jangle and bang go the pots and pans,
As he throws them all around;
And the plates and mugs and dishes and jugs,
He flings them all to the ground.

Madly the ghost tears up and down
And screams like a storm at sea;
At last the old wife stirs in her bed—
And it's "Drat those mice," says she.

Then the first cock crows and morning shows
And the troublesome ghost's away.
But oh! what a pickle the poor wife sees
When she gets up next day.

"Them's tidy big mice," the old wife thinks.
And off she goes to Hitchin.
And a tidy big cat she fetches back
To keep the mice from her kitchen.

This amusing verse should stimulate all kinds of ideas for dramatization, characterization, and movement. It can be done entirely in mime or with improvised dialogue. Why not have the entire group work on the ghost's movement and activities? They will enjoy it, and many ideas will be expressed within the security of the group. Music and sound effect are helpful and add atmosphere. This is a good poem for Hallowe'en, but it has a strong appeal for young children at any time of year.

I HEAR AMERICA SINGING
WALT WHITMAN

I hear America singing, the varied carols I hear.
Those of mechanics, each one singing his as it

should be blithe and strong,
The carpenter singing as he measures his plank
    or beam,
The mason singing his as he makes ready for
    work, or leaves off work.
The boatman singing what belongs to him in his
    boat, the deckhand singing on the steamboat
    deck,
The shoemaker singing as he sits on his bench,
    the hatter singing as he stands,
The wood-cutter's song, the ploughboy's on his
    way in the morning, or at noon intermission or
    at sundown,
The delicious singing of the mother, or of the
    young wife at work, or of the girl sewing or
    washing.
Each singing what belongs to him or her and to
    none else.
The day what belongs to the day—at night the
    party of young fellows, robust, friendly.
Singing with open mouths their strong
    melodious songs.

"I Hear America Singing" is a splendid poem for both choral speaking and dramatization. The various characters and their occupations suggest pantomime to participants of all ages. If playing in a large room, the characters can be scattered about the circle, with any number taking part. Pantomime and speaking may be done simultaneously or separately, as the group prefers. This is a poem that is particularly appealing to older students, who are often stimulated to further reading of the poet's work. The mood is powerful and usually acts as a unifying element.

An imaginative program combining puppets and poetry was devised by two artist/teachers in New Jersey a few years ago. Its popularity attests the effectiveness of the method, which is described in their brochure as follows:

> More and more puppets are used in education to add dimensions to learning. A puppet can add clarity and motion to difficult teaching problems and abstractions, demonstrating to the students a living picture of the offered material.[2]

2. Leila Weisholz and Lois Koenig. *Poetry and Puppets in Education: A Learning Experience in the Language Arts* (Cedar Grove, N.J.).

The artist/teachers make the point that poetry and puppets have certain similarities: the words are the puppets of the poem, just as puppets are the materials of the puppeteer. In each case, total involvement is necessary. The idea is not to be construed as a gimmick but rather as another way of teaching the language arts. Lyric poems are handled with great simplicity in order to deepen emotional involvement and not distract by excessive movement. Narrative poetry, on the other hand, is presented differently; puppets mime the story as the poem is read aloud. Puppets demonstrate the basic exaggerations of poetry, the artists say. Results include not only enjoyment and a better understanding of the poetic form, but also the writing of original verse.

SUMMARY

Poetry, in conclusion, is an effective springboard for improvisation. The directness of verse motivates the players to a response that is direct and imaginative. For this reason, it is a good starting point for the beginner, though it can be used at any time with even the most advanced players. Because the sounds of poetry have as great an appeal as the content and mood, it is suggested that poetry be spoken as well as acted.

Choral speaking is a group art and can, therefore, be combined with creative dramatics if the teacher so wishes. Some of the reasons for including choral speaking are as follows:

1. It can be done with groups of any size and age.
2. It emphasizes group rather than individual effort.
3. It provides an opportunity to introduce poetry.
4. It offers the shy or handicapped child an opportunity to speak.
5. It promotes good habits of speech through enjoyable exercise, rather than drill.
6. It is a satisfying activity in itself.
7. It can be combined successfully with rhythmic movement and pantomime.

Just as action songs are used with very young children as an approach to creative rhythms, so may poetry be used with older children, to suggest mood, stimulate ideas, and begin the flow of creative energy. Chants, and the repetition of words, have a natural appeal. Thus poetry and nonsense verse may prove a successful method of introducing creative drama. Skill in movement, rhythms, and pantomime are increased as all children are given opportunities to participate.

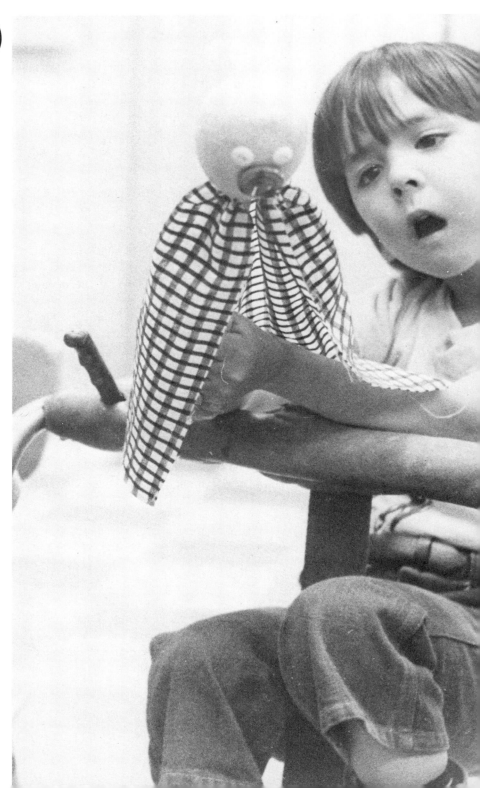

10

SPEECH
AND
SPEECH-RELATED
ACTIVITIES

As stated in an earlier chapter, improved speech is a shared objective of modern educators and teachers of creative drama. Although this book is not primarily directed toward speech and the language arts but is focused instead upon one aspect of dramatic techniques, the implications for improved speech habits are obvious. As the player, either child or adult, feels the desire to communicate orally with others, he will seek the words he wants and try to pronounce and articulate them clearly. This chapter explores some speech-related activities that may be carried on in addition to creative drama and may act as an incentive for improving oral expression.

Speech depends upon words. The more words one has at his command, the richer and more precise his communication. Children love words and enjoy learning new ones, given half a chance and some encouragement. Vocabulary building, moreover, is a never-ending process. Reading good literature is one of the finest ways of

179

George Latshaw, Puppet Project, the National Committee, Arts for the Handicapped, courtesy Wendy Perks.

meeting new words, and the improvisation of dialogue offers an opportunity for putting them into practice. Different characters speak in different ways. A person's manner of speech distinguishes him as much as his physical movements and behavior do. In assuming a role, the player learns as much as he can about the character he is playing: age, education, occupation, likes and dislikes, strengths, weaknesses, and other personal qualities. Knowledge of a character will help determine the words he uses as well as the way in which he says them.

The young or inexperienced player will not be able to delineate character at the outset, but he will slowly develop an awareness of the speech appropriate to a character, and in time will be able to handle dialogue, which conveys more than rudimentary information. Particularly effective in pointing out individual differences in speech and the possibilities of enriching them, is the discussion held after the first and second playing. The leader may ask the player some questions about his character: Would the character talk that way? Use those words? Use slang? Suggest his occupation by the way he describes it? Then the leader may proceed to some general questions about characters: How would a father speak? Would a child say the same thing in the same words and phrases? Children are quick to discern discrepancies. Moreover, they enjoy finding just the right words for a particular character and delight in using long words. Proof of this can be seen in the way in which very young children memorize repeated phrases and words from favorite stories; any deviation from the text on the part of a reader, in an effort at simplification, will bring an immediate correction from the listening child, who knows and loves the original.

As to clarity and audibility, no activity points up the necessity of being heard and understood any better than taking part in a play. The teacher need not—indeed, should not—stress such failings as indistinct or inaudible speech, but the other players will be aware of it. A far more effective way of telling a player that his voice is too soft is to raise such questions as: Would an angry man sound like that? What kind of voice do you think a giant would have? How do we know that the boy is calling to someone from a distance?

Too much attention to vocal projection and articulation frequently leads to an artificial manner of delivery, but attention to the reasons for a louder voice or clearer speech will accomplish the desired goals, though admittedly this approach takes longer. Observers are quick to comment when they cannot hear or understand a player. Peer criticism is a far more effective way of improving a player's speech than constant nagging by the teacher. If the player really wants to be understood, he will make the necessary effort. Again, he will not accomplish everything in the beginning, but with practice and encouragement as well as criticism, he will show improvement in time. Creative drama offers a unique opportunity to enlarge the vocabulary, promote more audible speech, and improve articulation.

In recent years there has been a conscious effort to improve the self-image of the speaker whose verbal skills are poor or for whom English is a second language. In order to accomplish this, voice and diction have been de-emphasized; in other words, *what* is said is considered of greater importance than *how* it is said. The objectives—encouragement of the speaker and the building of pride in a cultural heritage—have been given a priority. While no one would quarrel with this as the first step in language improvement, it is to be hoped that once a degree of self-confidence has been achieved, the student should be helped to move on to better habits of speech. Clarity, audibility, and a constantly improving vocabulary are still the goals for citizens in a democratic society. Freedom of speech is of little value without the ability to express oneself clearly and effectively. Today that means almost every facet of life and most jobs. Therefore, the speech arts are more important than ever before, and in the opinion of the author it is condescending to demand anything less than the best of students in this area as well as in others. What better place than the public school classroom to learn to communicate effectively?

Classroom activities other than improvisation provide work on oral communication. One of the oldest and best of these is storytelling, a favorite pastime in itself as well as a primary step in the preparation of a dramatization.

STORYTELLING

Storytelling is an ancient art that continues to be loved in spite of, or perhaps because of, our technical advances in communication. Television brings a vast array of entertainment into our homes, but it can no more replace the living storyteller than can film take the place of theatre. The reader-audience relationship depends upon the rapport between the one telling the story and the listeners: their involvement in the material and the way it is presented to them, which varies with each telling. The age, background, and interests of the audience, the physical surroundings, and even the time of day affect the development of that rapport. But the most important factor in storytelling is always the storyteller himself, his sensitivity and enthusiasm. Fortunate the boys and girls who are exposed to a good storyteller; fortunate, also, the one who possesses the skill to choose just the right story for the occasion and make it live again for his listeners.

Traditionally, stories were told for three purposes: to entertain, to teach, and to transmit the culture. These purposes have not changed essentially, though in an era of mass education the storyteller primarily provides entertainment and aesthetic pleasure. Folktales, myths, legends, fables, biography, and history offer a wealth of storytelling material. A lively tale, believable characters, and a worthwhile theme are the primary requisites; these are also the requirements for a good play, though not every good story can be adapted to the stage successfully, for a variety of reasons.

The storyteller has the freedom, however, to tell any tale he considers worthwhile and appropriate, for he will not have to cope with the problems of dramatization. A vast supply of good literature is available, but the good storyteller must first be able to find it. He must select material to which he responds and wants to share with others. He must then decide whether the story will be better read or told. Perhaps he will feel that the language and literary style of the author should not be sacrificed by putting them into the words of another. If this is the case, the story will be better if read. If, on the other hand, he decides that the material will be more effective told, the storyteller's preparation will be somewhat different.

He has already considered the age of his listeners; and he has thought about both the length of the story and the time at his disposal. Having satisfied himself that he has made a wise choice, he will familiarize himself thoroughly with all the details. For the beginning storyteller, making an outline is a good way to organize the material: the beginning, the action, the climax, the denouement. He should practice telling the story aloud, considering carefully the mood as well as the significant details.

Choice of words is important in storytelling. Often, certain words or phrases are repeated a number of times and are so important that the teller will wish to use them. He will not otherwise try to memorize the story, for this invariably leads to a stilted presentation and the risk of forgetting. Knowing a story so well that it can be told in one's own words is a far more satisfactory way of sharing it. Descriptive words create vivid pictures; words can suggest seeing, hearing, tasting, smelling, and touching, and can help the listener become more deeply interested and involved. Some impersonation makes characters come alive, though the storyteller's aim is to guide interpretation rather than to establish patterns for characterization. Facial expressions and gestures add interest only if they are natural and spontaneous. They should not be memorized and set, or sponteneity will suffer. Several rehearsals will be needed, however, for the storyteller to polish his sentences and achieve fluency.

Sincerity is a basic requirement in storytelling, for the child in the audience is sensitive to condescension and resents not being taken seriously. Humor, on the other hand, is enjoyed by everyone. A humorous tale, character, joke, or witty remark serves to draw teller and audience together. Indeed, one objective of storytelling is to develop a sense of humor, which is really a sense of proportion.

A pleasing voice and clear speech are to be cultivated, since the storyteller depends on his verbal communication exclusively, unlike the actor, who uses his entire body to convey his meaning. The storyteller is *not* an actor and must resist any temptation to become one. As interpreter, he guides the audience, helping it to create its own images through his words, vocal expression, and occasional well-chosen gestures. Finally, he must be able to forget himself in his preoccupation with the material. Rather than wondering how well he is doing, he will be checking constantly to see if the audience hears, understands, and seems to be appreciating the story.

This brief discussion of some of the aims and techniques of storytelling is directed to the teacher, but telling stories is also a good classroom activity for children. High school and college students not only enjoy the experience but often find use for it in working with camp or play groups. Children in the middle and upper grades take pleasure in sharing their favorite stories; at the same time, they are acquiring new skills in communication. If the group is small, each child may have a chance to tell a story of his own from time to time. If the group is large, then each child may be given a portion of a story to tell, one way of ensuring equal participation for all. Besides practice in recall and organization, storytelling is a splendid opportunity for work on vocabulary, syntax, and diction. Everyone loves a good story. Being able to tell one clearly and well is a way of providing pleasure for others as well as discovering the satisfaction of an attentive audience.

Joanna Halpert Kraus has coined the term, "sound and motion stories." This is a conscious use of the young child's natural impulse to participate in a story being read or told. Her collection of tales, suggesting places in the text where sounds and actions can be incorporated, is an excellent example of what the teacher can do to involve the group more actively in the experience. It is also a way of beginning a creative drama session, or of encouraging participation where time and space is limited. With a little practice, the storyteller can find places in a text where sounds and motions add a dimension and are fun to do.

Incidentally, because words grow out of sounds, this is a valid approach to the teaching of speech. Children enjoy the sounds of words, and this enjoyment of sound for its own sake should be encouraged. Small children love repetition; through correct repetition better speech habits are built. Difficult sounds can be practised in this way without the dullness of drill.

READERS THEATRE

Readers theatre, a relatively new concept in the speech arts, is particularly suitable for older children and high school students. The simplicity of production and effectiveness of result make it singularly desirable in schools with inadequate stage facilities and where rehearsal time is at a premium. More than that, it is a way of enjoying good literature through guided study, a mutually agreed-upon interpretation, and clear and expressive oral reading. Readers theatre may be defined as the oral presentation of drama, prose, or poetry by two or more readers, with characterization when necessary, narration if desired, coordination of material to constitute a whole, and the development of that special reader-audience relationship as an objective. Although traditionally a reader handled a single role, recent performances have permitted one person to read several. Readers theatre is neither lecture nor play; rather, it is a staged program that allows the audience to create its own images through the skilled performance of the readers.

The cast (whether large or small) usually remains onstage or on the designated area throughout, reading the various assigned portions. Generally, readers use little movement, suggesting action instead with simple gestures and facial expression. They must understand what the author has to say, the structure of the piece, and the development of characters; and they must be able to interpret a variety of roles in a matter of minutes, if called upon to do so. I have seen many presentations of readers theatre, ranging from some actual movement on stage to formal positions behind lecterns. Stools and steps are sometimes used to sit on, if an effect of informality is desired, or if the leader wishes to have the performers seated when they are not reading. Sometimes readers turn their backs to the audience to indicate their absence from a particular scene. The material, as well as the group's experience and preference, will determine how much or how little movement to include. In general, however, movement is minimal.

Readers theatre has grown in popularity in the past ten to fifteen years, and with this growth has come experimentation. Some groups have abandoned the lectern entirely and are now fully costumed. They use movement and have gone so far along the continuum that their results are scarcely distinguishable from theatre. Indeed, one of the criticisms of readers theatre is its indulgence in novelty for its own sake. I cannot share this concern because it seems to me that exponents of readers theatre are doing what is being done in all of the arts these days: consciously blending and mixing forms in the search for new ones. Sometimes they are successful; sometimes they are not. But I find experimentation that risks failure more interesting than rigid adherence to rules that were established by the originators.

One brilliant example of this mixing of forms is the New York production of *Colored Girls Who Have Considered Suicide/When the Rainbow is Enuf*. Described as a choreo-poem, it combines the oral presentation of poetry with choreographed movement. Simple but effective costumes are worn by the young actresses in the cast, and stage lighting is an important element of the production. First done experimentally, *Colored Girls* was moved uptown, where it is still drawing large audiences on Broadway.

Although a good deal of readers theatre has been done by adults for adult audiences (e.g., *John Brown's Body, Under Milkwood, Don Juan in Hell, Spoon River*), the Periwinkle Players of Monticello, New York, have for years been presenting highly effective programs for elementary school children. This company uses simple costumes to suggest character or period, and lighting effects to enrich the performance. With several programs in their repertory, they have proved that poetry—as well as drama and prose—has a strong appeal for children. Interest in words and writing were found to be an additional positive result. While these players are adult professional actors doing a professional job, their kind of program, on a simplified scale, could be done by children.

One particularly effective program was performed by high school students who selected and arranged a script with use of a group of the world's great love poems to celebrate St. Valentine's Day. In this instance, a narrator introduced each section of the program, giving some background material. A different but equally successful program for children was arranged by college students on the subject of the American West. Prose and poetry that told about the settlers and the frontier were combined with appropriate background music played on the guitar. When transitions were needed, folk songs were introduced. A chronological progression built interest, with the music adding a unifying colorful element. Children can select material they like and then decide as a group, just as these groups did, the questions of arrangement and sequence. Choral reading is often incorporated, if group speech is considered more effective than solo reading for some selections.

It should be mentioned that other kinds of literature can be used effectively: history, biography, letters, and various documentary materials. More than one program featuring the bicentennial celebration of American Independence featured American history and American essays. Black history has been the focus of other programs, whereas topics of current social and political interest have had powerful and dramatic content. Obviously, these materials require much more arranging and editing than do drama and short stories. On the other hand, they bring a new dimension to literature that is not usually read aloud.

This brings up the point that selections from separate works can be combined. It is not required that one text only be used. Thus there is a wide range of possibilities from which to choose, and the form is one that teachers consider rather than thinking always in terms of the play, traditionally staged and mounted. Readers theatre features the text, and, because it does so, can also serve as an extremely effective tool for learning.

New Canaan Country Day School, courtesy Mary Perrine.

Stories that are partially narrated, with readers assuming the various roles, comprise another way in which readers theatre makes literature come alive for an audience. Plays and scenes from plays can be performed in this way by students of all ages. For older children particularly, readers theatre is a viable activity for the classroom as well as an appealing vehicle for public sharing. Important to stress here is the fact that readers theatre does not require an audience beyond the class; indeed, the primary values are derived from the selection and interpretation of the material and the practice in reading aloud. Inasmuch as the result is so often worth sharing, this type of presentation is recommended for the opportunity it offers those engaged in it, an opportunity bearing much pleasure and no problems of production detail and lengthy rehearsals.

The following story of *The Musicians of Bremen* is included as an example of one way in which readers theatre was used by older students for children. If children do it, they should act the story creatively first, then read it aloud from the script, eliminating stage movement and business. Any story may be treated in this manner. Myths and legends, which often depend upon the supernatural, can be handled with ease, whereas difficulties are encountered when they are dramatized in the usual way. Appropriate music may be added, if desired, to suggest the passage of time, the movement from one scene to another, or changes of mood. Music is not necessary to this story, or to readers theatre in general, but it often makes the presentation more effective, just as background music and sound effects lend color and setting to a radio play.

Costumes may be suggested, if desired, but they need not, and, indeed, probably should not, be complete or literal. The same thing is true of settings, which, if merely suggested, make demands on the audience that lead to a clearer and more accurate understanding than any attempt to duplicate a place or scene. Platforms, stools, chairs, ladders, and benches do not connote particular places, which has been one reason for their popularity. Although material may be memorized, books or manuscripts are generally used to let the audience know at once that it is going to share literature, not see a play.

THE MUSICIANS OF BREMEN

(A folk dance dramatized by Nellie McCaslin)

NARRATOR	CAT
DONKEY	COCK
DOG	ROBBER

The six readers may stand throughout, reading from their scripts at lecterns or reading stands. Because the story is so simple and informal, they may prefer to sit on steps instead; they will probably be able to get more into the spirit of it if they are seated informally and close to the audience.

NARRATOR: There was once near the town of Bremen a farmer whose donkey was growing old and was every day less fit for work. The farmer knew that he should soon have to buy a new donkey and so he began to think of how he could get rid of his faithful old beast. Now the Donkey, who was not as stupid as the farmer thought, decided that he would settle the matter himself. So one day, when the farmer was in the house having his dinner, the Donkey took himself off and started down the road toward the city. "For there," he thought, "I may become a musician." He had a powerful voice which, in spite of his advancing years, could be heard for miles around when he put back his head and brayed. Yes, a musician was what he should be.

He had not gone far when he met a Dog, lying stretched out by the roadside. The Dog was panting as if he had just run a great distance. The Donkey stopped and greeted him.

DONKEY: Good morning, friend Dog. What may I ask are you doing out here all by yourself? And why are you panting so hard?

DOG: Ah, me. I have run away, but I am an old dog and my strength has all but given out.

DONKEY: Run away? Why should an old fellow like you run away? Pardon me for saying it, but I should think you'd be better off at home where you've someone to care for you than out seeking adventure.

DOG: I agree with you. But the truth of the matter is that my master no longer wants me around. I was a "fine fellow," a "good dog," as long as I was able to work. But now he grows angry when I trail behind and can no longer hunt or herd sheep.

DONKEY: (sympathetically) That is too bad.

DOG: That's not the worst of it. He even threatened to knock me on the head and thus be rid of me. Then, with me out of the way, he'll get him a puppy.

DONKEY: Your master is a cruel man, but I can understand how you feel, for the same thing has happened to me. My master is impatient with my slow steps and stiff joints and would replace me with a younger beast.

DOG: It's hard to grow old in this world. I suppose I may as well lie here till I die, for I am of no use to anyone anymore.

DONKEY: Nonsense, my friend. Listen, I have an idea. I'm on my way to the city. There I plan to become a musician. Why don't you join me and see what you can do? We may harmonize well together and anyhow, two are always better off than one.

DOG: I have nothing to lose by it. Yes, your words give me courage. I'll go along with you to the city.

NARRATOR: So the two of them set out. Before they had gone very far they came upon a Cat sitting in the middle of the road. They stopped to speak to her.

DONKEY: I beg your pardon, my lady, what is the trouble? You look as unhappy as my friend the Dog did less than an hour ago. Surely life is not all that hard.

CAT: And why shouldn't I look unhappy? You don't know what it is to grow old and no longer be welcome in your very own house.

DONKEY: Indeed? Do tell us what has happened. We, too, have suffered similar misfortunes. Perhaps we can help.

CAT: Very well, I'll tell you, though there's nothing either one of you can do.

DOG: (sympathetically) Sometimes it helps just to talk.

CAT: That is true. You see, I used to be loved very much. My mistress thought me the most beautiful cat in the world. She brushed my fur—it was soft and sleek in those days—and gave me cream in a saucer each morning, and meat at night. And she praised me to all the neighbors. She said I kept the place clean of mice.

DOG: Go on.

DONKEY: What happened next?

CAT: You wouldn't believe it! But because I no longer care to run about and catch mice and prefer to curl up by the fire, my mistress has said she would drown me. Is that the way to treat an old friend? I was fortunate enough to escape from her, but how I shall find enough to eat or a warm bed at night, I do not know.

DONKEY: Do not despair, old friend. We share the same sorrow. Instead of sitting here in the road, why not come with us to the city? You are a good musician, I'm sure. Perhaps we can work together. A trio is much more attractive than a duet. Wouldn't you agree, Master Dog?

DOG: Yes, indeed.

CAT: I hadn't thought of being a singer. But it's worth trying and I'm glad to have company, however it turns out.

NARRATOR: So the Cat got up and went with them. The three talked and exchanged stories of their youth and began to feel much better as they got acquainted. Presently they came to a farm yard where they saw a Cock perched on the gate. He was crowing with all his might.

COCK: Cock-a-doodle doo!

DONKEY: What a fine sound you make, Master Cock. Pray, what great event are you proclaiming?

COCK: Why, that it is a fair day and sunny and my mistress can safely hang out her wash.

DONKEY: She must depend on you very much.

COCK: Indeed she does. She would never know when the sun had come up if it weren't for my crowing.

DOG: You don't look pleased, somehow. What's the matter?

COCK: I've had a rude shock. Would you believe it, in spite of my years of service to her, I have just heard her say that she plans to cut off my head and roast me for Sunday dinner.

DOG: Oh, that is even worse than what has happened to us, friend Cock. Why don't you leave here at once?

COCK: Where can I go? And how do I know every other farmer's wife might not have the same idea?

CAT: Well, we have a plan. . . .

COCK: What kind of a plan?

CAT: Come along with us and we'll tell you.

COCK: Where are you going?

DONKEY: To the city. We are going to seek our fortune as musicians. With your fine strong voice, I'm sure you will have no trouble finding work.

CAT: And if we practice together, we may work up a concert. Four voices—do come along.

COCK: I'll join you. And I thank you with all my heart.

DOG: Anything is better than staying here, and who knows, things may turn out for the best after all.

NARRATOR: And so the four of them walked on together. The day was fair and their hearts were high, for they were certain that good luck was in store for them. As evening approached, they were still a distance from town, so they decided to stop at the edge of the woods for the night. The Donkey and the Dog made a comfortable bed under a tree and the Cat climbed up on a bough where she felt safer. The Cock, however, who was used to spending the night on a perch, flew to the very top of the tree and settled himself on a sturdy branch.

COCK: Everyone all right down there?

DONKEY: As right as my old bones can be on this hard ground.

DOG: This is better than being knocked in the head, though I shall be glad when we find proper lodging.

COCK: How about you, Mistress Cat? Are you comfortable?

CAT: Oh, I'm all right. The leaves keep out the draft and anyhow it's not a cold night.

COCK: Well, I'll say good night then and I'll wake you up first thing in the morning.

NARRATOR: Before tucking his head under his wing, however, he looked out in all directions, to be sure that nothing was amiss. As he did so, he noticed, not too great a distance anyway, something shining and bright. He called down to the others.

COCK: We can't be as far from the town as we thought. I see lights. There must be a house nearby.

DOG: Are you sure? It looks very dark to me.

CAT: Yes, I see it. It's a house or an inn.

DONKEY: Then perhaps we should push on. I could use a softer bed.

DOG: So could I. And, who knows, the master might throw in a bone and some scraps from his table.

CAT: Yes, indeed. I would willingly exchange this bough for a spot in front of a fire.

COCK: I'm game. Let's find out what it is.

NARRATOR: Having agreed, the four companions got up and followed the Cat, whose eyes served best in the dark. At length they came to a house. It was a very comfortable house, in which there lived a band of robbers. The four stopped outside the door, then the Donkey, who was the tallest, cautiously peered through the window.

COCK: Well, friend Donkey, what do you see? Do they look like kindly folk?

DONKEY: I see an astonishing thing. A table piled with good things to eat and a band of men sitting around it, counting their gold.

CAT: What do you take them to be?

DONKEY: If I'm not mistaken, I'd say they were robbers. This is no farmer's cottage.

COCK: Do you suppose they live here?

DONKEY: Either that or they've taken over the place.

DOG: Perhaps we can scare them away. I used to be good at that years ago. My master always said no robber could get within gunshot when I was around.

CAT: It looks like a fine lodging for us, if we can get in.

DONKEY: Let's think of a way.

DOG: I've got it. I'll get on the Donkey. You, Mistress Cat, jump on my back and the Cock can perch on your shoulders. Then we'll make music.

COCK: A capital idea! Let's do it.

ALL: (ad lib) All right—I'm for it—Good idea!

DONKEY: Is everyone in place? Good. Now, altogether. . . .
(Each animal makes his own noise at the same time.)

DONKEY: Now, then, stand back. I'll put my front feet through the window and we'll all go inside.
(Crash of glass.)

NARRATOR: The robbers, who had been startled by the concert, were terrified when the four musicians tumbled over the sill into the room. They were out of the door in a flash and scattered in all directions. The four old friends watched them go.

DONKEY: Well, it looks as if we have the place to ourselves.

DOG: And the dinner.

CAT: Will you see what's on the table! This is a feast.

COCK: It would be too bad to let so much good food go to waste. What say you? Let's eat.

NARRATOR: So the four gobbled up every crumb. Then, their hunger satisfied, each one sought a bed to his liking. The Donkey found a pile of straw outside the back door and bade the others good night. The Dog stretched out on a rug under the table. The Cat curled up on the hearth; and the Cock, who preferred a higher spot even indoors, perched on a beam in the ceiling. Warm and tired from their travels, they were soon fast asleep.

Later on that night, however, the robbers, seeing the house dark, and hearing no noise, crept stealthily back. The leader of the band was the first to venture inside. He struck a match on the fireplace and then out of the darkness blazed two bright eyes. The Cat was on her feet in a flash and flew at him and clawed him with all her might. (*Meiou.*) The robber yelled in fright more than pain. As he stumbled back he tripped over the Dog who bit him sharply in the leg. (*Bow-wow.*) Running out the back door, he bumped into the Donkey who woke up with a start and kicked him with both feet. (*Hee-haw.*) All this commotion roused the Cock who crowed at the top of his lungs. (*Cock-a-doodle-do.*) This was too much for the robber who ran off to his companions and told them what had befallen him.

ROBBER: A witch has got into the house. I saw her eyes in the dark. First she scratched me with her long nails; next she stabbed me in the leg. Then, when I tried to escape, I was struck with a club from behind and all the while someone on the roof was yelling, "Throw the rascal out! Throw the rascal out!" I tell you, the place is bewitched.

NARRATOR: Well, after that, the robbers never ventured inside the house again. The four musicians were so pleased with their lodging that they stayed right there. And I shouldn't be surprised if they're living there still.

The End

STORY THEATRE

Story theatre is closely related to readers theatre. According to Paul Sills, whose production by the same name, "Story Theatre," captivated audiences of all ages a few seasons ago, it evolved from readers theatre. Sills had worked in this medium, but in his search for a new form of expression, developed a technique that has become a genre. He defines this form as an oral story rather than as a piece of literature. In dispensing with the narrator, which he often does, the exposition is imbedded in the dialogue of the various characters. They may speak in the third person as in the short sketch that follows.

Like readers theatre, story theatre is hard to define because of its flexibility and because it is so new that no hard and fast rules apply. Actors are usually costumed and may speak or perform in pantomime, while a narrator tells the story. There may be musical accompaniment throughout, if desired, and the pantomime may approach dance, depending upon the wishes and abilities of the group. These may be conceived of as distinct and opposite forms, when readers theatre is kept motionless and books and lecterns are used. On the other hand, they may be quite similar when performers in readers theatre use stage techniques and story theatre is formalized. Inasmuch as both reflect the director's approach rather than any rigid set of rules, one can only enjoy and applaud the results, when they are successful.

The following short play is an illustration of what is usually meant by story theatre.

RIMOUSKI[1]

SHIRLEY PUGH

(*Music: "Gypsy Rover" melody used throughout.*)

MARCEL: A peasant named Marcel—

MADELEINE: —lived with his wife Madeleine—(*curtsies*).

JEANETTE: —and their little daughter Jeanette—
(*Madeleine cues Jeanette to curtsey.*)

MARCEL: —in the tiny village of St. Fabien. But he had it in his head to travel.

MADELEINE: Oh!
(*A sound of deprecation.*)
St. Fabien is good enough for me.
(*Mimes cooking and stirring.*)
I was born here and I'll die here.

MARCEL: Me. I want to see what is in the world. More than anything else, I want to see Rimouski.

MADELEINE: Rimouski! How can you think of it? So far away!

JEANETTE: Is Papa going to Rimouski?

MADELEINE: Papa is going nowhere, Jeanette. Stop pulling at my skirt.

MARCEL: Today I talked to the blacksmith. There's a good fellow—he has seen Rimouski.

MADELEINE: (*adds pepper to the pot*) That's very fine for the blacksmith.
(*She readies herself to sneeze—and the sneeze doesn't come.*)

1. Shirley Pugh, *In One Basket* (New Orleans: Anchorage Press, 1972).

MARCEL: (*sneezes without warning*) Ah-choo!

JEANETTE: Bless you, Papa.

MARCEL: Thank you. Listen—Rimouski is a town that could swallow St. Fabien. The blacksmith says that people crowd the streets there. Have you ever seen a crowd in St. Fabien? The blacksmith says—

MADELEINE: Then listen to the blacksmith and be satisfied.

MARCEL: No, listen—he says there are fine shops and large houses in Rimouski. He says—

JEANETTE: When is Papa going to Rimouski?

MADELEINE: Play with your doll, Jeanette. Papa is going nowhere.

MARCEL: No, listen. I am going, me myself, to Rimouski.

MADELEINE: Marcel, you are a peasant. We are poor people. Travel is not for you. So expensive!

MARCEL: I can't rest until I see for myself what is in the world.

MADELEINE: You certainly can't afford to ride such a distance!

MARCEL: Then I will walk.

MADELEINE: What? And wear out your boots? They aren't in good repair anyway.

MARCEL: Then I will walk without my boots.

MADELEINE: Barefooted! Hah! A fine sight he'll be in Rimouski with no boots on his feet.

MARCEL: Then I know what I'll do. I'll carry my boots in my hand. When I see the smoke from the chimneys of Rimouski, I'll put on my boots and go into the town.

JEANETTE: (*weeping*) Why must you go to Rimouski, Papa?

MARCEL: Don't worry, Jeanette. I will return.

MADELEINE: (*mimes packing a basket*) What can be done with such a man? Marcel, do you really want to go to Rimouski?

MARCEL: With all my heart.

MADELEINE: Go, then. Here's a basket with sausage and bread and beer—

MARCEL: Sausage and bread and beer—that will be fine. First I'll take off my boots—
(*Mime.*)
—and I'll be on my way.
(*Mimes taking the basket in one hand and his boots in the other, making ready to leave for Rimouski.*)

MADELEINE: Promise me you will stop to rest, Marcel.

MARCEL: Yes, well, I'll do that all right.

MADELEINE: And take time to eat your sausage and bread.

MARCEL: Sausage and bread. I will, I will.

MADELEINE: And whatever you do, Marcel, don't leave your boots at the side of the road or they'll be stolen.

MARCEL: I'm not a nincompoop. I'll keep them right here in my hand.

JEANETTE: How far is it to Rimouski, Papa?

MARCEL: Jeanette, it is a journey of one entire day.

JEANETTE: Oh, Papa! So far!

MADELEINE: And don't lose your way, Marcel. The road will be confusing.

MARCEL: All right! Jeanette, mind your Mama.
(Kisses her.)

MADELEINE: Oh, Marcel, it is such a distance!

MARCEL: *(He kisses her.)* Don't worry, keep well, and when I return I will tell you about the wonders of Rimouski.

MADELEINE: The wonders of Rimouski! Hah!
(Flounces off with Jeanette.)

MARCEL: *(Music. He walks.)* What a woman to worry, and the little one will be just like her. Do they think I can't keep my wits about me? She should see me now, on the road, a seasoned traveler.
(Music.)
The sun is high in the sky—it's getting hot. A little sausage and bread and a drink of beer will go down well. Here's a spot of shade.
(Music. Mimes eating.)
A swallow of beer—ah, that's good!—a bite of sausage—That's not so good—
(He finishes eating.)
Maybe now a small nap.
(He lies down, immediately sits up.)
But if I sleep, how will I remember which way the road goes? Ah, that's it! I'll put my boots on the ground—and I'll point the toes of them toward Rimouski.
(Mimes action.)
There. When I wake up, my boots will point the way.
(Lies down and snores gently. Threatening music.)

THIEF: Now a thief happened along the road. There's a pair of boots with no one's feet in them. I could use an extra pair of boots. He's asleep, all right.
(to audience) Should I, or shouldn't I? I'm going to do it anyway.
(Steals boots.)
These boots, they aren't much. Not worth the stealing. Full of

holes and all run down at the heels. They are no better than my own boots.

(*Puts boots down with toes pointing the wrong way.*)

And he put the boots down with the toes pointing back toward St. Fabien.

(*Music. Thief exits.*)

MARCEL: (*Wakes, yawns, scratches, stretches.*)

And now it's cooler and I'm on my way. But which way does the road go? See? I'm not such a fool. There are my boots, with the toes pointing to Rimouski.

(*Takes boots and basket and follows wrong direction. Music.*)

There's smoke! That smoke comes from the chimneys of Rimouski! Now to put on my boots.

(*Mimes action.*)

Well, so this is Rimouski! Looks a lot like St. Fabien! The blacksmith said it was so miraculous here. Why, this street could be a street in St. Fabien! These shops look no finer than the shops at home. And the houses—they aren't so large. I expected a town that looked better than this. Rimouski is not so grand!

(*Walks.*)

I'm really in Rimouski!

(*Madeleine appears, sweeping the sidewalk.*)

(*Jeanette appears, washing a window.*)

Ah, well, this street could be my own street. As far as that goes, look. This house could be my own house. See—an ordinary wife like my own wife. A little girl like my own daughter. If I didn't know I was in Rimouski, I'd swear I was in St. Fabien!

MADELEINE: Marcel! Come in the house and have your supper.

MARCEL: She calls me by my name!

JEANETTE: Did you bring me something, Papa?

MARCEL: It is exactly like St. Fabien! I've never heard of this, but it's true. Imagine—two places so far apart, yet with streets alike, houses alike—even the people are the same! Aha! Now I see! There is someone just like me who lives in this house, here in Rimouski. Maybe at this moment, he is visiting *my* house at St. Fabien.

MADELEINE: Marcel, stop talking to yourself. Go in and eat your supper.

MARCEL: Yes, I know. I know all about it. Tomorrow he'll come back

here. Well, I'll stay in Rimouski and wait until he comes.
(*Goes into house, sits and eats.*)

JEANETTE: (*puzzled*) And he's still waiting.

MADELEINE: And he still thinks he's in Rimouski.

(*A single minor note from the musicians.*) (BLACKOUT)

One other term should be mentioned: chamber theatre. In defining it, Robert Breen, the originator, calls it a method of preparing and presenting undramatized fiction, in which changes are made to accommodate time, space and number of characters. A narrator becomes dramatically involved in the story and speaks for the author. Chamber theatre, story theatre and readers theatre are similar in that the primary virtue is the text. All can be highly successful when used with children as they offer possibilities for inventive production and non-traditional content.

11

DRAMA AS A TEACHING TOOL

The use of drama as a teaching tool is not new; historically, both drama and theatre have long been recognized as potent means of education and indoctrination. The ways in which they are used today, however, are new, and they differ in a number of respects from the ways in which they have been used in the past.

Most familiar to us in the western world is the theatre of Ancient Greece, which developed from celebration and dance into a golden age of theatre. Athenian education in the fifth century B.C. was based on music, literature, and dance. Physical activities were emphasized, whereas music included the study of rhythms and harmony as well as the instruments of the time. As dance was basic to religious festivals, it was stressed, and the chorus of young people received a rigorous training subsidized by wealthy citizens. Dramatists were highly respected, and drama was a major educational force. Plato, in *The Republic*, advocated play as a way of learning. Aris-

199

Theatre in Education Performance by Creative Arts Team (CAT), New York University.

totle urged education in the arts, distinguishing between activities that were means and those that were ends.

The medieval church, in its use of mystery plays, taught through the medium of theatre, and, in so doing, helped to restore it to its proper place as a great art form. By the last half of the sixteenth century, drama was an important part of the curriculum of the English boys' schools. Not only the reading but the staging of classic plays flourished. We could go on through the centuries, nation by nation, and culture by culture, finding examples of the various ways in which drama and theatre have been used to inform, inspire, entertain, and indoctrinate.

The United States has only recently discovered the relationship between theatre and school. Indeed, the twentieth century was well advanced before the arts began to have any real impact on public education. Private schools often included them, but usually as extracurricular activities or as minor subjects, rarely placed on a par with the so-called "solids." On the secondary school level, they were given even less emphasis. All the arts tended to be what the teacher made them; thus they reflected her background, interests, and attitude. Drama was no exception, and, in fact, followed music, athletics, and the visual arts into the curriculum. In the minds of many, theatre and dance were even questionable as to their inclusion as part of a young person's education. Few today would argue against arts education; yet the inclusion, let alone requirement, of drama in the elementary school curriculum is far from widespread. In the high school there is still a greater emphasis on play production as an extracurricular and social activity than there is on drama as a serious subject, though recent publications of the Secondary School Theatre Association show progress in this area.

The first major curricular offerings in child drama and theatre in this country appeared in the twenties. College courses and textbooks on drama education and children's theatre followed. Since then there has been a steady increase in the number of colleges and universities offering courses and degrees in the theatre arts and in the teaching of drama and theatre. At the same time, there has been fluctuation in both quantity and quality of drama education in our public schools. Budget cuts and the lack of well-prepared teachers have been the most commonly given reasons for eliminating the arts or curtailing established programs.

Despite progress, however, the argument regarding the *function* of drama in education is still unresolved. Is it to be included in the curriculum as a means or as an end? Are we more concerned with its use as a teaching tool, or do we regard it as a discipline in its own right, to be taught for its own sake? Since the twenties, many of the foremost leaders have warned against the exploitation of drama/theatre to achieve other ends; that is, making it a "handmaiden" to other subject areas. This use, incidentally, has been of concern to teachers of the other arts as well. Are the visual arts, for instance, to be respected as art, or are they to be utilized for the preparation of school decorations, posters, party invitations, stage sets, etc.? This concern is not to be confused with integrated projects, in which the same activities might be done, but where they are related, often brilliantly, to a unit of study.

Integrated Projects

Projects integrating drama, music, dance, creative writing, and the visual arts with the social studies and literature have been popular since the early days of the progressive education movement. Even the most traditional schools have found integrated projects an effective way of teaching and learning. Arts educators have generally endorsed them because they placed the arts at the core of the curriculum rather than on the periphery. Accorded an importance equal to the academic subjects, the arts thus became a basic part of the educational system rather than a frill or something of fringe interest. Integrated projects continue to find popularity in schools where staff members are able and willing to work closely together. This is often more easily accomplished in small private schools, where the schedule allows for flexibility and where there is concern for student interest.

Projects tend to be part of school work, done in school time and seen by an audience of school children. Occasionally a project reaches into the community or is of such magnitude that a wider audience is invited to see the work. One such program was given in New York City early in 1979 in celebration of the International Year of the Child. This was an extremely effective project in which performers from Asia, Africa, and Latin America, children from the Third World Institute of Theatre Arts Studies, and children from the United Nations International School worked together on an ecumenical multiethnic pageant. Entitled *A Third World Litany*, it brought dance, chanting, music, and religious rites together, concluding with a pledge to observe the rights of children everywhere. The result was a deeply moving performance given for parents and friends in the community. This program, incidentally, which was conceived by the Childyear Culture Corps, had its beginning in 1978 in San Jose, California; the Pacific Peoples Theatre Arts Festival also brought performers from many lands together to heighten the understanding of our rich cultural diversity in celebration of the International Year of the Child.

Drama in Education

Since the first edition of this book, there have been some innovations in drama and theatre education which must be attributed to strong influences from England, where drama in education and theatre-in-education (T.I.E.)

programs and leaders have attracted wide attention. Best known of these British educators, because of their numerous visits to the United States, are Dorothy Heathcote and Brian Way. Dorothy Heathcote, who is on the faculty of the University of Newcastle-upon-Tyne, has given workshops and summer sessions in various parts of the country and has been the subject of three films made at Northwestern University.

Mrs. Heathcote's approach to drama is particularly appealing to classroom teachers, who find in it techniques that they can use in their own teaching. She works, as she says, from the inside out, and her concern is that children use drama to expand their understanding of life experiences, to reflect on a particular circumstance, and to make sense out of their world in a deeper way. Her goal is not the teaching of drama alone but of other subjects as well. In fact, there is no area of the curriculum in which she has not used drama. She begins with process, and in time moves to a product that may take an audience into account, though this is not her major concern. Her intent is always the depth and breadth of learning, which excites the class and brings satisfaction to the teacher.

In lieu of putting on plays and dramatizing literature, Heathcote prefers to help children find the dramatic moment in an event or unit of study. She believes in helping the teacher use drama to teach more effectively, not by exploiting it to sugarcoat nondramatic material, but to work with children as a guide and resource person. Where there is a drama specialist in the school, Heathcote advocates having the classroom teacher, or generalist, follow up the lesson with his suggestions. Where there is no specialist, the teacher must learn how to discover the tension, conflict, or point of greatest interest in a topic; how to collect relevant source materials; and how to guide the class through an original piece of work. This process may last for a few periods or for an entire semester, depending on the scope of the study and the interest of the children.

Dramatizing an event, Heathcote believes, makes it possible to isolate and study it. Like most creative drama teachers, she starts with discussion. She uses the children's ideas and encourages their making decisions. Once the direction is clear, she suggests a choice of procedures: analogy, simulation, and role. Of the three, Heathcote prefers the last because she believes it fixes an emotional reaction. She will, therefore, assume a role. She frequently steps out of role, stopping the drama where she believes clarification is needed, and taking time for further discussion. She will then resume the improvisation. It is said that this technique most differentiates her work from that of the majority of American creative drama teachers. The children, because of their interest in the situation, are able to stop, enter into discussion, and then continue playing.

Meanwhile, the teacher is collecting the best reference materials, literature, and artifacts she can find. The children are encouraged to spend much time studying them in order to build an original drama. Social studies, current events, moral and ethical problems become grist for the mill because Heathcote is concerned with both cognitive and affective learning. Possible topics for drama might be: the study of a particular community, industry, energy, pollution, transportation, immigration, a disaster with social implications, or a great or well-known person like Martin Luther King. The possibilities are endless and may come from any area of the curriculum, but the point is that by employing drama in this way, children are helped to see below the surface of an event or topic and thereby gain a better understanding of it.

The Heathcote approach has been hailed by many as meeting objectives that were not being met by other methods. Classroom teachers are especially comfortable with her goals, for they are directly related to the curriculum. The emphasis on learning also appeals to some drama specialists and supervisors who are concerned with budget cuts and demands for teacher accountability. They suggest that arts programs might be saved or strengthened, if it could be said that drama stimulates and enhances other learning.

The major difference between creative drama as traditionally taught in this country and drama in education as here described, lies in emphasis and techniques. There are, of course, as many different approaches to the teaching of drama as there are teachers, but the Heathcote approach has been discussed because it is the best known of the newer methods and has had the greatest impact to date on American classroom teachers. Betty Jane Wagner's book, *Dorothy Heathcote—Drama as a Learning Medium*,[1] provides the most detailed description available of this dynamic leader's philosophy and methods.

Brian Way, on the other hand, is best known for his textbook, *Development through Drama*, and for his theory of participatory theatre briefly described in an earlier chapter. Brian Way shares with Mrs. Heathcote a concern for the participant, making the same point, but in different words; he says that he is not interested in training actors but in developing people. For the past few years he has been giving lectures and workshops of varying lengths throughout the United States on the subjects of creative dramatics and participatory theatre. In both areas he has brought new ideas and ways of working, though it is in the use of audience participation that his most original work has been done. Here formal theatre and creative drama are combined to create a new form, which is being used by a number of children's theatre companies. His years as director of the Theatre Centre in London have given him a wealth of experience, particularly with inner city children. This has won him a ready

1. Betty Jane Wagner, *Dorothy Heathcote—Drama as a Learning Medium* (Washington, D.C.: NEA Press, 1976).

Theatre in Education Performance by Creative Arts Team (CAT), New York University.

and receptive audience in the United States. Where Heathcote's following includes many classroom teachers, Way tends to attract producing groups, both professional and amateur, who work with children in schools. The changes that have taken place in England in the past twenty-five years are clearly summarized in the following statement:

> There has been a shift in direction from an interest in the personal development of the individual pupil through the acquiring of theatrical and improvisational skills, to the recognition of drama as a precise teaching instrument, which works best when it is seen as part of the learning process, and when it is embedded firmly within the rest of the school curriculum. Drama is no longer seen only as another branch of art education, but as a unique teaching tool, vital in language development, and invaluable as a method in the exploration of other subject areas.[2]

Except for a few fears regarding the exploitation of drama for the purpose of teaching other subjects, some questions regarding the relevancy of creative drama today, and occasional misunderstandings about the nature and function of audience participation, I believe that there are more similarities than differences involved. Drama, when it is used in education, is, as opposed to formal theatre, primarily concerned with process and the growth of the individual. Both means and ends are involved, however, because they are inseparable. In

2. Cecily O'Neill, Alan Lambert, Rosemary Linnell, Janet Warr-Wood, *Drama Guidelines* (London: Heinemann Educational Books, 1976), p. 7.

the final analysis, we must each discover our own way and create our own teaching methods. We may find imitating the methods of others a necessary and valuable first step, but we are strengthened by trusting ourselves and risking failure in the beginning in our search for success.

Artists-in-the-Schools

A different approach to drama/theatre education is through the use of the Artists-in-the-Schools Program, which brings performers into the classroom for a morning, a day, a week, or sometimes a much longer period of time. Here actors perform, demonstrate, or work directly with the children. This provides an opportunity for the teacher to learn new techniques which help her to continue on her own after the actors have gone. It also exposes children to the creative artist, whom they would otherwise probably never meet. Throughout the United States, actors, dancers, musicians, painters, puppeteers, and poets have been brought into schools through funded programs. Information on available artists (both groups and individuals) is available through state arts councils and state departments of education. Although not every school has made use of either the program or the concept, many have, and children have had their education enriched as a result.

The Theatre in the Schools Program of the National Endowment for the Arts was described recently in *Theatre News* by its coordinator, Sr. Kathryn Martin. Beginning first with pilot projects, the program was opened to all state arts agencies in the mid-seventies through the Artist-in-the-Schools Program. By 1978, twenty states had theatre components. Basic structures varied from state to state because of geographical and educational needs. Three entirely different models were described in the account. These were:

Alaska This state utilized four performers, who accepted two-week residencies in metropolitian and rural areas. They combined work in drama, mime, movement, and technical theatre.

Florida The Asolo Touring Theatre was assigned residencies in school districts with students bussed to central locations. The company was available for classroom workshops and prepared study guides for teachers.

New York Three different professional companies were used in the structuring of this component. Both elementary and secondary schools were served in a variety of ways, including attendance at performances, meeting with the professional staff, teacher workshops, and planning sessions.[3]

3. *Theatre News*, summer 1978, vol. x, no. 9, p. 6 (Pub. by American Theatre Association, Washington, D.C.).

Theatre-in-Education

One of the newest types of performing groups is the Theatre-in-Education touring company. The concept of T.I.E. originated in England in the mid-sixties. The first company was established in Coventry, and was rapidly followed by a number of other companies of actor/teachers, who took plays based on curricular material or topics of current interest into the schools. Performers were required to have certification as teachers, and to hold Actors' Equity cards. T.I.E. companies have several plays for different age levels in their repertories and receive funding from government and local education authorities. The pedagogue is the established link between education and theatre. Although many teams are attached to regional theatres, there are also T.I.E. groups in the academic community, and some grants are available only to academic theatres. Standards and goals vary widely among the teams. Some are highly political; others are not. All, however, research and develop their own material and create original projects they consider relevant to young people in school and social situations. Emphasis is on the learning involved, though enjoyment and appreciation of theatre are essential. The classroom teacher. is a key person in helping children derive maximal benefit from a Theatre-in-Education visit.

T.I.E. is described as "based on an extension of children's play and a combination of theatricality and classroom techniques to provide an experience in its own right, with the glamour of strangers in dramatic role and costume providing both a stimulus and a context which are not normally available to the teacher."[4]

The children are often expected to enter into the situation and asked to make decisions or to solve problems. In this respect they become much more deeply involved than they do in a production which is merely entertaining. Small audiences and preparation or follow-up work are a part of a T.I.E. presentation. A great variety of plays, designed for different age levels, has been presented since the inception of T.I.E. Some pieces are humorous, some serious; all are thought-provoking. A class may even be given an assignment between visits; in this case, the teacher, with the help of the materials prepared by the team, sets the stage for the next meeting. In its use of improvisation, relevant themes, audience involvement, and education rather than entertainment as the major involvement, and education rather than entertainment as the major thrust, T.I.E. represents an entirely new concept in drama/ theater as a teaching tool.

The United States has a growing number of such companies, some patterned after the British model. A professional company that has been in existence for a number of years is the Looking Glass Theatre of Providence, Rhode Island. Looking Glass sends educational materials to school in advance of a visit; then, on arrival, members of the cast go into the classrooms indi-

4. John O'Toole, *Theatre in Education* (London: Hodder and Stoughton), Preface, p. vi.

vidually to prepare the children for the active part they will take in the performance. Participatory theatre techniques are used in the belief that they enhance the experience. The company tours schools in the region during the academic year. Looking Glass states that its plays grow out of improvisation and address themselves to the needs of children, both rural and urban, poor and affluent. The company also provides a summer street theatre, a creative drama library series, a workshop school for children and teenagers, and workshops and consultant service for area teachers.

The Creative Arts Team of New York University, on the other hand, is an example of a professional company of actor/teachers attached to an educational institution. C.A.T. defines itself as a "new kind of provocative and challenging theater which questions, probes, involves, and finally motivates personal response and action . . . a catalyst for thought on social and curricular issues, enriching the lives of both young people and adults by the vitality, immediacy, and pertinence to the concerns of today's society."

The team does its own research, and through improvisational techniques develops its own material and teachers' packets. C.A.T. offers workshops for students of all ages, as well as for teachers and community organizations. It has a repertory of several theatre pieces, which it performs in a tri-state area, and farther afield on occasion.

A quite different type of organization is represented by the Performing Arts Foundation (P.A.F.) of Long Island. This resident and touring company has been a community resource since 1963. It gives performances in schools, but its program differs from the preceding two in several respects. It is, first of all, a community project that from the beginning has included dance and music as well as theatre. It is one of CEMREL's (Central Midwestern Regional Educational Laboratory, Inc.) eleven centers committed to research and the development of aesthetic education. P.A.F. calls its company members artist/actors, rather than actor/teachers, and it is primarily interested in integrating theatre arts techniques into the ongoing classroom curriculum. "The program concentrates on activities related to the arts process— perceiving, understanding, responding, creating, evaluating, and developing—and how these actions can be incorporated into education in all subject areas."

A recent feature of P.A.F. was a funded program for children with special needs. Classes in acting, mime, and theatre arts for adults as well as children are also offered throughout the year, including the summer. P.A.F. operates on the conviction that the arts are basic to learning and that experiential learning is just as important as analytical. This is a point made by some of our most concerned educators and psychologists. Dr. Jean Houston, Director of the Foundation for Mind Research in Pomona, New York, states that "a child without access to a stimulating arts program is being cut off from most of the ways in which he can perceive the world."

Theatre of Youth in Buffalo, which also describes itself as a nonprofit T.I.E. company, offers a repertory of plays for school and public performance. These include traditional, original, and participatory scripts. T.O.Y. has also presented two international artists-in-residence and summer street theatre. T.O.Y. stresses the literary value of the plays, their potential for enhancing the child's understanding of his world, and interaction between performers and audience.

There are other companies throughout the United States with theatre-in-education programs, designed according to their own interests and backgrounds and planned to meet the needs of their communities. The ones mentioned were selected because they represent distinctly different types of programs and have been in operation over a long enough period of time to have established stability and continuity. All attempt to lift the performance above the level of mere entertainment. All work with the schools, some more closely than others. All obtain subsidy from state arts councils, the federal government, or private foundations. Services usually include teacher workshops and the preparation of study guides for teachers to use with children either before or after the visit.

Some companies use participatory theatre techniques and improvisation as a way of developing programs; others do not. Despite individual differences, however, they share a common belief in a new kind of children's theatre, one that meets the needs of the schools, the children, and the teachers of today. In this respect, T.I.E. represents a radical departure from children's theatre of twenty years ago. A visit from the latter is generally intended as an entertainment or a treat. Theatre-in-education, on the other hand, is conceived as a dynamic force, geared to tackling specific areas of learning. The school, as well as the producing company, must have a clear understanding of its purpose and procedures in order for it to be effective.

Special Arts Projects

Special arts projects have been funded by the United States Office of Education in fifteen states to promote intercultural and interracial communication for students, teachers and community members. Any school with a twenty percent black student population is eligible to participate in project programs. An example of the way in which this operates is illustrated by the Special Arts Project in the Jefferson County schools in Kentucky. The Kentucky Arts Commission outlines the following areas of concentration.

1. Artist-in-residence. This is the foundation of the project. Prior to each residency, the artist holds a workshop with teachers about his craft. Artists include a poet, a dancer, a media specialist, a visual artist, a dramatist, and a musician.
2. Special series program. In this area there are performances by actors, orchestras, ballet, mimes, and puppet theatres.

3. Speakers and field trips.
4. Arts camps.
5. Publication. A cultural calendar and newsletter.
6. School-community relations. The aim is to involve more parents and community organizations in the purpose and implementation of the program.
7. Teacher training. Workshops to help teachers in an ongoing program.
8. Project replication. Visits to other school systems and preparation of helpful materials.

What are increasingly evident are the strong forces that are attempting to change the direction of education from a purely intellectual emphasis to one that recognizes our latent potential and therefore includes the arts as a basic component. What is also apparent is the growing interest of many teachers in using the arts as a tool for teaching, as well as a discipline in its own right— not to sugarcoat other subject areas, but to illuminate and interpret them. This is less a change, however, than it is an expansion of goals. The many and varied approaches to these concepts represent a new vitality.

Circumstances rather than specific methodology, however, should be our guide. Leaders share certain common objectives; but they assign priorities according to their situations, strengths, and needs. In other words, although there have been significant changes in the philosophy and the methods employed by teachers of creative drama, there is perhaps less difference than there appears to be on the surface. All subscribe to a primary concern for the child; all place process above product; all hold certain educational goals in common.

In the foreword to a publication released by the State University of New York in 1978, a strong stand is taken regarding the place of the arts in education. "The arts are a means of expressing and interpreting human experience. Quality education of individuals is complete only if the arts are an integral part of the daily teaching and learning process. The integration of the arts in the elementary, secondary and continuing education curriculum is a key to the humanistic development of students."[5]

It is such statements of purpose that distinguish the attitude toward arts education today from that held in the past. The hundreds of agencies and foundations, federal, state, and private, which contribute to the arts, are a further expression of support. Though we still have far to go before we can point with pride to a curriculum in which the arts and the academic areas have equal emphasis, progress has been made. In this respect the picture in 1980 is brighter than at any other time in the history of American education.

5. *The Arts as Perception (A Way of Learning)* Project Search, The University of the State of New York, The State Department, Division of Humanities and Arts Education, Albany, New York, 1978 Foreword, p. iii.

12

CREATIVE DRAMA FOR THE SPECIAL CHILD

This chapter considers creative drama in one of the newer areas of education: special education, or the education of the exceptional child. Special education may be defined as any program of teaching techniques designed to meet the needs of children whose abilities deviate markedly from those of the majority of boys and girls of their age. Included in this group are the intellectually gifted as well as the mentally retarded, the physically handicapped, the emotionally disturbed, the culturally and economically disadvantaged, children for whom English is a second language, and the underachievers, whose problems may not have been identified.

Until recently very little has been done to help these children, whose basic needs are the same as those of so-called normal children but whose individual needs require special educational services. A difference of opinion until recently has existed as to whether, or when, these children should be integrated into regular classrooms; but

211

The National Committee, Arts for the Handicapped, courtesy Wendy Perks. Photograph by John Reynolds.

there is recognition of the fact that their special needs must be met and that they should be helped to take their places with their peers in as many areas as possible, and as soon as they are able to do so. One of the greatest obstacles to this goal has been the widespread notion that these children are "different" from normal children. Modern educators and psychologists have pointed out the values of getting these boys and girls into regular classrooms while they are receiving remedial help, therapy, or, in the case of the gifted, additional enrichments. The remediation should be an aid to their instruction, rather than a separate program of instruction.

MAINSTREAMING

This is the term used to define the integration of exceptional children with the so-called normal. The major objective is social: to assist both groups in working and living together. To this end, the following practices may be followed.

Speech therapy, remedial reading, language classes for non-English-speaking children, psychological counseling, and special classes for the partially sighted, blind, or deaf may be included in the school day without removing a child from the group for more than a period or two at a time. Most schools do not have this extensive a program of special services, but many schools have set up some programs to meet the more urgent needs of the school or community. In some instances special activities have been added as enrichment for the culturally disadvantaged as well as for the gifted. In all of these programs there is an opportunity to use creative drama as a therapeutic process. As used here, the term therapeutic does not imply psychodrama or sociodrama, but rather an art form in which children find pleasure, emotional release, mental stimulation, personal satisfaction through success, and, most of all, a chance to use and stretch their imaginations.

THE GIFTED CHILD

One group of children that has received very little attention, perhaps because they are able to move ahead on their own, is the intellectually gifted. Only recently have educators and parents taken constructive steps to enrich the curriculum so that these gifted boys and girls may receive the stimulation they need by participating in extra classes and following individual interests. One of the areas that has been used most successfully for enrichment is the arts. This is not to imply that *all* children should not have wide and continued exposure to the arts, but because this is an area with endless possibilities, it has been selected often for use with the gifted. Arts programs have been designed both as afterschool activities and as additional classes during school time. Some programs include field trips to museums, theatres, and concerts, although funds given for this purpose are generally allocated for the use of all children rather than for one specially selected group. Classes in drama, dance, music, and the visual arts offer gifted children a chance to use their abilities in putting on plays—often written by the children themselves—and in designing and making costumes and scenery.

Gifted children have the ability to think of many things at a time; therefore, drama, with its wide range of responsibilities, is an ideal choice. When dealing with gifted children, the leader must always present a challenge. Drama, by its very nature, does this.

Programs outside the school day can be somewhat different from those presented during the school day. One particularly interesting program set up specifically for the gifted was described in a recent issue of the *Children's Theatre Review*.[1] In Pennsylvania the Lackawanna County Schools established a program for sixty fifth- and sixth-grade children whose IQs ranged from 130 to 165. A sixteen-week series of Saturday morning classes was held on the Marywood College campus in Scranton, although funds came from the Pennsylvania Department of Public Instruction in Harrisburg. Believing that all children have creative power, the faculty offered a variety of experiences aimed at stimulating this power and giving the participants a chance to express it. Literature was chosen as the focus of the program. During the eight Saturdays of the fall semester, the accent was on the development of the creative process; during the eight weeks of the spring semester, the accent was on the academic, with each child selecting, as an outgrowth of the first semester's activities, work in special areas in which he was most interested. The central theme, which coordinated all activities of the second eight-weeks' period, was "What kind of world would I like to live in?"

No homework was required, but the Marywood Children's Library facilities were available and the children were encouraged to withdraw books each week. A librarian and three teachers, aided by college students, were responsible for the four groups of fifteen children. Films were shown and specialists in the areas of pantomime, creative drama, dance, and puppetry were engaged to come to Scranton to work directly with the children on ideas sparked by the films selected for the day. Specialists came from the Museum of Natural History in New York City, the Woods Hole Oceanographic Research Center, colleges, and art studies. Trips to New York City and the Roberson Arts Center in Binghamton, New York, further enriched the program. The Marywood Readers Theatre interpreted selections from *Alice in*

1. Jeanne R. Spillane, "Stimulating Creativity in the Gifted Child," *Children's Theatre Review* 19, no. 1 (1970): 10–13, 18–19.

Wonderland and *The Wind in the Willows*, which the children had read and enjoyed. A documentary film showing each of the children's experiences was made during the first year as a record of the project. Plans for the following year included more subject matter in depth, with particular emphasis on creative drama as one of the most successful means of stimulating creativity.

The Lackawanna County project is not unique; it is cited here because it recognized the needs of the gifted for opportunities beyond the classroom and because it emphasized creative drama in its program.

Another experiment, designed for a doctoral study, was conducted at the same time in La Crosse, Wisconsin.[2] Creative drama classes were held for two semesters in three schools for groups of gifted seventh-graders. The results confirmed the hypothesis that creative drama is an effective learning experience in promoting the growth, development, and functioning ability of the imaginative capacities of gifted junior high school pupils. The favorable results of the research indicated that this approach to education is deserving of far more consideration than it has had in the past.

A different type of program for gifted youth was recently established by the Hunter College Center for Lifelong Learning in New York City. Here Saturday classes in science, the arts, and social studies are given regularly for young people aged twelve to sixteen who are designated as gifted. Drama workshops are among the offerings, and instruction is by highly qualified and experienced leaders.

A concern for the education of gifted youth in Cleveland, Ohio, led to the formation of a still different type of program designed for both teachers and students. The first such program had been established in the twenties but it was subsequently dropped for budgetary reasons. Spearheaded by former teacher and community leader, Elizabeth Flory Kelly, whose workshops in "curriculum dramatics" for Cleveland area teachers have attracted national attention, an interest in the gifted was rekindled. In 1979 through special funding she was able to secure as consultant Dr. Dorothy Sisk, formerly head of the Office of the Gifted and Talented in Washington, D.C., to help establish a series of workshops and seminars. This is cited as yet another example of the awakened interest in one of our most valuable resources, the gifted child, and the ways in which drama can serve his or her interests and needs.

THE MENTALLY RETARDED CHILD

Mental retardation describes a condition rather than a disease. Although it can refer to any degree of retarded mental development, the classifications

2. Sister Dorothy Prokes, "Exploring the Relationship Between Participation in Creative Dramatics and Development of the Imaginative Capacities of Gifted Junior High School Students" (Ph.D. dissertation, School of Education, New York University, 1971).

most commonly used are the following: the educable mentally retarded, the trainable mentally retarded, and the dependent mentally retarded. This discussion of creative drama in the education of the mentally retarded child centers on the first category. It is with this group that play can be most rewarding both as a teaching tool and a pleasure. Inasmuch as play constitutes an important role in the all-around development of the child, it has a special significance for the mentally retarded.

According to a survey taken in the early 1960s,[3] the major objectives of teachers using creative drama in the education of the mentally retarded child were to stimulate language and to promote social development. The nature of drama makes it a versatile tool in working with these handicapped youngsters. Rhythms, dramatic play, and pantomime are activities that are widely used by many teachers of the educable and trainable mentally retarded. Adaptations of the techniques used with normal children and developed over a longer period of time can bring both immediate satisfaction and lasting benefit. According to one teacher who has used creative drama successfully with mentally retarded groups, some of the best material comes from the very social situations that cause the retarded child to be stared at and shunned: entering a restaurant; ordering food and eating it; going on a bus, train, or plane trip; and dressing—simple daily activities that the average child of his age has mastered.

Like all children, the retarded child wants to be a member of a group, to contribute to it, and to have his contribution accepted. Drama offers this opportunity. One characteristic of the retarded child is his slowness to use his imagination or to deal with abstract ideas. Some teachers believe that the retarded child becomes more imaginative when placed in a class with normal children. Whether he is in a regular classroom or a special class, however, his pace is slow. Recognizing this handicap, the teacher can guide his dramatic play and stimulate his response. Frequently the leader errs in expecting too much too soon. The retarded child needs more help and encouragement than other children; he needs to repeat experiences more often; and finally, he must learn self-confidence and feel the satisfaction of having his contribution, however small, accepted. The game of "pretending" can help him learn to use his imagination, to prepare for new experiences, and to lay a firmer foundation for oral communication. Experienced teachers state that dramatic activities help to develop the skills of listening and looking. In this way, attention is engaged.

Rhythms and movement games are excellent beginning exercises. They aid the development of large muscles while they motivate use of imagination. The acting out of simple stories comes much later. At first, the retarded child

3. Geraldine Brain Siks, *Children's Theatre and Creative Dramatics* (Seattle: University of Washington Press, 1961), chap. 17.

National Theatre of the Deaf, courtesy Mary Beth Miller. Photograph by Ann Raychel.

will be more comfortable participating in a group than working individually. He has probably experienced frustration and the sense of being different; his need for praise and encouragement, therefore, will be greater than that of a normal child. When he shows an interest in moving out of the group to become a specific character—someone other than himself—he is ready for the next step. Now, instead of general group activities, individual roles may be undertaken. The teacher will need to provide not only stimulation at this stage but must also give clear and simple direction: Who is the character? How does he walk? What is he doing? How does he do it? What does he say?

If social ease and a sense of security are our first consideration, oral expression is the second. Guided dramatic play is a way of introducing oral vocabulary and developing concepts that prepare the child for reading. A variety of experiences will help to provide him with a better understanding of his world, and acting out words that describe this world will give them meaning. Action words such as jump, run, skip, skate, throw a ball—teach by doing. Nouns such as farmer, mailman, mother, or grocer can become the basis for dramatic play and pantomime. Mentally retarded children who have been guided carefully and slowly through dramatic play will eventually be ready to dramatize simple stories. By this time they will have achieved some personal freedom and mastered a functional reading vocabulary. The procedure of planning, playing, and evaluating is the same as that followed in the normal classroom, except that with these children, the task and the process must be simpler and will take longer.

One particularly important point to remember is that adjustments in all activities for the retarded child should be made on the basis of his interests and needs. Stories selected for dramatization should, in addition to being clear and simple, reflect the interests that give meaning to his life. As his interests widen, a greater variety of stories may be introduced, with new words to express and describe them.

Not only literature but other subjects as well can be taught through the medium of improvisation. For example, one teacher had the children in her arithmetic class be plus and minus signs and pieces of fruit; through acting out simple problems of subtraction and addition, the children were able to see the correct answers. So-called "creative walks," on which children became trees, flowers, stones, birds, and animals, helped them to observe and recall what they had seen after they returned to the classroom. Such use of creative drama is not generally sanctioned; and, indeed, it was discouraged in an earlier chapter. With these children, however, communication and social development are the primary goals; art is secondary. The potential in drama for motivating and reaching these primary goals validates its use. In time, other objectives can be established, but these are not possible until the child has developed a sense of security, has acquired some freedom of expression, and has mastered a working vocabulary that will enable him to take on the role of another.

Participation by the retarded child in the formal play is to be discouraged. A continuing program of creative drama, on the other hand, offers an opportunity for social growth, emotional release, and a way of learning. As one teacher put it after using creative drama techniques successfully for many years: "These children need to be crawled with first—then they can walk." When they have reached the walking stage, they often astonish us with what they have learned.

THE EMOTIONALLY DISTURBED CHILD

It is in this area that the classroom teacher must exercise the greatest caution. We know so little about these children and the causes of their problems that the possibility of doing harm is greater than with any other group.

Indeed, it is often difficult to distinguish between the emotionally disturbed child and the mentally retarded child because of the frequent similarity of behavior. Frequently repeated testing must be done in order to determine the nature of the condition. What might be a rewarding activity for the retarded child might not be good for the child who is disturbed. Psychodrama and play therapy are accepted techniques in the treatment of emotionally disturbed children, but they can be damaging in the hands of the lay person, regardless of his background and skill as a teacher of creative drama. The seriously disturbed child will probably not be found in the regular classroom, but will be enrolled in a special class or special school, where he is provided with special services. These services may or may not include psychiatric help and play therapy. Often children in special schools are referred to outside clinics or therapists, and drama may be part of the treatment.

Remedial Drama

Remedial drama is an umbrella term used here to cover several specific techniques. As was stated earlier, drama/theatre has historically been an essential part of human development. In preventive and therapeutic work we are primarily concerned with communication and therefore in helping individuals and groups build better relationships. According to Sue Jennings, author of *Remedial Drama*, " —(it) does not differ in content or technique from other types of drama, although great care must be taken in selecting and applying drama techniques to remedial work."[4] Her emphasis is on experience, and the goals of drama, used in this way, are *socialization, creativity,* and *insight.*

Drama therapy, role playing, psychodrama, and sociodrama are the terms most frequently heard. They differ both as to technique and thrust. David Johnson of Yale University, a leader in this new field, defines drama therapy as "the intentional use of creative drama toward the psychotherapeutic goals of symptom relief, emotional and physical integration, and personal growth."[5] Drama therapy, like the other arts therapies, applies a creative medium and establishes an understanding or contract between the client and the therapist. Thus it is differentiated from creative drama in an educational setting.

Psychodrama is a psychoanalytic approach through drama. It is a structured technique which works on the individual and ends in a catharsis. A program of training is required before the therapist is ready to practice. It deals with the real life situations of the participants.

Sociodrama, as the name implies, deals with the group and group problems or conflicts. A class in creative drama may become a sociodramatic ex-

4. Sue Jennings, *Remedial Drama* (New York: Theatre Arts Books, 1974), p. 4.
5. David Johnson, Unpublished duplicated material, 1978.

perience when a real life situation is employed and leads into discussion with benefits to all the participants. Classroom teachers and recreation leaders sometimes use sociodrama in a limited way to help solve problems that arise and persist with a damaging effect on the group. Though individuals are involved, it is the group and the group relationships that are the primary concerns.

Indeed, there is a difference of opinion as to the desirability of drama for the emotionally disturbed child. Some teachers believe that role playing is beneficial; others, that the child's problems present difficulties that may make this form of expression less desirable than participation in the other arts. The seriously disturbed child needs to make sense out of his own environment before he can enter another; moreover, until he knows who *he* is, he will have difficulty being someone else. His greatest needs frequently include the ability to interact and to develop language. Until he can express himself, he will find it difficult, if not impossible, to enter into the simplest form of dramatic play. According to Dr. Haim Ginott, "The playroom behavior of immature and neurotic children is characterized by an excess of inhibition or aggression."[6] Inasmuch as play therapy requires special training techniques, we shall confine ourselves to the consideration of appropriate activities for the child with emotional problems who is to be found in the regular classroom.

The child who functions well enough to be in a class with normal children may derive great benefit from dramatic play and dramatization. Under these circumstances, engaging in creative drama may be both an emotional release and a socializing experience. Bear in mind, however, that because the child's language and speech are frequently poor, he is likely to meet with frustration and difficulty in the oral expression of ideas and the improvisation of dialogue. An inhibited child cannot be expected to function at as high a level as his classmates, and needs much more support and encouragement. The aggressive child, on the other hand, needs to be restrained in his tendency to take over or to distract others. The attention span of children with emotional problems is apt to be shorter than that of other children their age, yet some teachers report highly creative work on the part of children who have demonstrated poor attention in other classes.

According to some experienced teachers, dramatic play, when first introduced to the child with emotional problems, should include reality-based situations rather than fantasy. Highly imaginative situations may cause young children who are not in touch with reality to meld with the idea or to identify too closely with the characters played. All children tend to become deeply involved in their dramatic play. The normal child can suspend his disbelief for the duration of the period, then return to reality. The disturbed child may not

6. Haim G. Ginott, *Group Psychotherapy with Children* (New York: McGraw-Hill Book Co., 1961), p. 40.

be able to shake off the role so easily, however, and may continue to be the character long after the play period has ended. As said earlier, however, we are dealing here with the child who is able to be in a normal group and therefore may be helped by his more reality-oriented peers.

There is a general agreement that dance, rhythms, and ritual movement are excellent for disturbed children. Physical activity gives them a sense of the body; and large movements, such as skipping, galloping, stretching, and moving the arms, are wonderful exercises for those who are poorly coordinated. "Reaching for the sky or pushing away the clouds," "feeling big," "growing tall," all are movements which contain an element of drama. The Dance Therapy Center in New York City works for release through the improvisational method, whereby the student is made conscious of new insights through bodily action. The philosophy of this unusual center is based on the "restoration of spontaneous movement to break the tenacity of the neurotic hold of body memory and on the experience of new psychophysical action as health is regained."[7] This is a relatively new field, and it is interesting that it recognizes movement as a specific therapeutic technique in dealing with emotional problems.

Many teachers have reported that the nonverbal child can develop the ability to express feelings and knowledge through the use of movement and pantomime. In this he finds a means of communication, and from it he may find motivation for speech. The teacher may also discover capabilities and awareness that remain hidden in the usual classroom situation.

A good exercise for any group of children but particularly good for the disturbed is the following:

One child begins a pantomime. This might be a man shoveling snow. Another child, who knows what he is doing, steps up and joins him. The second child may also shovel snow or do something that relates to it. The pantomime is kept up until the whole group has entered into the activity, one at a time. This is an excellent means of focusing attention and assisting each to "join" the group in a natural and logical way. If the class is large, two smaller groups can be formed, each taking a turn at the same exercise.

Another suggestion is a variation on the old game of "statues." One person comes into the center of the room and strikes a pose. She freezes as another person joins her. Each one stays in a pose until the entire group has come together, forming a large sculpture. This exercise is not drama therapy but is pantomime with possible therapeutic benefits, inasmuch as it encourages both observation of others and movement that relates to them.

Although it is suggested that all groups benefit from starting a session with movement, it is essential for children with problems. Through ritual, they find security; through warm-ups, use of the body; through moving as a

7. Dance Therapy Center brochure, New York, 1972–73.

group, a lessening of self-consciousness. It is further suggested that dance involving physical touch is often helpful, and patterned dance with its structure is a better starting place for some children than freer dance forms. Under any circumstances, rhythms that involve the whole body, clapping the hands, and making sounds to a beat are all good ways of getting and holding attention. Sue Jennings warns against imposing "end of session" discussions on children with problems. "Let them happen," she advises. The first job is to establish trust and security. Verbalization may be slow, and any analytical discussion should be a future goal.

Both finger puppets and hand puppets have been found to work successfully with children too inhibited to assume roles themselves. Such children usually have a poor self-image; thus it takes longer to build interest and ego strength to the point where they are able to move out of the group to assume roles and sustain them through improvised situations. Again, we are speaking of the child with knowledge of himself and his reality. When they reach the point where they can enter into dramatic situations with relative ease, they will begin to derive some of the same benefits found by other children. In terms of objectives, interaction with the group, ability to concentrate, ability to express themselves orally, and ability to take the part of another come first on the list. After these objectives have been met, the child should be able to work with joy, accomplishing as much and sometimes more than the others in the group. His sensitivity, if properly guided, can be an asset to his understanding of a character and creation of a characterization. Drama, because of its total involvement—physical, mental, emotional, and social—offers a wealth of activities, all of which have therapeutic value, if properly handled.

A new professional organization, The National Association for Drama Therapy, was formed in 1978, to set standards and goals. Both specialist and generalist should benefit from this formalization of principles and practices.

THE PHYSICALLY HANDICAPPED CHILD

In many ways the physically handicapped child presents fewer difficulties to the classroom teacher than the emotionally disturbed or the mentally retarded child. His handicaps are visible and his limitations obvious. His problems are easier to identify, and depending upon the seriousness of the disability, decisions have already been made as to whether he can function in a regular classroom or not. As with all exceptional children, the physically handicapped child is thought to be better off in a normal situation rather than segregated; if the disability is so severe that he requires special services, however, he may have to be enrolled, at least for a time, in a special school or in a hospital.

For our purposes we shall consider the physically handicapped to include the deaf, the partially sighted or blind child, as well as the child unable to function normally because of some other physical disability. Frequently the child with physical problems has emotional problems as well; for both of these reasons he will need all the support and encouragement that the teacher can give him as he struggles to reach his goals. Because of the conspicuousness of his handicap, however, he is generally treated with more compassion and understanding than his classmate with emotional problems whose behavior is inappropriate or immature. The person whose psychological problems cause him to behave in a socially unacceptable manner is often criticized or ridiculed, prompting the comment, "Why must he act that way?" The person on crutches, on the other hand, never gets this reaction, for we know he is walking as well as he can. In spite of, or perhaps because of, his physical limitations, the child who cannot hear, see, or speak clearly, or who lacks physical coordination or cannot walk, needs an opportunity to escape the walls of his prison on the wings of his imagination. Creative drama offers this opportunity, though admittedly the goals must be modified.

The Little Theatre of the Deaf, which achieved national prominence at the end of the 1960s, is a shining example of what can be done by actors for children who cannot hear. Because oral communication is emphasized in early education, the deaf child is at a disadvantage when attending theatrical performances, just as he is in ordinary classroom situations. Pantomime is the obvious means of reaching the hard-of-hearing, and it is in this form that *The Little Theatre of the Deaf* has succeeded so brilliantly. A cue can be taken from this experiment: pantomime is an area of drama in which the child with hearing loss can participate as well as enjoy as a spectator. Incidentally, we have recently become accustomed to seeing interpreters using sign language on television to bring important programs to nonhearing viewers.

Again, movement is an ideal way to begin activities. Large physical movements comes first, then rhythms and dance. Small muscle movements follow. Sensitive to the deaf child's keen visual perception, the leader can move from dance into pantomime. There will be motivation for speech in drama, but the easiest communication will be through pantomime, in which the deaf child can achieve success. Stories may be told in this medium, giving pleasure both to player and observer. My observation of creative drama classes in a school for the deaf revealed remarkable possibilities for learning and emotional release.

Graduate students from the New York University Deafness Center frequently share some of their techniques and experiences with my classes. On a recent occasion, a cast of hearing and nonhearing students, using mime, sign language, and a speech choir, presented a program of unusual artistry. One of the greatest values of the production was the opportunity it offered the actors and the audience to share ideas and insights.

The blind or partially sighted child faces different problems. He is at home with speech, so storytelling is an excellent beginning activity. Choral speaking, like music, is also an art in which he can excel and at the same time find pleasure. Original poetry composed by the group offers him a chance to express feelings and personal responses. Free movement is more difficult for him than for the sighted child, but it is not impossible. Carefully guided improvisation may be attempted, although the formal play, where movement is predetermined and not changed in rehearsal, is by its nature easier. One director who has had great success with a blind drama group stresses the fact that she never moves scenery or props once the placement has been established. A knowledge of where things are enables the players to move freely and easily about the stage. For the blind or partially sighted player, formal drama offers greater security than improvisation.

Children with physical problems that prevent them from running, walking, or even using their arms or legs easily, have also found drama to be within the range of their capabilities. Group participation while the children are seated is an excellent way of involving everyone in pantomime, choral speech, and puppetry. In preparing a dramatization, the roles of narrator and storyteller are highly regarded and can be handled by a child who may not be able to engage in more active participation. The imaginative teacher can find a place for the handicapped child, where he is able to add his bit to the group endeavor, thus enhancing his self-image and giving him a sense of achievement. The philosophy of all therapeutic recreation includes this sense of pride in a job well done and the joy of creative accomplishment.

There have been some major developments in this country since the publication of the first edition of this book in 1968. One of these was the founding of the National Committee: Arts for the Handicapped. In June 1974 the John F. Kennedy Foundation provided funding for a national conference on arts for the mentally retarded. As a result of the interest engendered by the Alliance for Arts Education, the Department of Health, Education, and Welfare, and the Bureau of Education for the Handicapped, a new national committee was formed. The purpose of this committee was to plan and coordinate an arts program for all handicapped children.

The committee's belief in the creative arts experience as a powerful means of bringing joy and beauty into the lives of children burdened by physical, emotional, or mental handicaps has resulted in a strong, ongoing program. The other and much more comprehensive development that is affecting arts programs, as well as others, inasmuch as educational institutions are involved, is the Rehabilitation Act of 1973 regarding Handicapped Persons.

Section 504 states: "No otherwise qualified handicapped individual in the United States . . . shall, solely by reason of his handicap, be excluded from the participation in, be denied the benefits of, or be subjected to discrimination under any program or activity receiving Federal financial assistance."

In 1977 a final Section 504 regulation was issued for all recipients of funds from HEW, including elementary and secondary schools, colleges, social service agencies, and hospitals. Already the results of this legislation have been felt in numerous ways, and they are bound to increase in the future. The arts will be affected as part of the educational system; and, as with any changed condition, so will public attitudes. "Mainstreaming", mentioned earlier, will be strengthened and, it is also to be hoped, the quality as well as the quantity of arts experiences for all children and youth. Indirectly, drama/theatre education will be expanded.

Related but not germane to this text is the current interest in and recent legislation regarding the aged. It is mentioned here only because some creative drama teachers and group leaders have successfully applied the same techniques that they have used in the classroom with senior citizens and nursing home patients. This opens up a new area and one in which very little has been done as yet. Funds are becoming available for programs for the senior adult, however, and it would appear that teachers of the arts, particularly those experienced in working with children and the arts therapies, will have much to offer. Texts and articles dealing with the arts and this population are beginning to appear; meanwhile, the basic principles and practices of creative drama are finding a new use.

THE CULTURALLY AND ECONOMICALLY DISADVANTAGED CHILD

Since the advent of the Head Start program, we have been hearing much about the culturally disadvantaged child, or the child in the disadvantaged urban area. This is not a new problem in our society but one which, for a variety of reasons, is currently attracting wide attention, with funds allocated for the establishment of educational and recreational programs. The arts, including dramatic play and creative drama, are emphasized in many of these programs. The values cited in Chapter 1 have tremendous implications for these children, who have been born into an environment lacking books, playing space, supervision, the arts—and, in many cases, language itself. According to one group of leaders at a conference on the subject of Creative Drama in Special Education, the problems of these children are manifold. For example, poverty may preclude treatment of a physical handicap; the handicap causes feelings of inadequacy, and this results in emotional disturbance. Hence, we

National Theatre of the Deaf, courtesy Mary Beth Miller. Photograph by Ann Raychel.

have a combination of problems requiring understanding and skill beyond the qualifications of the average well-prepared teacher.

The need for special training is recognized, and many universities and organizations are offering it. Because this is a subject of specialized interest and content, it is beyond the scope of this book; but for those teachers and recreation leaders who are interested in working in disadvantaged areas, let it be said that creative drama and theatre are approved and exciting techniques.

Nevertheless, the classroom teacher can do much for ghetto children. Actually, the first work in children's drama in this country was intitiated in the settlement houses of our large cities at the turn of the century. It is significant that the first children's theatre in America was established at the Educational Alliance in New York City in 1903 for the children of immigrant families of the lower East Side. This enterprise attracted wide attention, and in the next twenty-five years many settlement houses and playgrounds introduced storytelling and drama to the children of the poor. Most of the classes were conducted by social workers and Junior League members, some of whom had had theatre training but all of whom realized the potential of drama in teaching the language, brightening the lives of the boys and girls, and bringing strangers together socially in a new land.

Since that time the schools have taken up the challenge, although the social settlements have by no means abdicated their responsibilities. The 1960s and '70s have seen the phenomenon of street theatre in our cities: free performances of drama, music, and dance in ghetto neighborhoods, where strength is drawn even as it is given. Some of these productions have been subsidized by state arts councils, some by municipalities, others by churches and universities. Some have been part of a two-pronged program, involving both participation and spectator enjoyment. Many school districts have reported pilot projects in the arts for culturally disadvantaged youngsters, and drama is a frequent inclusion.

The schools have been concerned in recent years with bilingual education and the teaching of English as a second language. Particularly in large urban areas has the need been felt for teachers with a knowledge of Spanish and the ability to teach English in the early grades to children who enter school speaking a foreign language. One technique used and discussed today involves movement and pantomime.

For over a century, body movement has been recognized as bearing a relationship to the acquisition of a second language. Indeed, several methods making use of mime, rhythm, and sign language have been devised for teaching foreign languages. Movement is, therefore, not a new technique; rather, it is now recognized as an integral part of the learning process. Movement plus oral activities offer a great variety of opportunities for learning on any level.

The child who is learning a second language is faced with a problem not unlike the others we have discussed. It is therefore suggested that the procedures be much the same. Dance is recommended as a beginning because it forces more concentration than does pure verbal exercise. Folk dances involve a physical response to oral commands. Pantomime makes the spectator guess what the performer is doing and thereby ties the word to the act. Choral speech, on the other hand, has great value because it offers practice in talking, pronunciation, and interpretation. It is, in addition, an enjoyable exercise which does not single out the less able speaker.

A number of experiments have been conducted to determine the value of movement in the learning of language and to create new teaching procedures. One research project conducted at New York University merits special mention, since it revealed that daily participation in oral language activities derived from children's literature expanded skill significantly. The study was conducted with 500 black children in twenty classrooms—kindergarten through third grade—over a period of one year. Selected books were read aloud; this was followed by sessions in creative drama, puppetry, role playing, and storytelling. The objective was to teach standard English without negating the dialect spoken by the children. One important finding was that the earlier the program was begun, the more susceptible children were to language expansion. The research team recognized the importance of self-image to the nonstandard speaker, a point of view which differs from that commonly held a generation ago. The acquisition of language is not an isolated aspect of intellectual development but is rather a part of the process of socialization.

Bilingual children

Creative drama with bilingual children does not differ from creative drama with other groups except in the matter of vocabulary. The most common error in dealing with these children is underestimating their ability and overestimating their verbal skills. By giving them very short but interesting activities they can be successful and thus at the same time improve their self-image.

One gifted young drama teacher, whose work with a bilingual sixth grade I observed recently, used television commercials as assignments. Each child wrote and performed a commercial for a well-known product. These were clear, brief, and, in some cases, humorous; in every instance they were within the capabilities of the youngsters, who enjoyed creating and improvising them. An activity of this kind could be done on almost any level and can be assured of being understood.

A particularly interesting experiment was originated by Jearnine Wagner of Trinity University for nonachieving children in San Antonio. Called "Learning about Learning," it is based on a philosophy of the consideration of the whole child—at school, at home, at church, in the neighborhood: his world. Federally funded, a staff of twenty-five worked for two and a half years on a special curriculum directed primarily at the fourth, fifth, and sixth grades. Special books relating to the child's world were written and used to stimulate his interest in himself, his problems, and the people around him. The first objective was to develop a more positive attitude toward himself. This accomplished, the child was free to learn, and an exciting program of community-oriented activities was set up. Creative activities, including drama, formed an important part of this curriculum, which was aimed at helping children discover who they were and to value this discovery.

The need for special training in working with the disadvantaged is widely recognized, and many universities and organizations are offering programs toward this end. Because of the emphasis on the urban child, there has been less recognition of the disadvantaged rural child. In both instances, experienced teachers urge beginning with the child's own experiences and interests rather than forcing preconceived ideas on him. Encouragement of his efforts helps build confidence and motivate interest in exploring new ideas and new interests.

Funding programs giving support to professional and community theatre groups benefit the economically deprived by making performances and workshops available. Drama experiences that would otherwise not be available to the inner city child are now possible, if school administrators take advantage of artists-in-the-schools programs, theatre-in-education teams, and professional and highly competent nonprofessional performers in the community. Free and half-price tickets to plays in cities where live theatre exists provide enrichment for older students. CETA money, recently cut back, was designed for a different purpose, though audiences were composed of children who would otherwise not have been able to attend the theatre.

It is to be hoped that all the agencies and organizations that have taken such positive action in establishing programs will be able to continue and to expand. Only through ample subsidy can all children be provided with regular arts experiences of quality.

SUMMARY

Obviously, the exceptional child merits individual attention, and each teacher knows the capabilities as well as the disabilities of the various children in the group. While we are not here discussing the special services school, we are concerned with the exceptional child in the regular classroom and the ways in which creative drama techniques can be utilized to meet his needs and potential. Although he cannot do everything that the normal child does, the exceptional child can do some things well, and from this experience he can move forward, thus gaining pleasure and a sense of accomplishment. One successful teacher stresses *listening* as the first and most important element of the teaching process. What is the child trying to tell about himself, his desires, his frustrations? What is unspoken and why? Important cues are there to be picked up by a sensitive ear.

Every teacher recalls with clarity those handicapped children and college students who have been able to meet the challenge of learning and succeed beyond all expectation. The child with muscular dystrophy who participated in the enactment of an Indian legend sitting around an improvised campfire with the rest of the braves. The boy with the broken leg who beat a drum because he could not walk, yet was able to lead the group. The child labeled "slow," who memorized a lengthy part in a play although she was failing in her academic work; after that, she improved in all areas—was it, perhaps, because of increased self-confidence? The high school stutterer who was able to perform without hesitation in her class play. The college student with an arm partially paralyzed by polio, who not only participated actively in workshop drama but who later went on the professional stage as a singer. Not all will attain this degree of success, but all can achieve in some measure if we hold the belief articulated by the late Emily Gillies in an article describing the Institute of Physical Medicine and Rehabilitation in New York: "Here is a child's world where we can concentrate on the abilities, not the disabilities, which brought him here. Hopefully, if given enough sense of accomplishment, he can come through to a discovery and recognition of himself as a person."[8]

This is a goal we hold. The classroom teacher does not presume to be a therapist, but by knowing the exceptional child in the class—his problems and needs—the teacher may apply the techniques of drama to effect growth, strengthen abilities, and build a more positive self-concept. Moreover, the teacher can work with the therapists to their mutual benefit.

No one has stated this goal more eloquently than Thomas Carlyle, when he wrote the following lines: "Let each become all that he was created capable of being: expand, if possible, to his full growth; and show himself at length in his own shape and stature, be these what they may."

8. Emily Pribble Gillies, "The Katherine Lilly Nursery School," *IMPR* 2, No. 3 (1962), 11.

13

SHARING
A PLAY
WITH
AN AUDIENCE

The formal play in contrast to creative drama, is primarily audience-centered and has, from the beginning, public performance as its goal. A script is selected in advance and memorized by the players. It does not matter whether the lines were written by a playwright or the teacher, or composed by the children themselves. The use of a script distinguishes the formal play from creative drama, and supplies the structure—plot, theme, characters, dialogue—that will be followed.

It would be unwise to attempt to cover both informal and formal dramatic techniques in one book, whatever its length. It is hoped that teachers of young children will confine their efforts to creative drama exclusively. But for teachers of older children, and junior high school students, a few elementary suggestions are offered as to the smoothest way of moving the play to the stage.

This transition should come easily and naturally to the group that has spent many hours in improvisation. For

231

Older students perform for children.

boys and girls who have played together informally over a period of time, the result is more likely to be one of "sharing" than "showing," and to this end the teacher should be able to help the players achieve their goal—successful communication with an audience. Public performances, regardless of their popularity, should be infrequent, however, and then planned only for other classes or parents. This chapter has been included to help the teacher move, if she must, from informal classroom drama to the sharing of an experience with others, or to experience performance as the natural outcome of creative playing.

Unless the teacher has had some theatre training, directing the formal play can be a difficult experience. That is the reason for emphasizing simplicity: a long script, requiring elaborate scenery and costumes, poses problems for the most seasoned director. The average teacher does not have the background, time, or facilities to cope with such problems, but she can support and help enthusiastic young players prepare and demonstrate their work. In guiding beginners of any age, the most important single element is the approach of the leader. Enthusiasm and guidance help young players to cross the bridge between self-expression and successful communication.

Creativity is less dependent upon training and past experience than it is upon a special way of feeling, thinking, and responding. It is, therefore, quite possible for the teacher to be a highly creative person without having specialized in the theatre arts. Nevertheless, the formal play does make technical demands, which the teacher must realize; an audience is involved, and, therefore, a product. She must be prepared to take an additional step by supplying showmanship and maintaining discipline.

CHOOSING THE SCRIPT

It is to be hoped that the play presented by children in the lower and middle grades will be one they have written themselves. When the script comes as the result of enthusiasm over a good story or the culmination of their study of a subject, it is much more likely to have meaning for the class. If, for example, a class has been studying another culture (the American Indian, China, the Middle Ages), and they dramatize material relating to it, the play emerges from the background as a natural result. They may decide they want to dramatize one of the stories or legends they have read. After playing it creatively a number of times, they will be ready to write, or have the teacher write, the dialogue as they suggest it. The results will be childlike and crude, but the story itself has stood the test of time and, therefore, serves as a good scenario.

Sometimes a group wants to try an original plot. This is infinitely more difficult. Again, if it comes as the result of great interest in a subject they have been studying, they will know something of the background (time, place, occupations of the people, beliefs, superstitions, education, food, housing, folk or tribal customs). Their very enthusiasm is the primary requisite. Beyond that, they will need the guidance of the teacher in planning a story and developing characters who motivate the action. Inexperienced playwrights of any age cannot be expected to turn out well-made plays. What they *can* do is demonstrate their understanding of the subject matter about which they are writing, and show believable characters involved in the story. The play that comes as the result of integrating drama with social studies, music, literature, dance, or art will have its greatest value to the players. Another class will enjoy seeing their work, and perhaps be stimulated to try a play of its own. These are sufficient reasons for deciding to share the project, but unless the children are older and the teacher has had considerable experience in drama, it should probably not go beyond the school-assembly audience.

Occasionally, however, a class of older children will want to do a play that is not related to class work. When this request comes, the problem is somewhat different. There is the question of a good script that will offer as many opportunities as possible, without featuring three or four talented players. There is a scarcity of such material, though there are some good short plays available which have been written with the class or club group specifically in mind. The values cited in an earlier chapter should be considered when making the decision. Is it worthwhile material? Are the characters believable? Does the dialogue offer enrichment? Is the play interesting to the players? Beyond that, we must ask if it has enough parts to involve the whole group in some way.

Often a play written expressly for classroom use will have several major characters, and groups of townsfolk, or a chorus. This gives everyone a chance, makes double casting possible, and may even offer an opportunity to add music or dance. Production problems are another consideration. What are the staging facilities? Or will the play be performed in the classroom? If so, will it be in the round, or proscenium style? Are scenery and costumes essential, or can the script be simply performed with the tables and chairs that are available?

Sometimes the teacher will find a play based on a favorite story. Other times, the children will want to work on a particular kind of play—for example, a mystery. Whatever the choice, it should be a short script, requiring as little time as possible for rehearsals; long periods spent in rehearsing difficult scenes rarely make for a lively experience. If the group does a play for an audience, the choice of a script is the first important consideration.

THE DIRECTOR

The teacher moves from being guide to being director during the rehearsal periods. Some directors are permissive and allow much opportunity for individual interpretation. Others plan action carefully in advance and supervise every detail. The director of inexperienced casts often finds his greatest success in an approach that is somewhere between the two extremes: she gives enough direction to make the cast feel secure but provides enough leeway for individual interpretation and inventiveness. Regardless of method, however, the use of a script and the anticipation of an audience automatically place the emphasis on product rather than process.

Production also implies scenery and costumes; hence time and effort must be given to their design and construction. These need not be elaborate; indeed, they seldom are, in school or club situations, but the mounting is an important aspect of the formal play. When children can assume some responsibility for scenery, costumes, and properties, additional learning experiences are provided, as well as the opportunity for integrating arts and crafts with drama. Cooperation between the players and the backstage crew is essential to success, and is certainly one of the greatest satisfactions a group can experience.

For younger children, however, these values are all too frequently outweighed by anxiety, or boredom, or both, and the results tend to be wooden, lacking freshness and charm. For the child in the middle grades, however, there is occasionally reason for producing a play, provided the script is not too demanding or the direction too rigid. For the older child, on the other hand, the produced play is frequently of great value in teaching dramatic techniques and sharing an art with an audience. For the seventh- or eighth-grader, there are values to be found in the sustained work of production. Older children delight in the sharing of an activity and enjoy the discipline required to bring the performance to a high level.

It is suggested that before any work on the play is begun, the director have the group play the story creatively. Improvisation helps the players become familiar with the plot, get acquainted with the characters, and remain free in their movement. When the cast is thoroughly acquainted with the story, it is a relatively easy matter to rehearse more formally.

FLOOR PLANS

The director should make a floor plan or diagram of the playing space in advance. On this she will sketch in the essential pieces of scenery, or furniture, and indicate the entrances. This is not a picture of the set, but rather a careful diagram of the floor area, which indicates where each piece of scenery will be placed, its relative size, and the space left on the stage for easy movement. She will be careful to put entrances where the actors can use them most comfortably and effectively. Although the scenery will probably not be available much before final rehearsals, she will try to find pieces of comparable size so that the cast becomes used to the plan and will have as little trouble as possible adjusting to the setting when it appears.

UP RIGHT	UP CENTER	UP LEFT
RIGHT CENTER	CENTER	LEFT CENTER
DOWN RIGHT	DOWN CENTER	DOWN LEFT

WINGS   WINGS

APRON

This is a diagram of the areas of the stage. Left and right always mean the actor's *left and right.*

The director will also want to list all pieces of scenery so that she can check them off as she collects or makes them. The beginner will find that the simpler the setting, the fewer the problems, and, incidentally, the more effective the stage will probably be. Children can be involved in all the details of the production; they will enjoy it and learn from the experience.

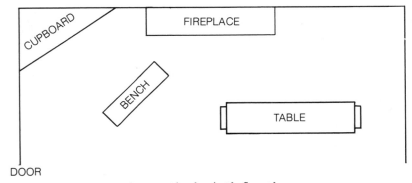

CUPBOARD

FIREPLACE

BENCH

TABLE

DOOR

An example of a simple floor plan.

THE STAGE MANAGER

This is an important job, and one that a responsible boy or girl can do and enjoy. He should be appointed at the same time the cast is selected and given a script of his own. He attends all scheduled rehearsals and keeps a record of all cuts, action, and business. It is a good idea for him to sit at one side of the stage where he can not only see and hear but also call the actors for their entrances.

Under most circumstances, he will be able to pull the curtains and handle or give cues for the lights. He works closely with the director and assumes as much authority as the director feels he can when the play is presented. The stage manager has a chance to grow in his job, for he is important to every aspect of the production and learns, by doing, the meaning of the word "responsibility."

CASTING THE PLAY

This preliminary work done, the director is now ready to give his attention to casting the play. In creative drama the cast changes with every playing. In the formal production, however, there is one cast that rehearses each scene a number of times in preparation for the performance. The matter of casting is therefore, important. The director tries to get the best possible cast together, and usually does it by means of tryouts. He is obligated to do a certain amount of type-casting. For example, a giant must be played by a very large child; a dwarf, or elf, by a child who is small; other characters who may have certain specified physical characteristics, by children with similar characteristics. To cast for any other reason than theatrical effectiveness is a questionable practice.

The audience must believe in the reality of the characters, and if they are too obviously different from the description or implications in the script, an audience cannot find them acceptable. Likewise, older players will feel uncomfortable if they realize that they are not believable, and so the good that the experience may do them is negated by their own feelings of inadequacy. This, of course, is one of the strong arguments against public performance by children. An actor cannot grow if he is constantly cast in the same type of role; yet he cannot experiment with a part, for which he is conspicuously miscast, in front of an audience.

Casting should be done carefully, for a mistake made in the beginning may be fatal later. Some directors like to have two casts. This is a good idea, provided there is sufficient time for a double set of rehearsals. It is a precaution against illness and accidents, and gives the entire group a feeling of security. It also provides twice as many opportunities for participation, and should work out well, if there is time enough to rehearse both groups equally. It goes without saying that both casts must be given a chance to perform.

STAGE MOVEMENT

Stage movement is the movement of actors about the stage. The director who plots it in advance will find that he saves valuable time in rehearsal. Writing notations in his script, or even making diagrams, will help him see at a glance where the various characters are. Although most published scripts have action included, it seldom works, for the simple reason that no two stages are alike. For example, an important entrance, which the script indicates should be from the right, may have to be reversed if the wing space in the school auditorium cannot accommodate it.

If the movement is memorized along with the lines, and not changed, it is an advantage. Once the general movement is set, the cast is free to develop appropriate business (action) and work on characterization. Early memorization of lines also helps the group move ahead, giving attention to the rhythm of the play, the building of climaxes, projection of voice, and general polishing. Perfection is never the aim when working with children, but their satisfaction will certainly be greater if they can feel well-prepared, comfortable, and able to enter into the performance with a sense of security. Encouragement, plus necessary constructive criticism, helps to make the rehearsal period one of pleasure and learning.

SCENERY

Scenery means the large pieces that suggest the locale of the play. There is always controversy as to the difference between scenery and "props." Scenery is background, whereas properties are those items used by the actors.

The trend today (and a fortunate trend it is for inexperienced and young groups) is toward curtains rather than box sets, and toward suggested rather than realistic settings. For example, a bench, a table, chairs, stools, perhaps a fireplace or a hutch—if available—will suggest a peasant's cottage, without the necessity of building flats, putting in doors, or painting an elaborate representional background. Some of the most effective settings, both on Broadway and off, have been abstract, or so simple as to focus all the attention on the play and the players.

Platforms and steps are helpful in creating different levels, thus adding variety in appearance and making for interesting movement. A bright tablecloth, a few large flowers, two or three benches or stools can often provide all that is needed. Children have wonderfully imaginative ideas for suggesting scenery; what they do need is practical help in constructing it, and supporting the pieces. If the director works closely with the art department of the school, most backstage problems can easily be solved. And, best of all, the stage crew or scenery committee will have an ideal opportunity to learn techniques of painting and handling materials.

Scenery is usually not needed until the final rehearsals. It is suggested that if it can be ready a week in advance of the first dress rehearsal, the players will have a chance to get used to it, and not have to add that adjustment to costumes and other last-minute details. A few *dos* and *don'ts* may be helpful:

1. Scenery should enhance, not distract.
2. Scenery should be firm, not flimsy.
3. Scenery should unify the production.
4. Scenery should be in keeping with the mood of the play.
5. Scenery should suggest the time and place of the story and the circumstances of the characters.
6. Scenery and costumes should be planned together.
7. Scenery should help the players, not get in their way.

PROPERTIES

Very little needs to be said about properties. They are all the objects (usually small) used by the players. If the school has a property closet, many commonly used items can be kept and brought out when needed. Baskets, canes, wooden bowls, china, swords, and the like are basic equipment. Some things must be borrowed, some made. It is a challenge to the ingenuity of the committee when, for example, such things as a "golden goose," a "snowman," a "roast chicken," or a "birthday cake" are called for. Papier-mâché and styrofoam are excellent materials for the unusual item, but, again, the young or inexperienced committee needs help in construction.

One other word regarding props: The property committee learns what responsibility is all about, for objects are often needed at particular moments in the play, and the absence of them can ruin an otherwise excellent scene. Properties should be checked before and after every rehearsal and performance, and if damaged or missing, replaced. It is a good idea to begin gathering the properties as soon as the play goes into rehearsal so as to give the actors ample time to get used to handling them.

COSTUMES

Costumes, like scenery, can be a source of worry and frustration to the teacher whose group is too young or inexperienced to assume responsibility for them. Sometimes parents take a hand with the costumes, and sometimes the art department offers assistance. The former may be a satisfactory arrangement, but all too often it builds what should have been a simple performance into a major production. Too much emphasis is put on the mounting, and the public performance with adult contributions takes precedence over the learning. The second arrangement—assistance from the art department—is decidedly preferable, since it keeps the play within the framework of the school, and may give the class an opportunity to help design or even make some part of the costumes. If neither type of cooperation is available, the teacher should try to solve the matter of clothing by merely suggesting it, or adapting easily obtainable garments to the play.

For example, aprons, hats, vests, capes, boots, and shawls are easily acquired and go a long way toward suggesting various kinds of characters. Children accept simple suggestions readily, and do not demand complete or authentic outfits. Blue jeans, tights, and colored T-shirts are in the wardrobes of most children and young people today, regardless of economic circumstances. If these can be chosen with a color scheme in mind, they can be used as costumes for many folk tales, or for plays with historical backgrounds.

Paper should be avoided. It tears easily and so is hazardous. It is suggested that all good costumes, whether made for a particular occasion or given to the school, be saved and kept in good repair. The collection of basic garments should be a continuing project; as time goes on, it will provide many, sometimes all, of the costumes needed for future productions.

It is generally better not to put old and authentic garments and inexpensive, newly made costumes on the stage at the same time. The effect is usually that of making the old look faded and dirty, and the new—cheap, and too bright. Occasionally the two can be combined, but, in general, it is better to use one or the other for a unified overall impression.

Here, also, a few suggestions are offered as to the function of costumes:

1. Costumes should suggest the personality, age, occupation, and financial circumstances of the characters.
2. Costumes should belong to the period and setting of the play.
3. Costumes should be appropriate to the season of the year, as suggested by the story.
4. Costumes should help to unify the production.
5. Costumes should be planned with the scenery in mind; they should carry out the color scheme and look well against the background.

6. Costumes should not distract for reasons of brightness, richness, or design, unless, of course, there is a reason for it.
7. Costumes should fit the wearers and be clean and well pressed.
8. Costumes should be secure, neither carelessly made nor too fragile to be safe.
9. Costumes should make the wearers feel appropriately dressed and comfortable, not self-conscious.

REHEARSALS

In the beginning, the director, regardless of the group, will have many decisions to make and many details to organize. Once he has cast the play, decided upon the floor plan, and has made arrangements for settings and costumes, he can get down to the serious business of rehearsing. As stated earlier, time spent on improvisation will be time well spent; the cast will become thoroughly acquainted with the characters and the plot. Better yet is the play that evolves from a comprehensive unit of study. When children have been deeply immersed in a situation, a period, or a place for a long time, the play they build will have much greater meaning for them and for the audience.

The director is now ready to set up a rehearsal schedule. It is hoped that, for the teacher or director of children, this will be an informal procedure. Even though a performance date has been set, and the work planned, he must try to avoid the anxiety and boredom that mar rehearsals of so many nonprofessional productions. For this reason, rehearsals should be frequent but short. Scenes, rather than the entire play, should be rehearsed first; complete run-throughs come later.

Early memorization of lines is advocated, since it frees the players to move and develop pertinent business. People memorize at different rates of speed, but the sooner it is done, the more productive the rehearsal periods will become. Most important is probably interpretation. Discussions along the way help the actors to learn who the characters are, and why they behave as they do. Such questions as these should be answered:

1. How would you describe the character you are playing?
2. What is his motivation?
3. How does he relate to others?
4. What are his individual qualities? (Personality, temperament, age, occupation, background, likes, dislikes, education, beliefs.)

Blocking the scenes comes next. If the director plans movement in advance, he will be able to approach a rehearsal, knowing when characters enter and leave, by what door, and where they sit or stand. It is a good idea to note all movements on a master script. Often, when a few days have passed between rehearsals, there is disagreement as to what was done before. A careful record will answer the questions so that the rehearsal can proceed.

Business, which is individual action in keeping with the character, can be developed next. For example, knitting, sweeping, eating, and so on add to the reality of the characters and give young players something definite to do. The more times business is repeated, the more natural it becomes. As was mentioned earlier, if properties are available at the beginning of the rehearsal period, the players grow used to them, and can handle them with ease and naturalness.

Composition, or "stage picture," is another thing for the director to bear in mind. Even an experienced actor cannot see the grouping on the stage when he is part of it; hence the director, who is watching closely from the front, must be aware of the composition. Are the players hiding each other? Can important business be seen? Are entrances blocked? If there are several players together, do they make a pleasing picture? Does one composition flow into another? All of this pertains much more to the play designed for an outside audience; yet, even under the most informal circumstances, it is important that the players be clearly seen and heard.

If dances or songs are included, they should be rehearsed and integrated as early as possible. It is always a temptation to let them go, but the director will find that this makes for a weak spot, or a slow transition. Such business should appear to spring from the play and belong to it; it should not be imposed for the purpose of adding more people or relieving monotony.

As with scenery, any cooperation between the drama and music teachers is an advantage. The more a staff can work together on a project, the better the learning and the better the production. If a player is absent, the stage manager or another person should step into the part. When the director reads the lines from out front, the cast is at a disadvantage; for, while the lines are delivered, the space is empty, and the scene very often breaks down. Incidentally, this is another good reason for double casting. It assures each group of a substitute at a moment's notice.

As the rehearsal period proceeds, the play should grow in feeling, understanding, technical competence, and unity. Smoothness will come as lines are learned, the business perfected, and the actors develop rapport with each other. Rough spots should be ironed out in the beginning, rather than left to the end for polishing. And, finally, if the director can maintain a spirit of fun, the rehearsal period will be a source of pleasure as the cast shares the satisfaction of building something together.

As in creative drama, the director occasionally finds a show-off, or clown, in the cast. He does not want to inhibit inventiveness but he cannot afford byplay, which disrupts the rehearsal and takes the attention away from the script. Clowning must be stopped at once, for it can jeopardize the entire performance. Most children and young people, if approached constructively, will see that practical and private joking are out of order and, for the good of the production, their energy must be used to build, not break up, a scene. For children of junior and senior high school age, this experience may be the highlight of the year and leave a lasting impression.

Teamwork is both a necessity to a good performance and a source of deep satisfaction to the players. There is probably no experience comparable to the camaraderie that develops during rehearsals. A special feeling binds a group together when it shares the hard work, the creative effort, the interdependence, and the fun of rehearsing and presenting a play.

THE DRESS REHEARSAL

The dress rehearsal can be either a day of confusion or a satisfying culmination of weeks of group effort. When details have been well planned, and the scenery and costumes are ready, there is no reason why it should not be the high point of the rehearsal period. The old adage, "a poor dress rehearsal makes a good show," is fallacious. It is true to a degree only when the dress rehearsal is so bad that the cast makes one last mighty effort to prevent the play from being a disaster. This always involves work that should have been done weeks before; with this work completed, the cast is ready to add the final details with a sense of security.

Two, or even three, dress rehearsals are desirable, and should be planned from the beginning. At the first one, the scenery should be finished and in place. At the second and third, costumes should be worn, so that by the time the play goes on, the cast and backstage crew have mastered all the problems. After each dress rehearsal and performance, costumes should be hung up carefully and properties checked. This not only helps to keep things in good order but also instills a sense of responsibility in the players. Even in the most informal of plays, the actors should remain backstage and not mingle with the audience. Food and other refreshments have no place in a dressing room. They are a risk to the costumes, and divert the players.

If makeup is used (and with children it is nearly always unnecessary), it should be tried out first for effectiveness. Teenagers like working with makeup; therefore, for them, another learning experience is provided. Again, makeup extends or enhances a character; it does not create one. Sometimes a player will say, "I'll be all right when I'm made up and get into my costume." He will be better, perhaps, but if he has not succeeded in creating a character by that time, costumes and makeup cannot do it for him.

Children at the Salt River Indian Reservation, A2, courtesy Lin Wright. Photograph by John Barnard.

If there is a curtain call, it should be rehearsed so that the players are ready to come out and take a bow to the audience. One curtain call is sufficient for the audience to show its appreciation. Although there is some difference of opinion about this, the curtain call is a convention of the formal theatre, and an audience should be given a chance to observe it.

THE PERFORMANCE

Once again, let it be stated that a performance by beginners or children should be simple and informal. The director has the greatest responsibility here, for his attitude of calm encouragement will be contagious. If he regards the play as a good piece of work, which the cast and crew take pleasure in sharing, they will view it much the same way. They will look forward to the performance with anticipation rather than with anxiety. Both excessive criticism and excessive praise are as harmful at this stage as at any other. The most satisfying response a group can be accorded is the appreciation of the audience. The players will know that they have succeeded in achieving their goal: successful communication.

THE AUDITORIUM

One aspect of producing a play that is frequently overlooked is that of the auditorium. Ushers may be members of the class, who have worked on committees and so are free when the dress rehearsals are over. Ushering is an excellent way for them to perform a necessary function. If there are programs, they may hand them out, though in an informal situation, a narrator is a preferred way of imparting necessary information to the audience.

Attendance should be by invitation only, rather than by ticket. When tickets are sold, there is an added emphasis on perfection, and a felt obligation to make elaborate settings and costumes. Young players feel the strain, and the "sharing with" too often turns into "showing-off." Publicity, also, should be restricted to posters made by the group and oral announcements. The greater the participation of the class in every aspect of the production and the fewer contributions from outside, the more positive values the experience will have.

SUMMARY

To summarize: the presentation of a play for an audience should be done only when older children are involved, and then infrequently. Informality and simplicity should be stressed if the basic values of communication and sharing are to be realized. There is real difference of opinion as to whether children should ever appear before an audience, for fear of destroying their spontaneity and naturalness. This is a valid argument, but the contention here is that performance will probably do no harm if it is done without pressure, thus avoiding drudgery. The teacher must become director, supplying showmanship, and making certain decisions. As teacher, however, she tries to involve every member of the group so that the procedure is as democratic as possible. Most important, children should not be exploited to show the value of the content or of the instruction.

In the school, club, or camp play, the educational and social values comes first. The product will hold interest for the viewers if they are properly oriented, and their appreciation is the natural consequence of a successful attempt at communication. If these emphases are preserved, the leader and group will find producing a play a rewarding experience. There is probably nothing that binds a group together more closely than the production of a play; and no joy more lasting than the memory of a play, in which all the contributions of all the participants have dovetailed so well that each has had a share in its success. This can and should happen, when exploitation does not enter the picture.

Finally, theatre is a performing art. Let us not forget this. The suspicions that have surrounded it in our country from the beginning are still here, if masked. When we cut the arts from the budget in times of depression and deemphasize *acting* in favor of the word *learning*, we are giving tacit acceptance to an old prejudice. Some funding agencies request a product as proof of the effectiveness of the programs to which they have given support. A product need not be interpreted as a full-fledged production, however; in fact, a good demonstration can meet the requirement just as well, often better. You may find a production desirable, but if not, consider a demonstration of creative drama or an open class by showing what it is, what it does, and how it works. If there is one thing that recent experimentation in the arts has shown us, it is that there are few, if any, rules that must be obeyed. Children experiment freely, mixing media, ignoring conventional forms, being "horse and rider" simultaneously, and erasing the line that exists between actor and audience. Therefore, an opportunity to observe children working creatively may satisfy the funding agency and be a far more effective presentation than the traditional school play.

14

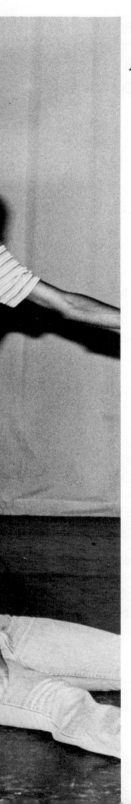

CHANGES
AND
CHALLENGES

PIONEERING PROGRAMS

The preceding chapters have dealt with creative drama as part of a curriculum or, at least, an art to be included whenever time and curriculum permit. Although the focus of this text is the classroom, mention must also be made of some of the other areas where creative drama programs exist. These include community and recreation centers, and churches. As recreation and leisure time activities, drama classes and clubs have always enjoyed great popularity. I believe that these programs are important for a variety of reasons, not the least of them being that they are elected "for fun." Many leaders hold degrees in recreation or theatre and are doing outstanding work; some volunteers are teachers and graduate students who lead workshops in the arts because they, also, enjoy them. The first recognition of drama as an educational and social tool came from such centers as the Educational Alliance, the Henry Street Settlement, Christadora House, and Greenwich House in New York; Hull

247

"Creating Statues." Howard University Children's Theatre Workshop, courtesy Kelsey E. Collie.

House in Chicago; Goodrich House, and the Karamu Theatre in Cleveland. Many other settlements, from Boston to the West Coast, included classes in storytelling and informal dramatics under the guidance of social workers and the Junior League. The American Community Theatre Association and the National Recreation Association, to mention only two national organizations, offer help and support. True, the demand for qualified leaders and directors still exceeds the supply, but with the consciousness of our increasing leisure time, government agencies and universities are endeavoring to help communities set up programs to help people live richer and more satisfying lives. Experiences in the arts are an important inclusion.

The little theatre movement of the 1920s brought dramatic activities to the children of other communities, but it was not until the 1940s that the major responsibility was assumed by educational institutions. Notable for its pioneering efforts in this field since 1925 is Northwestern University which, in cooperation with the public schools of Evanston, under the distinguished leadership of Winifred Ward, first demonstrated what town and gown can do, working together. There have been other ventures, too numerous to mention, some of which have resulted in permanent programs, contributing both to the children of the community and the training of teachers. Many colleges and universities offer work as a curricular inclusion or an extracurricular activity, with a touring program or campus performances of plays for children's audiences.

The Adelphi University Children's Centre for the Creative Arts is a unique program serving both students and area. Founded in 1937 as a community service, it now includes an extensive program of Saturday classes for children aged six to twelve, evening classes for teenagers, and classes for adults. In addition, graduate students may earn a master's degree in speech arts and educational theatre or elementary or secondary education with a concentration on aesthetic education through participation in the activities of the children's centre. Throughout, attention is devoted to the process rather than the product and to all the arts instead of drama only. There are many instances of university and community cooperation in this country, but the Adelphi program is cited because it has been in successful operation for over forty years and provides the same strong leadership for both groups of participants.

Libraries and playgrounds have introduced drama to some communities, and individual teachers, particularly in the private schools, have made valuable contributions. The Children's Theatre Association of America, first established in 1944 as a committee dedicated to the promotion of children's theatre and creative drama, became a full-fledged division of the American Educational Theatre Association in 1951. Its membership, interestingly enough, has always included teachers and leaders from universities, colleges and schools, community theatres, settlement houses, the Association of Junior Leagues of America, the professional theatre, and interested citizens. National conventions, held every August, provide programs demonstrating work done in the various regions of the country, as well as talks, symposia, and panel discussions on topics of current interest. Workshops in creative drama and puppetry, under the direction of outstanding leaders, have often been planned prior to the opening of the conference, in response to the members' demand for further training. While the principal interest at the present time is the introduction of creative drama into the school curriculum, there is a growing enthusiasm for its inclusion in camp, hospital, and special education programs. Reports on research in the field indicate the effectiveness of this aspect of drama as a social and educational technique.

During the last two decades a number of experimental and pilot projects have been initiated in the arts. Some of these have been funded by state arts councils, some by private foundations, and some by interested organizations such as PTAs. All have had a common goal: to bring the arts to the children of communities in which little has been done or where more exposure to the arts is desired, and to bring the arts to the handicapped. Such projects have not been confined to any particular regions; they have been nationwide. Nor have they followed identical patterns. An example of a particularly extensive project was the Arts in General Education, financed by the John D. Rockefeller III Fund, for the 8000-pupil school system of University City, a suburb of Saint Louis.

In this program, painting, music, photography, dance, poetry, drama, and other visual and performing arts were integrated into the curriculum from kindergarten through the twelfth grade. The major objective of the program was to give children experience in the arts and to increase their knowledge of the arts. In-school participation, field trips, and exhibitions were among the experiences offered. One problem discovered by the evaluators was a general feeling of inadequacy on the part of the educators. Because few teachers have had enough training and experience to feel comfortable with the arts, they have not introduced a variety of activities into their classrooms on any regular basis. Moreover, arts education, particularly in the upper grades, is often considered a separate area and is segregated from other studies, if not neglected.

Through the financial support of the JDR III Fund, the community support of the University City School Board and the staff and resources of CEMREL (Central Midwestern Regional Educational Laboratory, Inc.), an extensive program was carried on over a three-year period. Both specialists and classroom teachers participated in an effort to realize present and long-term goals with the result that many of the ideals and objectives have become a part of the University City Arts Program.

CEMREL'S long-range curriculum program, which includes drama/theatre for children, was founded in the hope that the materials and philosophy will have a lasting effect on education throughout the United States. CEMREL is reported to be the first educational laboratory established under ESEA that included all the arts in its program.

An example of one of the newer kinds of programs offering creative drama experiences for children and workshops for teachers is Pennsylvania's Plays and Creative Ways Ensemble. This pilot project involves a group of actors from Pennsylvania State University and is funded by the Department of Education in Harrisburg and the various subscribing school districts. A typical day's plan includes a relevant play for a children's audience, followed by periods in classrooms with teams of actors and leaders working with the classroom teacher in directing improvisational responses to the performance. Further opportunities are offered for teachers and administrators at the close of the day to continue work as well as special in-service programs and lecture-demonstrations. The reaction to both content and format has indicated high enthusiasm for an ongoing program designed to meet the needs and interest of school districts throughout the state.

Many other imaginative projects have been undertaken in other communities, some of which have set patterns that have continued. While the arts in this country are still not generally accepted as a significant part of public education, such efforts as these indicate a growing concern for a neglected area and positive steps in the direction of constructive change in the curriculum. Drama, a relative newcomer to the schools, is finding recognition as an art that contributes to the emotional, intellectual, and social development of the child, with values to be derived from active participation on all levels.

THE MEAD SCHOOL

The Mead School in Byram, Connecticut, attracted national attention in 1977 when it was featured in an article entitled "Why Children Should Draw" in the *Saturday Review*. The unique character of this school lies in its belief in the arts as basic to education. The Mead catalogue states that learning is multisensory. "Children need to touch, taste, see, talk," and to that end should follow a curriculum that gives the arts and traditional subjects equal status. "Indeed, art gets the largest space here," according to Mead's director, who explained that a child uses her mind in concert with hands and eyes. Through experiential learning (the arts), the child reaches the symbolic (traditional). This small private school, after ten years, is able to point to scores at or above Standard Achievement Test (SAT) averages in every subject.

The article also cited some other schools that have embarked on innovative arts programs. Project IMPACT, begun in 1970 and located in five different areas, lasted only a few years but developed into other institutions like the Magnet Arts School in Eugene, Oregon, and The Eastgate School in Columbus, Ohio. In these and in The Magic Mountain School in Berkeley the emphasis is on the role of the arts in the development of human capacities, rather than on arts education as traditionally taught.

CREATIVE DRAMA IN THE CAMP

Except for the arts camps, drama/theatre is rarely one of the more important activities of the camp program. Camps exist primarily to give city children an experience in group living in an outdoor setting. An opportunity to engage in a variety of sports is provided, with nature study, music, arts and crafts, and drama, as well as other activities from which to choose. Because of this emphasis, children should not be expected to spend long hours indoors, in rehearsals, but rather to enjoy drama and share the results of their work in occasional informal programs. Creative drama is, therefore, an ideal activity for campers of all ages and backgrounds. Pantomime, improvisation, and simple, out-of-door pageantry can contribute both to the participants and to those occasions when the group comes together for programs. Full production with scenery and costumes would seem to have no place in the average camp; the drama counselor might better prepare herself by studying creative drama techniques so that she is able to work informally with campers of all ages, rather than formally for an audience. Class periods should be short and flexible. This, however, does not mean that time should be wasted or misspent; quite the contrary. No activity brings satisfaction unless it is looked upon with respect; hence, informal drama, seriously undertaken, has as much to offer the camp as it has the community center or school.

AN EXPERIMENT IN LEARNING

One reportedly successful experiment in creative drama was carried out in a workshop for teachers held at a mountain camp in Switzerland.[1] A leader with twenty-five participants (all kindergarten and elementary school teachers) lived and worked together for a week. The members of the group did not know each other beforehand, but became well acquainted through the close association of informal classes, discussion groups, and meals taken together in the dining hall. The first classes were conducted in a large room,

1. Fraulein Brigitt Streuli, 2 Hauptlehrerin, Kantonales Kindergartnerinen, Semenar, Umiken, Switzerland.

bare except for a carpet on the floor and a piano. Participants wore informal clothing and soft shoes, or rhythm sandals. On the first morning, they were asked to walk around, to get used to the space they would work in. Movement and rhythms followed, with piano accompaniment. Next came simple exercises in pantomime.

The Grimm tale of *Frau Holle* was introduced the next day, but for several sessions only portions of the story were played. The leader then took the group outdoors and had them try the scenes in the woods under the trees. In pairs they enacted the scene of Frau Holle's trying to pull the girl into the cottage. This was followed by the scene in the doorway with the shower of gold, and the dripping of tar. By the end of the week, they had played the entire story outdoors, in a setting appropriate to the tale and conducive to physical freedom.

Mornings began with singing, movement, and dance. Evenings included readings from modern literature and group discussion. These, and Bible stories, were enacted by the participants so that they had the experience of approaching material as children might, but making ultimate use of literary works that challenged them on an adult level. According to one member of the group, the greatest values of the workshop were the sense of freedom it engendered, the loss of self-consciousness that ensued, and the concept of creative drama as an art form which emerged by the end of the week. This illustration is cited because of the unusual opportunity it offered for group work in a simple yet ideal setting. While the camp program is filled with a variety of different activities, it does offer the same advantages of plenty of space, an outdoor setting, and freedom from the usual daily distractions.

DRAMA IN THE CHURCH

Historically, it was the church that was responsible for the rebirth of the western theatre through its use of plays as a teaching device in the Middle Ages. The popularity of these early plays led to an eventual separation of theatre and church. It was a relationship that has never been fully restored. Perhaps in future we shall see a reunification as the arts become more central to our lives. At any rate, creative drama is being used in some church settings by some of our most experienced leaders.

Dramatic activities in the church fall into two categories: that in which the church is used as a community center with drama classes and the performance of plays of a secular nature; and when the purpose is religious education with creative drama and plays based on Bible stories or material containing ethical and moral problems. In both cases, the procedures are the same as in the classroom; it is the content only that differs. Experienced leaders of creative drama and theatre have told me that the same activities take place in the church setting as in the school; the stated goals are education and social development.

Children exposed to the Bible as literature have actually improved their habits of speech and their vocabularies because of the use of excellent language. The material, skillfully presented, captures the children's interest, and the problems provide challenging topics for discussion. Religious drama at one time was likely to be little more than a pageant or an occasional program presented to an audience; today there is a movement to upgrade both the content and the methods of handling it. For several years now the Children's Theatre Association of America has had an active committee on religious drama. It has assembled bibliographies and scripts in this area, and it is represented on the program for the national convention each year.

WORKSHOPS AND TRAINING

Many workshops in creative drama are held in the United States each year under a variety of sponsorships. Some are part of the summer school offerings of universities and colleges. Others are sponsored by such organizations as the Children's Theatre Association (both national and regional), the Association for Childhood Education International, the National Recreation Association, and the National Catholic Theatre Conference. Still others are among the in-service courses for public school teachers, held after school or on Saturdays. The Junior League, women's clubs, religious and recreational organizations, the Head Start program, as well as individual community theatres and churches, have instituted programs for the training of their drama leaders. Surveys have been made from time to time in an effort to determine the amount and kind of training being offered by educational institutions throughout the country, but it would be difficult to list or assess the numbers and types of workshops conducted by the other institutions and organizations mentioned. It is significant, however, that they seem to be on the increase, and that hundreds of teachers and leaders take part in them each year for the purpose of broadening their own backgrounds and adding another dimension to their programs.

Most successful seem to be the workshops that include demonstration, actual work with children, and participation in acting on the adult level. Reading, lectures, and discussion are to be taken for granted, but practical laboratory experience is essential for any study of the arts. It has been my experience that the members most reluctant to participate in the beginning have always mentioned it first when evaluating the course. Only a concentrated workshop, or a semester's class, permits enough hours to include all these activities. The acquisition of fine technical skills should not be expected, for techniques are a developmental process, attained over a much longer period of time spent in practice and study.

The Naropa Institute Teacher Re-Training Program in Boulder, Colorado, is one of a number of recent programs designed to bring the teacher into a closer and more comfortable relationship with the arts. Despite such excellent resources as Young Audiences and Artists-in-the-Schools, the classroom teacher often feels personally alienated and inadequate when it comes to continuing the programs they have initiated. Administrators, farther removed from these programs, have even greater difficulty relating to them; hence, a good start all too often dies out before it has accomplished its purpose. At the Naropa Institute, the objectives are (1) to change the attitudes of nonarts teachers and administrators, and (2) to introduce the arts to this population through direct personal experience in the arts. In its first summer session in 1977, eighty-five students from throughout the United States were immersed in the performing arts; during the following summer, the visual arts were added.

The aim is not to provide either "recipes" or workshops in sensitivity training. Rather, it is to try to develop awareness and appreciation of the arts that will enable nonarts teachers to continue on their own after the summer is over. This includes the development of greater self-confidence; a basic understanding of the elements of the arts; an appreciation of the interrelatedness of the arts; a belief in the creative spirit in all human beings, not just the artist; and a desire to relate all of this to education.

A number of American universities have brought visiting lecturers from abroad and have established overseas study programs for credit. Among the universities which have done extensive work in the area of drama/theatre education are Northwestern University, which has brought Dorothy Heathcote and Gavin Bolton for summer sessions on the Evanston campus; and New York University, which has conducted a program for the past several years at Bretton Hall College of Education in England. In Cleveland, in-service courses for area teachers have been held for the past few winters under a joint sponsorship of Cleveland State University, the Cleveland Playhouse, and the Board of Education. Many other colleges and universities in the West, the South, and in New England have sponsored teacher workshops and exchange programs for students.

Brian Way has spent much of the past four years traveling throughout the United States, lecturing and giving workshops on creative drama and on participation theatre. In addition to these leaders, there have been other educators who have come for conferences and short-term engagements. Among them are Donald Baker of Weymouth College of Education in England, who has also worked closely with the A.C.E.I. (Association for Childhood

Education International); Margaret Faulkes, cofounder with Brian Way of the Theatre Centre in London, and now on the faculty of the University of Alberta, Canada; John Hodgson of Bretton Hall; Gerald Tyler, former drama advisor in Yorkshire and a founder of ASSITEJ; and Billie Lindquist of Sesame in London. There have been additional programs in other foreign countries, but the ones cited are among the very successful because of their content, common language, and duration.

With improved travel, American teachers have been able to meet with colleagues overseas and, on occasion, to lecture, give workshops, and to attend conferences and festivals—in short, to extend the perimeters of their own experience as no generation of educators has until now been able to do. This appears to be a trend in drama/theatre education, which can only enrich our offerings.

At the time of this writing, a *Theatre Resources Directory/Handbook* is being prepared by the Education Division of the National Endowment for the Arts. It is designed to help Artists-in-Schools coordinators for state arts agencies in locating and selecting theatre companies and resource persons who are capable of providing successful in-school theatre residencies. The fourfold purpose of the Directory is to:

1. Provide descriptive information about those companies who have developed or are willing to develop programs for residencies in schools.
2. Provide lists of individual theatre artists willing to participate in artist-in-residence programs in schools or communities.
3. Provide companies with sample educational materials of a preperformance and postperformance nature.
4. Provide in-school coordinators with examples of schedules for planning residencies and suggestions for curriculum materials related to theatre artists and performance groups.

More than mention must be made of the 334-page Rockefeller Report released in spring 1977. Entitled *Coming to Our Senses: the Significance of the Arts in American Education*, it is by far the most comprehensive survey ever made in this country. A panel of experts, over a period of two years, studied arts education in elementary schools, secondary schools, and colleges with funding from the Office of Education, the National Endowment for the Arts, and several private foundations. Professional organizations assisted in the research, which revealed a widespread belief in the arts in education, despite inadequate programs in many areas. Among the ninety-eight recommendations that were made, the panel called for the creation of a National Center for Arts in Education, a federal agency to coordinate information about artists, funding, programs, and research, and also recommended that the existing Federal Council on the Arts and the Humanities carry out a ten-year strategy for arts in education, in cooperation with states.

The panel also suggested that school districts allow students to earn credit for work done in community arts programs and that curricula should be expanded to include dance, film, drama, poetry, and design. In the area of teacher education and in-service training, the panel urged that all prospective teachers have experience in a variety of arts and learn how to relate them to each other and to other disciplines. The reception of the report was generally favorable, and some results have already taken place. One is the formation, in 1978, of a new agency called Arts, Education, and Americans, Inc., which has as its aims:

1. To organize several regional conferences, in which there will be an opportunity to discuss the report, develop specific plans for local or regional implementation, and to make recommendations toward the national plan.
2. To maintain a speakers bureau which will include panel members and others connected with the report.
3. To establish a central communications center in the New York office.
4. To promote the distribution of the report.
5. To participate in developing a national plan for the arts in education.

As a private organization, it will seek all possible means to foster the development of a national program for strengthening the role of the arts from kindergarten through college. One chapter, incidentally, suggests cooperation between schools and nonacademic institutions as a way of increasing funds that are available for the arts. In addition, by making use of community resources such as museums, theatres, studios, film libraries, and local artists, children's experiences could be enriched.

Federal Programs

By 1976 the seven principal programs among which the federal government efforts were divided were:

1. The Alliance for Arts Education
2. The Office of Education Arts in Education Program
3. The Office of Education Special Arts Project
4. The Educational Program of the National Endowment for the Arts
5. The Educational Research and Development Program of the National Institute of Education
6. Educational Innovation and Support Program of the Office of Education's Bureau of School Systems

7. The Division of Education Programs of the National Endowment for the Humanities
8. The National Committee/Arts for the Handicapped[2]

THE TEACHER OR LEADER

With so much interest in creative drama, is it not appropriate to raise some questions regarding the teacher? What special qualifications should he have? What kind of education best prepares a person to teach creative drama? Is a pure theatre background a disadvantage? Is a workshop experience sufficient preparation? Dare the teacher embark on a program without some specialized training? Is certification necessary?

Without discrediting academic preparation, what seems most important are those personal attributes that make him a good teacher. If a person already possesses the qualities of sympathetic leadership, imagination, and respect for the ideas of others, he has the basic requirements. Sensitivity to the individuals in a class is necessary to an activity that is participant-centered with the growth of each child an objective. In other words, although he is teaching an art and should therefore have some knowledge and appreciation of it as a form, a genuine concern for the players is of equal importance.

The successful creative drama teacher guides rather than directs. She is able to work with others, offering and accepting ideas. To her, sharing is more important than showing; thus her satisfaction will come through the process as well as from the product. When she does show the work of her group, she will be clear as to what is demonstration and what is performance. Unless she is working with groups over the age of ten or eleven, she will avoid the latter, in favor of informal class demonstrations.

The teacher of creative drama finds her own way. No methods courses can prepare her perfectly, for no two groups are alike. What works well with one class does not work with another. Materials and methods that arouse a response in one group may be totally inadequate in a second, whose cultural background, age, and experiences are different. Knowledge of the neighborhood in which she is working is just as important as a knowledge of literature and drama. She must find out for herself what stimulates and what fails to elicit a response. Familiarity with techniques is an invaluable asset, but the imaginative leader will, in the end, create her own methods.

A sense of humor helps her over those periods when nothing goes right. Her ability to laugh with the group, as well as at herself, enables her to carry

2. Junius Eddy, *Arts Education 1977 in Prose and Print (An Overview of Nine Significant Publications Affecting The Arts in American Education)* Washington, D.C. 1977 (prepared for The Subcommittee on Education in the Arts and the Humanities of the Federal Interagency Committee on Education).

on, in spite of failures and frustrations. Because she is interested in all kinds of things, she will have an expanding background of information on which to draw. She learns constantly from her pupils. She must also learn not to expect good results each time the class meets. Many efforts will be pedestrian and disappointing, but, as Hughes Mearns points out: "Those who work with children creatively are compelled to discard or ignore a hundred attempts while they are getting a mere half-dozen good ones."[3] It is these "good ones" that inspire others, and encourage the leader to keep on trying.

He maintains high standards, knowing that what he accepts in the beginning is what the group is capable of at the time, but that he can expect more from them later. By establishing an atmosphere in which all feel important, he will challenge his class to give only their best; the teacher waits for this, without demanding or pushing. For this reason, it is more difficult to teach creative drama than formal theatre. The absence of a basic structure, or script, demands flexibility, judgment, a willingness to accept the efforts of the shy and inarticulate, patience, and the confidence that something of value is eventually forthcoming. This is not easy for the teacher whose only previous experience has been with the formal play, or whose theatre background has conditioned him to expect technically perfect results within a stipulated period of time.

The teacher must, at the same time, set limits. The establishment of boundaries does not limit freedom, but, rather, gives a sense of security to the young or inexperienced player. As in any class, discipline must be maintained at all times in order to ensure, for each member, the freedom to experiment. In his book *Child Drama*, Peter Slade has observed that "The manner of handling is what matters, and, because of this, some of the best work with children is done by experienced teachers who really understand what they are doing and yet, strangely enough, have very little knowledge of drama."[4]

All of this is not meant to imply that specialized training is unnecessary; what is meant is that the successful teacher of creative drama seems to possess certain attitudes and qualities of personality that distinguish and qualify him. A background that includes both education and theatre is ideal, but the interested leader, whatever his preparation, may acquire, through course work and reading, additional information and techniques. Some knowledge of music and dance is invaluable and should be part of the teacher's preparation. Classroom teachers, professional actors, and social workers have all achieved notable results. Because of their belief that creative drama has a contribution to make, they have adapted their own individual skills to its use, with intelligence and imagination.

3. Hughes Mearns, *Creative Power* (New York: Dover Publications, 1958), p. 33.
4. Peter Slade, *Child Drama* (London: University of London Press, 1954), p. 271.

SUMMARY

In conclusion, creative drama may be viewed as an art form, a way of learning, a means of self-expression, a leisure-time activity or a therapeutic tool. In each instance, learnings include self-knowledge, a knowledge of others, information acquired through the process of drama, and aesthetic appreciation.

Self-Knowledge

Through drama, the player thinks, plans, and organizes. He feels deeply but learns to channel and control his emotions. His communication skills are involved as he speaks and expresses his ideas. Through rhythms and physical movement, he makes use of his body. Working with others teaches him the meaning of cooperation. He comes to understand his own strengths and weaknesses. Benedetti calls acting self-extension rather than self-expression, which describes in a word what we are talking about.

Knowledge of Others

By trying on characters, the player learns about other people. Acting a variety of parts helps him to think and feel like persons different from himself. Being part of a group not only teaches him something of teamwork but sensitizes him to the feelings of those with whom he is working. And, finally, through the material the teacher brings in, he is exposed to other people's customs, to ideas and values that may be foreign to his own.

Intellectual Development

Play has long been recognized by nursery educators as experimentation that offers unlimited possibilities for learning. Jean Piaget has written extensively on the function of play in the intellectual development of young children. He sees conceptual thinking as originating in spontaneous play through manipulation of objects and social collaboration with other children. Recent research indicates that an appropriate balance between spontaneous and more structured play is desirable.[5] No activity provides a greater variety of opportunities for learning than creative drama, regardless of the level.

5. Millie Almay, "Spontaneous Play: An Avenue for Intellectual Development." Reprint from the *Bulletin of the Institute of Child Study* (University of Toronto, 28, no. 2, 1966).

A NEW DIMENSION

Recent research indicates that there may be an important connection between the arts and learning. Dr. Jean Houston, director of the Foundation for Mind Research in Pomona, New York, has produced some new and challenging questions in the past few years. She goes beyond the integration of subject matter into methods of enhancing concentration and freedom from distraction. She advocates a holistic approach to education; in other words, if a start is made from a deep aesthetic base, everything related to the subject at hand can be learned more quickly, easily, and thoroughly. A richer sensory perception, kinesthetic thinking, and the use of rhythms and movement to facilitate learning form an important part of her theory.

Her workshops in discovering latent human capacities are being offered to teachers on elementary and secondary school levels, to religious leaders, and to social workers. Dr. Houston's goal is a fuller development of the human being, and she is convinced of the important role the arts play in this.

CONCLUSION

A basic requirement of any activity is that it be a satisfying experience for both leader and group. The more successful the project, the greater the degree of satisfaction. As the leader grows in experience, he will recognize the possibilities in a variety of materials and methods, and his group will likewise grow in security and the ability to tackle problems more imaginatively. This is true of the creative drama leader and her group on any age level, whether in a school or recreational setting.

Through the spread of our mass media, we have become known as a "spectator society." Our lives have become increasingly programmed and our experiences packaged. Participation in any of the arts is, therefore, more needed today than at any other period in our history. Drama, of all the arts, demands of the practitioner a total involvement. By offering an opportunity for participation in drama, we are helping to preserve something of the play impulse in all of its joy, freedom, and order.

Educational and social goals are closely related in drama; therefore a climate in which the player feels good about him or herself and others is conducive to learning. Although the word *child* is used throughout this text, the basic principles apply to all ages, and the concept of a warm and supportive environment as a positive influence is applicable everywhere. It is this kind of environment that we should try to create, an environment in which all persons can grow. Robert Benedetti, in a text written for the adult actor, puts it most succinctly when he says, "Acting is neither seeming nor being; it is becoming."[6]

6. Robert Benedetti, *Seeming, Being and Becoming* (New York: Drama Book Specialists, 1976), p. 87.

A SELECTED
BIBLIOGRAPHY

On Creative Drama, Movement, and Puppetry

Allen, John. *Drama in Schools: Its Theory and Practice*. London: Heinemann Educational Books, 1979.

    The author of this book is both well-known and well qualified to write on drama education. After a brief history of the subject in England, he proceeds to discuss current practices and to take a strong stand on a number of controversial issues. This should be required reading for every specialist and recommended for the generalist.

Barlin, Ann and Paul. *The Art of Learning Through Movement*. New York: Ritchie Ward, 1971.

    The authors have had wide experience in public school teaching. They present their material clearly with enthusiasm and practicality.

Barnfield, Gabriel. *Creative Drama in Schools*. New York: Macmillan, 1971.

    A British publication with an emphasis on the secondary school. It gives ideas that the author has used and found successful. He begins with movement and rhythm and dance and describes the use of music as a technique for encouraging imagination.

Burger, Isabel B. *Creative Drama in Religious Education*. Wilton, Ct.: Morehouse-Barlow, 1976.

    One of the few books on the use of creative dramatics in religious education. Mrs. Burger's years of successful teaching make this a practical and authoritative text for leaders in this field.

263

Burger, Isabelle. *Creative Play Acting*. New York: A. S. Barnes, 1950.

 This is a practical book written by a leader of long and wide experience. It includes many practical exercises and techniques for acting and movement.

Byers, Ruth. *Creating Theatre*. San Antonio: Trinity University, 1968.

 This is a handsome book with a focus on a creative approach to playwriting with children and teenagers. Pantomime and improvisation lead to exercises in writing. Many beautiful photographs and nine scripts illustrate the work done in classes under the guidance of the author, who is director of the Teen-Children's Theatre and assistant professor of drama at Baylor University in the Dallas Theatre Center.

Chambers, Dewey W. *Storytelling and Creative Drama*. Dubuque, Iowa: William C. Brown, 1970.

 This is an invaluable little book for the teacher, librarian, or group leader who wants to learn something of the ancient art of storytelling. Clear and succinct, it guides selection of material and offers simple techniques for effective presentation.

Cheifitz, Dan. *Theatre in My Head*. Boston: Little, Brown, 1971.

 This book describes an experimental workshop in creative drama conducted by the author in an inner-city New York church. Mr. Cheifitz communicates the need to look *into* the child, not merely *at* him, as he reports the successes and failures he met.

Coger, Leslie, and White, Melvin. *Readers Theatre Handbook*. Chicago: Scott, Foresman, 1967.

 Here is an excellent text on this new technique written by experts in the field. Directed toward the adult reader, it is nevertheless equally useful to the high school teacher or to any teacher interested in trying this new concept of theatre.

Cole, Nancy. *Puppet Theatre in Performance*. New York: William Morrow, 1978.

 What distinguishes this book is its emphasis on performance. Whereas many texts on puppetry offer detailed instructions for making puppets, Nancy Cole gives ideas and clear directions for handling them. An unusually good book for advanced as well as older puppeteers.

Coming to Our Senses: The Significance of the Arts for American Education. Panel Report, David Rockefeller, Jr., chairman. New York: McGraw Hill, 1977.

 This long-awaited survey of the state of arts education in America will be of greatest interest to the specialist and the administrator. It represents years of collecting, compiling, and writing down information gathered from many sources, both persons and organizations.

Conner, Norma, and Klebanoff, Harriet. *And a Time to Dance*. Boston: Beacon, 1967.

 This is a sensitively illustrated book that explains, encourages, and shows the reader how to involve children in creative dance. Simply written, it also shows what can be done with the mentally retarded.

Courtney, Richard. *The School Play*. London: Cassell and Co., 1966.

 This book is of greatest interest to the teacher of older children. The author's wealth of experience and depth of understanding make it much more than a "how-to" text.

Courtney, Richard. *Play, Drama and Thought*. New York, Drama Book Specialists, 1974.

 There are many useful sections in this British publication directed toward the philosophy and practice of drama in the school.

Crosscup, Richard. *Children and Dramatics*. New York: Scribner's, 1966.

 A recent addition to the literature in the field, Mr. Crosscup's book is an autobiographical account of his twenty-seven years' experience in one school. Of greatest value is the view he gives of a gifted teacher, able to stimulate the creativity of his pupils. Social values are stressed.

Cullum, Albert. *Aesop in the Afternoon*. New York: Citation, 1972.
This is a most usable collection of Aesop's fables which can be played creatively by children of all ages.

Cullum, Albert. *Push Back the Desks*. New York: Citation, 1967.
The author has written an account of some creative projects and techniques he has used in the public school classroom to enhance learning. History, reading, vocabulary, and math are included units of study.

Cullum, Albert. *Shake Hands with Shakespeare*. New York: Citation, 1968.
Eight of Shakespeare's plays are adapted for children. The results are filled with action and are relatively simple to produce. They do require time to prepare but could also be improvised, if desired. The value of using Shakespeare is the richness of the language and is a further recommendation for this text.

Cummings, Richard. *101 Hand Puppets: A Guide for Puppeteers of All Ages*. New York: McKay, 1962.
This is an extremely comprehensive book offering step-by-step instruction for making every conceivable kind of hand puppet, from the simplest to the most elaborate. It includes scripts and has over sixty diagrams and illustrations. For older and more experienced classes.

Dodd, Nigel, and Hickson, Winifred, Eds. *Drama and Theatre in Education*. London: Heinemann, 1971.
This is a collection of essays by well-known British experts including Gavin Bolton, Dorothy Heathcote, Veronica Sherbourn, and others. Of interest to the more experienced leader.

Dorian, Margery. *Ethnic Stories for Children to Dance*. San Mateo, Cal.: BBB, 1978.
Here is a second book by the author of *Telling Stories Through Movement*. It includes stories from around the world with suggestions for rhythmic accompaniment on drums and other instruments. Years of experience as a dancer and as teacher of dance give the author knowledge and insight. The choice of material is a valuable addition to the resources available to teachers in lower grades.

Dorian, Margery, and Gulland, Frances. *Telling Stories Through Movement*. Belmont, Cal.: Fearon, 1974.
This is an invaluable little book for creative drama teachers working with young children. The authors bring a rich background in dance, education, and drama to the task, and the result is practical and clear. Creative movement and rhythms are used to tell stories from many lands.

Ehrlich, Harriett, and Grastry, Patricia. *Creative Dramatics Handbook*. Philadelphia: School District of Philadelphia Instructional Services, 1971.
This handbook offers a wealth of ideas for the teacher wishing to include creative drama in the curriculum. Since the material grew directly from the authors' experiences, it is fresh and practical.

Engler, Larry, and Fijan Carol. *Making Puppets Come Alive*. New York Taplinger, 1973.
This is a charming and practical text for the beginner of any age. To be used by the teacher, it offers help in making and handling puppets, including exercises to develop the skills needed to produce a show. Beautifully illustrated.

Fitzgerald, Burdette. *World Tales for Creative Dramatics and Storytelling*. New York: Prentice-Hall, 1962.

In this book the author introduces a wide variety of stories not usually found in collections of this sort. She has drawn from the folklore of countries rarely represented in anthologies of children's literature, thus making an interesting contribution to the field.

Gillies, Emily P. *Creative Dramatics for All Children*. Washington, D.C.: Association for Childhood Education International, 1973.
This is a welcome addition to the scanty supply of material on dramatics in special education. Mrs. Gillies, whose years of experience qualify her to speak authoritatively, discusses drama for the emotionally disturbed and physically handicapped child as well as its use in the education of children for whom English is a second language.

Gray, Vera, and Percival, Rachel. *Music, Movement and Mime for Children*. Oxford: Oxford University, 1962.
The emphases in this book are on music and movement and the authors give a good basic introduction to those planning to teach in these areas. It is clear and concise with many exercises and procedures suggested.

Haaga, Agnes, and Randles, Patricia. *Supplementary Material for Use in Creative Dramatics with Younger Children*. Seattle: University of Washington, 1952
This outline of lessons, planned and evaluated by the authors, is of great practical value to teachers of younger children. It is unique in describing the activities of each session in detail, the music and literature used, and the children's reactions.

Haggerty, Joan. *Please Can I Play God*? Indianapolis: Bobbs-Merrill, 1967.
Mrs. Haggerty's book tells of her first teaching experience in a ghetto school in London. Throughout her account, which is both amusing and touching, runs her concern for these disadvantaged children as she guides them in creative dramatic activities. It is not a textbook but a sympathetic account of a beginning teacher's classroom experiences.

Hanford, Robert Ten Eyck, *The Complete Book of Puppets and Puppeteering*. New York and London: Drake, 1976.
A 157-page paperback concentrating on an overview of puppetry—past, present, and to come; the tools of the trade; the production; and techniques and tips from the pros. An excellent book written in clear, definitive style with simple, yet complete instructions on all aspects of puppets and puppet productions.

Heinig, Ruth, and Stillwell, Lydia. *Creative Dramatics for the Classroom Teacher*. Englewood Cliffs: Prentice-Hall, 1974.
The authors' years of experience make for a practical text for nonspecialists. Pantomime, improvisation, songs, and games are among the activities suggested; they are arranged so as to guide the teacher through simple to more advanced techniques.

Hodgson, John, and Richards, Ernest. *Improvisation*. London: Methuen, 1967.
This book on improvisation is not directed exclusively to work with children. The aim is to utilize two elements from everyday life: spontaneous response to unexpected situations and the employment of this response in controlled conditions. Exercises are given.

Jennings, Sue. *Remedial Drama*. New York: Theatre Arts, 1974.
The message in this book is that the experience of drama can enrich everyone's life, whether one is mentally or physically handicapped, or socially disadvantaged. For nonspecialists. It is clear and easy to read and will help the teacher to work with the therapist.

Kase, Robert, *Stories for Creative Acting*. New York: Samuel French, 1961.

Professor Kase has collected stories recommended to him by experts in the field. All the stories have been used with success, thus making this a valuable addition to any teacher's library.

Kelly, Elizabeth. *Dramatics in the Classroom: Making Lessons Come Alive*. Bloomington, Ind.: Phi Delta Kappa Educational Foundation, 1976.
This small pamphlet gives, in a nutshell, a philosophy of education as well as practical help in showing how drama can be used to teach curricular material effectively. Of greatest value to the beginning or general classroom teacher.

Keysell, Pat. *Motives for Mime*. London: Evans, 1975.
This little paperback is divided into three parts: the first deals with beginning activities for children from five to seven; the second, with development for the seven-to nine-year-olds; and the third, application for those aged nine to twelve. Starting with real objects, the author progresses to mime. She works for aware-ness of size, weight, shape, and the use of space. Although the material is or-ganized according to age levels, it also follows a logical progression from simple to complicated and is, therefore, a useful text on any level.

King, Nancy. *The Actor and His Space*. New York: Drama Book Specialists, 1971.
This book explains the importance of movement in an actor's training. Many exercises are given. It is probably less useful to the elementary and secondary school teacher than her other text, *Giving Form to Feeling* but is good material nevertheless.

King, Nancy. *Giving Form to Feeling*. New York: Drama Book Specialists, 1975.
This is a sound and useful handbook with many exercises and ideas. The author says that it is a book of beginnings. This is true, but it is not necessarily written for the beginner; the actor, dancer, and teacher on any level will find help in expressing ideas and feelings through movement, rhythm, sounds, and words.

Koste, Virginia Glasgow. *Dramatic Play in Childhood: Rehearsal for Life*. New Or-leans: Anchorage, 1978.
Anchorage gives us this delightful book directed particularly toward the teacher of young children. The author's appreciation and understanding of her subject are infectious; moreover, she writes with simplicity and clarity.

Kraus, Joanna Halpert. *Sound and Motion Stories*. Rowayton, Ct.: New Plays, 1971.
Although not a textbook, the way in which sounds and actions can be used to capture attention and stimulate the imagination of younger children qualifies it for inclusion in this bibliography. The reader can learn from the author's suggestions how to use other material in this way.

La Salle, Dorothy. *Rhythms and Dance for Elementary Schools*. (Revised) New York: Ronald, 1951.
This collection of rhythms and dances should be extremely useful to the teacher of dramatic play and creative drama, or to the children's theatre director. It contains movement fundamentals, singing games, and folk dances, ranging from simple to advanced.

Lowndes, Betty. *Movement and Creative Drama for Children*. Boston: Plays, 1971.
First published in England, this practical and stimulating book should find en-thusiastic readers in the United States as well. The author, an experienced teacher, explains the value and use of improvised movement and follows with chapters on body awareness, locomotion, mime, sensory awareness, and creative movement.

Maclay, Joanna Hawkins. *Readers Theatre: Toward a Grammar of Practice*. New York: Random House, 1971.
This is an excellent text on the subject. It covers a definition of readers theatre,

gives a selection of material, and also describes performance techniques. It is most useful to teachers of upper grades.

Maynard, Olga. *Children and Dance and Music*. New York: Scribner's, 1968.
This book includes material not usually found in texts on creative drama. A good supplement to any text.

McCaslin, Nellie. *Children and Drama*. New York: Longman, 1975.
This is a collection of essays on creative drama written by fourteen different experts in the field. A variety of viewpoints are represented and different methodologies suggested. It is of greater interest to the experienced teacher than to the beginner.

McCaslin, Nellie. *Puppet Fun (Performance, Production and Plays)*. New York: McKay, 1977.
This juvenile text, directed to the child from seven to ten, can be used equally well by the inexperienced teacher or recreation leader who wants to include puppetry but who has never worked with it. Diagrams and illustrations show the rudiments of making and manipulating hand puppets.

McGregor, Lynn, Tate, Maggie, and Robinson, Ken. *Learning Through Drama*. London: Heinemann, 1977.
Here is another book for the specialist, particularly if he knows something about drama education in England. It represents a comprehensive survey done by three well-qualified young educators. An important contribution to the field.

McIntyre, Barbara. *Informal Dramatics: A Language Arts Activity for the Special Child*. Pittsburgh: Stanwix, 1963.
This book is a useful guide for teachers of special education and is one of the few directed toward this new area.

Pereira, Nancy. *Creative Dramatics in the Library*. Rowayton, Ct.: New Plays, 1974.
While the content is not substantially different from other books on the subject, the consideration of the neighborhood library as a location for dramatic activities is. The author offers suggestions for starting points, games, use of time and space, the handling of groups, visual aids, and culminating activities.

Peyton, Jeffrey, and Koenig, Barbara. *Puppetry: A Tool for Teaching*. New Haven: P.O. Box 270, 1973.
Simplicity and economy characterize this 100-page guide to puppetry for the curriculum. Originally prepared for the New Haven Public Schools, it is adaptable to other systems and a variety of subject areas.

Polsky, Milton, and Gardner, Joan. *Creata-Play (Pandora's Box)*. New York: Westwood, 1975.
Here is a kit designed by two experienced teachers for the classroom teacher who wants to use dramatic techniques for the teaching of subject matter. Games, exercises, and activities are printed on sturdy cards in a large box made to stand up under heavy use over a long period of time.

Prokes, Sr. Dorothy. "Exploring the Relationship Between Participation in Creative Dramatics and Development of the Imaginative Capacities of Gifted Junior High School Students." Ph.D. dissertation, School of Education, New York University, 1971.
This is one of the few studies made in the field of the arts for the gifted child and is unique in its focus on creative dramatics. The study is available in microfilm and at the New York University Library.

Schattner, Gertrud, and Courtney, Richard. *Drama in Therapy*. Vol. 1. New York: Drama Book Specialists, 1979.
The editors have collected and assembled two volumes of essays written by a

large group of experts in a variety of specialized areas. The first books of their kind, *Drama in Therapy* should be of enormous interest and value to teacher and student as well as to specialist and generalist in drama education.

Schwartz, Dorothy, and Aldrich, Dorothy, Eds. *Give Them Roots and Wings*. Washington, D.C.: American Theatre Association, 1972.
This is a guide to drama in the elementary school, prepared by leaders in the field and edited by Dorothy Schwartz and Dorothy Aldrich as co-chairmen of a project for the Children's Theatre Association. Published in workbook form, it offers the classroom teacher goals and dramatic activities with check lists for rating children's development. Usable and attractively illustrated.

Shaw, Ann M. and Cj Stevens. *Drama, Theatre and the Handicapped*. Washington, D.C.: American Theatre Association, 1979.
This collection of articles is the work of a comittee of the American Theatre Association, funded under a Special Project Program Grant of the National Committee, Arts for the Handicapped, and chaired by the editor. Contributors are experienced in their respective areas and address themselves to the potential of the arts for handicapped persons, the removal of barriers, programs that have already been established and a review of the existing literature. This is recommended reading for all teachers and recreation leaders.

Shuman, R. Baird, Ed. *Educational Drama for Today's Schools*. Metuchen, N.J.: Scarecrow, 1978.
This collection of articles came about as a result of workshops given in this country by Dorothy Heathcote, who has written the lead chapter. Drama in education is defined as "anything which involves persons in active role-taking situations in which attitudes, not characters, are the chief concern . . . at this moment, not memory based." Each chapter, written by a different person, deals with values clarification, language development, moral education, etc.

Siks, Geraldine Brain. *Children's Literature for Dramatization*. New York: Harper & Row, 1964.
This is a collection of stories and poems, old and new, for the classroom teacher and group leader. The introductions to the stories make the book particularly valuable to less experienced teachers, but it is useful to anyone working in the field.

Siks, Geraldine Brain, and Dunnington, Hazel, Eds. *Children's Theatre and Creative Dramatics: Principles and Practices*. Seattle: University of Washington, 1961.
This volume, edited by Geraldine Siks, was written by a group of experts on the various aspects of children's theatre and creative dramatics. It contains much factual information, which should have its greatest value for the student who wishes to become generally informed on the subject.

Siks, Geraldine Brain. *Drama with Children*. New York: Harper & Row, 1977.
This latest book by a well-known creative drama leader and author of other texts in the field is of particular interest to the more experienced teacher or graduate student. It is divided into three parts: the philosophy, the teaching of drama, and individual experiences and uses of drama. She discusses what she calls the "process-concept structure approach" and includes a selected bibliography and a few short plays.

Slade, Peter. *An Introduction to Child Drama*. London and Toronto: Hodder and Stoughton, 1976.
All the fundamental principles of Slade's methods are here. Children, if unhampered by adult imposition, can find self-expression and reach toward full human development. It is simply written, short, and to the point. Highly recommended for the beginner.

Slade, Peter. *Child Drama*. London: University of London, 1954.
    Written by an expert in children's dramatics in England, this lengthy book presents a philosophy and way of working. It is detailed and informative and should be of interest to all leaders and teachers of creative dramatics. The author takes an unequivocal stand against children in public performances.

Slade, Peter. *Natural Dance*. London: Hodder and Stoughton, 1977.
    This is particularly recommended for the teacher of creative drama. In it Slade discusses "natural dance," or dance that is improvised, as opposed to formal dance techniques. It deals with all ages, levels of experience, and levels of ability; the therapeutic aspects of dance are also included.

Spolin, Viola. *Improvisation for the Theatre*. Evanston: Northwestern University, 1963.
    This is a comprehensive handbook of teaching and directing techniques, not specifically designed for use with children but nevertheless appropriate and useful to the more experienced teacher. It contains a variety of exercises and theatre games.

Stanistreet, Grace. *Teaching Is a Dialogue*. Garden City, N.Y.: Adelphi University, 1969.
    This is an unusual book in that it is a collection of letters from the author in reply to questions asked of every teacher of acting. Her philosophy is clearly stated as to the values of creative playing: in essence, the growth of human beings as opposed to the external assumption of roles. Exercises, which offer a means of reaching this goal, are also given.

Tynas, Billi. *Child Drama in Action (A Practical Guide for Teachers)*. Toronto: Gage, 1971.
    This is an instructor's manual, which opens with a brief but clear introduction, then moves directly into a series of lesson plans. Each of these plans follows a theme and gives the activity to be emphasized. This very beautiful book will be of most use to teachers with a background in creative drama rather than to beginners.

Van Tassel, Katrina, and Greimann, Millie. *Creative Dramatization*. New York: Threshold Division, Macmillan, 1973.
    Here is a book with special value for the teacher of very young children. Based on sound educational principles, it is a guidebook for the stimulation of creativity through music, mime, movement, and language arts. It is clearly written and presented in an attractive format. Illustrated. Highly recommended.

Wagner, Betty Jane. *Dorothy Heathcote (Drama as a Learning Medium)*. Washington, D.C.: National Education Association, 1976.
    The author has done a masterful job of describing the methods of this distinguished English drama teacher. Ms. Wagner explains how Heathcote finds material, helps children build an imagined situation and leads them to see and feel the elements of human experience. Most important, she shows how the learning takes place. It is apparent from this book why Dorothy Heathcote has so great a following among elementary school teachers.

Wagner, Jearnine, and Baker, Kitty. *A Place for Ideas: Our Theatre*. (Revised) New Orleans: Anchorage, 1978.
    This is a unique book in that it describes with appreciation and beauty the theatre in which the authors work. It is not a children's theatre in the usual sense but rather a "place for ideas," where the arts can be explored and experienced. Illustrations show children experimenting with color, movement, and music, as well as creative drama. This is less a textbook than an inspiration to others who work with children in the arts.

Ward, Winifred. *Playmaking with Children*. New York: Appleton-Century-Crofts, 1957.
    This book, by a distinguished leader is a landmark text. It is arranged both as to age levels and use, including dramatics in school, recreation, religious education, and therapy. Highly readable, it is valuable both for the beginning and the experienced teacher.

Ward, Winifred. *Stories to Dramatize*. Anchorage, Ky.: Anchorage, 1952.
    In this collection, the author includes a rich variety of stories, and some poems, for use in school and recreation groups. It is arranged for children on various age levels (from six to fourteen) and contains material that the author tested and found rewarding in her many years of experience.

Way, Brian. *Development Through Drama*. New York: Humanities, 1972.
    The development of the whole child is the thesis of this book, directed particularly to teachers of older children. Many practical exercises in improvisational drama are included. Highly recommended.

Wethered, Audrey, G. *Drama & Movement in Therapy*. London: Macdonald and Evans, 1973.
    The therapeutic use of movement, mime, and drama are covered in this short text. It is simple, clear, and should be useful to both nonspecialist and specialist.

Wilder, Rosilyn. *A Space Where Anything Can Happen*. Rowayton, Ct.: New Plays, 1977.
    The author brings a wealth of experience to this text, directed to the teacher of older children. Challenges, projects, descriptions of her own classes and students, discipline, and clear guidelines for leading modern youngsters in creative work are the most valuable aspects.

A Selected List of Books on Choral Speaking

Abney, Louise. *Choral Speaking Arrangements for the Lower Grades*. Boston: Expression, 1937.

Gullan, Marjorie. *The Speech Choir*. New York: Harper & Row, 1937.

Huckleberry, Alan W., and Strother, Edward S. *Speech Education for the Elementary Teacher*. Boston: Allyn & Bacon, 1966. Chapter 6.

Rasmussen, Carrie. *Choral Speaking for Speech Improvement*. Boston: Expression, 1942.

Rasmussen, Carrie. *Let's Say Poetry Together and Have Fun*. Minneapolis: Burgess, 1962.

Teaching and the Related Arts

Aronoff, Frances Webber. *Music and Young Children*. New York: Holt, Rinehart and Winston, 1969.
    A widely used text for music teaching, this book has much to offer both specialist and generalist in drama. Ways in which music can enrich the lives of children are suggested and explained. An excellent resource.

Baker, Donald. *Understanding the Under Fives*. London: Evans, 1975.
    The author combines background and expertise in early childhood education as well as theatre and drama education. It is a unique, practical, and highly readable text.

Behrn; Snyder; and Clopton. *Drama Integrates Basic Skills, Lesson Plans for the Learning Disabled*. Springfield, Ill.: Charles C. Thomas, 1979.

The material in this book is based on the authors' work at the Kingsbury Laboratory School (for learning disabled children) in Washington, D.C. They present a convincing argument for a drama curriculum to help integrate basic affective and cognitive skills. These include behavioral sensory, motor, verbal, and conceptual skills. This is a practical and unique text for any teacher.

Creative Dramatics. Washington, D.C.: American Alliance for Health, Physical Education and Recreation, 1977.

Creative drama with handicapped and non-handicapped children and adults is described. Games, activities, story drama and role playing are included for the purpose of expressing one's own feelings and helping one to work cooperatively with others.

Doyle, Donald P. "An Investigation of Elementary Teacher Education Related to the Preparation of Teachers in the Use of Creative Drama in Teaching Language Arts." Unpublished Ph.D. Dissertation, University of Minnesota, 1974.

The findings of this study advocate the use of creative drama as an aid in teaching of language arts in the elementary grades; research showed preparation inadequate and in general not required.

The Eagle Soars: The Artist, the Teacher, and the Handicapped. Chappaqua, N.Y.: New York State Poets in the Schools, 1977.

Activities used in an interdisciplinary arts program with both moderately and severely handicapped students are described. Objectives, procedures and lesson plans are included.

Hartley, Ruth; Frank, Lawrence; and Goldenson, Robert. *Understanding Children's Play*. New York: Columbia University, 1964.

Linderman, Earl W., and Heberholz, Donald W. *Developing Artistic and Perceptual Awareness*. Dubuque, Iowa: William C. Brown, 1964.

Materials on Creative Arts (Arts, Crafts, Dance, Drama and Music) for Persons with Handicapping Conditions. Washington, D.C.: American Alliance for Health, Physical Education, and Recreation, 1975.

This guide provides information on resources for use in the arts for persons with various handicapping conditions. It suggest activities, guidelines, and implications for programming in art, crafts, dance drama and music; materials, references and suppliers of equipment add to the usefulness.

Mearns, Hughes. *Creative Power*. Second rev. ed. New York: Dover, 1958.

Tiedt, Iris M. *Drama in Your Classroom*. National Council of Teachers of English, 1974.

Written by and for the teacher of English, the text advocates drama as an aid to more effective classroom teaching.

Some 16-mm. Films for Use in Teaching Dramatics

Creativity: A Way of Learning.   11 min. color, sound.
NEA Distribution Center
The Academic Bldg. Saw Mill Rd.,
West Haven, Ct. 06516.

This film explores creativity, how it is related to life in and out of school, and how it can be encouraged.

Creative Dramatics: The First Steps   29 min. sound, color
Northwestern Film Library
614 Davis Street
Evanston, Illinois 60201

This is an outstanding film that demonstrates the teaching of creative dramatics to a group of fourth-grade children. Guided by an experienced teacher, the group moves from the faltering first steps to the creation of a drama.

Dorothy Heathcote Talks to Teachers—Part I.   30 min. color
Northwestern University Film Library
1735 Benson Avenue
Evanston, Illinois 60201

Dorothy Heathcote Talks to Teachers—Part II.   32 min. color
Northwestern University Film Library
1735 Benson Avenue
Evanston, Illinois 60201

Everyman in the Streets   30 min. color
Channel 13 NET—New York (no charge)
304 W. 58th Street
New York, New York 10019

One of a Kind   58 min. color, sound.
Phoenix Films, Inc.
470 Park Ave., S.
NY, NY. 10016
    Intended for audiences of all ages, this powerful film deals with the relationship between a child and a troubled mother. Through participation in a traveling puppet show, the child is able to express her anguish and needs. The film can be used effectively for classes in special education, psychology, creative drama and language arts.

Playing: Pretending Spontaneous Drama with Children   20 min. b/w
Community Services Department
Pittsburgh Child Guidance Center
201 De Soto Street
Pittsburgh, Pennsylvania 15213
    This film, by Eleanor C. Irwin, describes a number of different forms of spontaneous drama with primary and elementary-age children. Activities showing creative movement, puppetry, role play, and improvisation are demonstrated. The nature of creativity; the developmental roots of drama; the importance of impulse control as well as impulse expression; the individuality of children and their fantasies; and the value of dramatic play for children in both cognitive and affective learning are discussed.

Three Looms Waiting   52 min. color
BBC Production
Time-Life Films, Inc., Distributor
43 W. 16th Street
New York, New York 10016
    This film shows Dorothy Heathcote, one of the leading British teachers of creative drama, working with a group of children. An excellent demonstration of her method.

Take 3.   70 min. 16-mm, color, sound.
National Audio-Visual Aids Library,
Paxton Place, Gipsy Rd.,
London SE27 9SR.
    This English film describes the work of three drama teachers and is intended to provoke thought and raise questions about the nature of drama, assessment, and evaluation. Although not available in the U.S.A. at the time of publication of this book, it is recommended because it shows three different teachers at work in three entirely different situations, each using individual techniques.

THEATRE FOR CHILDREN
A SELECTED BIBLIOGRAPHY

Breen, Robert. *Chamber Theatre*. Englewood Cliffs, N.J.: Prentice-Hall, 1978.

Broadman, Muriel. *Understanding Your Child's Entertainment*. New York: Harper & Row, 1977.

Chorpenning, Charlotte. *Twenty-One Years with Children's Theatre*. Anchorage, Ky.: Anchorage, 1955.

Corey, Orlin. *Theatre for Children —Kids' Stuff or Theatre?* Anchorage, Ky.: Anchorage, 1974.

Fisher, Caroline, and Robertson, Hazel. *Children and the Theatre*. Palo Alto: Stanford University, 1950.

Forkert, Maurice. *Children's Theatre that Captures Its Audience*. Chicago: Coach House, 1962.

Goldberg, Moses. *Children's Theatre: A Philosophy and a Method*. Englewood Cliffs: Prentice-Hall, 1974.

Healy, Daty. *Dress the Show*. Rowayton, Ct.: New Plays, 1976.

Johnson, Richard. *Producing Plays for Children*. New York: Rosen, 1971.

McCaslin, Nellie. *Children's Theatre in the United States: A History*. Norman: Oklahoma, 1971.

McCaslin, Nellie. *Theatre for Young Audiences*. New York: Longman, 1978.

O'Toole, John. *Theatre in Education*. London: Hodder and Stoughton, 1976.

Ward, Winifred. *Theatre for Children*. Anchorage, Ky.: Anchorage, 1958.

Whitton, Pat Hale. *Participation Theatre for Young Audiences*. Rowayton, Ct.: New Plays, 1972.

A NOTE ABOUT THE AUTHOR

Nellie McCaslin teaches in the Program in Educational Theatre and directs the University Without Walls Program, both at New York University. After she received her Ph.D. from New York University, she went on to do post graduate work with Madame Maria Ouspenskaya in Hollywood, and then taught at the National College of Education in Evanston, Illinois, Teachers College of Columbia University, and Mills College of Education.

She is a Fellow of the American Theatre Association. The Children's Theatre Association elected Professor McCaslin their president in 1973 and she served in that post until 1975. She has lectured and written extensively on children's theatre and her books include a history of the movement in the United States and two books also published by Longman, *Children and Drama* and *Theatre for Young Audiences*. In addition, she is the author of a number of children's plays and three juveniles, *Act Now!*, *Puppet Fun*, and *Shows on a Shoestring*. She has been a guest on CBS educational television, coordinator of children's programs on WABC radio, and producer of two records for children. Nellie McCaslin lives in Greenwich Village with a friend, a cat, and a poodle named Coco.

INDEX

277